Money in Politics

Lexington Studies in Political Communication

Series Editor: Robert E. Denton, Jr., Virginia Tech

This series encourages focused work examining the role and function of communication in the realm of politics including campaigns and elections, media, and political institutions.

Recent Titles in This Series

Money in Politics

Campaign Fundraising in the 2020 Presidential Election

Cayce Myers

LEXINGTON BOOKS
Lanham • Boulder • New York • London

Published by Lexington Books
An imprint of The Rowman & Littlefield Publishing Group, Inc.
4501 Forbes Boulevard, Suite 200, Lanham, Maryland 20706
www.rowman.com

86-90 Paul Street, London EC2A 4NE

British Library Cataloguing in Publication Information Available

Library of Congress Cataloging-in-Publication Data

Names: Myers, Cayce, 1982- author.
Title: Money in politics : campaign fundraising in the 2020 presidential elections / Cayce Myers.
Description: Lanham, Maryland : Lexington Books, 2021. | Series: Lexington Studies in Political Communication / series editor, Robert E. Denton, Jr., Virginia Tech University | Includes bibliographical references and index. | Summary: "Money in Politics explores the political fundraising of the 2020 presidential election from the primaries through the General Election, illustrating the importance of campaign fundraising and examining how campaign contributions are now a political topic in the 2020s"— Provided by publisher.
Identifiers: LCCN 2021042638 (print) | LCCN 2021042639 (ebook) | ISBN 9781793640277 (Cloth : acid-free paper) | ISBN 9781793640291 (paperback) | ISBN 9781793640284 (ePub)
Subjects: LCSH: Campaign funds—United States—History. | Presidents—United States—Election—2020. | Politics, Practical—United States. | United States—Politics and government—2017-2021.
Classification: LCC JK1991 .M89 2021 (print) | LCC JK1991 (ebook) | DDC 324.7/80973—dc23/eng/20211015
LC record available at https://lccn.loc.gov/2021042638
LC ebook record available at https://lccn.loc.gov/2021042639

For my daughter Cayce Anne Myers.

Contents

List of Tables

Acknowledgments

This book has been written with the help of many people. I want to thank Lexington and its editors for their help in publishing this book. I want to especially thank Nicolette Amstutz for her help and patience during this process and Robert Denton Jr., the editor for this series in Political Communication and the director of the School of Communication at Virginia Tech where I am a faculty member. Special thanks to the staff of Virginia Tech's Carol M. Newman Library for their assistance in finding books and other items to make this work complete. I also want to thank the reviewers for this book, especially Ruthann Weaver Lariscy, Melissa Smith, and Lisa Burns for their kinds words.

As with any major project, I want to especially thank my family, particularly my wife, Anne Myers, and my mother, Linda Myers, who encouraged me throughout the writing process. During this difficult time of a global pandemic, I wrote this book surrounded by my family, especially my daughter Cayce Anne. Appropriately this book is dedicated to her.

Introduction

The presidential election of 2020 was unique in many ways. It was held during a pandemic, it featured an incumbent who had undergone impeachment, it featured the matchup of the two oldest presidential candidates, it was the first time an African and Asian American woman appeared as a major party nominee, it featured the largest primary field for the Democratic Party, and it cost more than any presidential election in the history of the United States. To be accurate, the presidential election of 2020 was a multibillion-dollar affair, with the Federal Election Commission (FEC) stating that all presidential candidates raised a combined $4,021,221,646 and estimations of all money raised from all sources being even higher.[1] That also does not include all of the House and Senate races held in 2020, which set records as well. All of this cash in elections begs the questions: What is the effect of campaign dollars on elections in the United States? How much did the candidates raise, and how much do political action committees (PACs) and super-PACs play within the political system? Perhaps more importantly, how did the American political system get to this point?

All of these questions are important because they address an underlying issue within American democracy—is there such a thing as too much money in the political process? In an opinion from the 1976 U.S. Supreme Court case, *Buckley v. Valeo*, it says, "The concept that government may restrict the speech of some elements of our society in order to enhance the relative voice of others is wholly foreign to the First Amendment."[2] That sentiment has been at issue for over a century in American campaign finance laws and reform efforts. The net result of the wrangling over this issue is the multibillion-dollar presidential election of 2020.

This book seeks to examine both the amount of money that was raised and spent in the 2020 presidential election, but it also contextualizes it within

1

the law, history, and current events of campaign finance. Using legal cases, historical news accounts, contemporary news coverage, and FEC filings from campaign committees, PACs, super-PACs, parties, and joint fundraising committees, this book presents an overview of the money in the 2020 election. More broadly, however, this book shows the reality of campaign fundraising during an election and how the American campaign system got to the point it is today. From that overview, this book concludes with an overview of what campaign finance in American politics will be in the coming years and its potential impact on the American political system.

Chapter 1 begins with an overview of campaign finance laws and regulations beginning in the nineteenth century with the campaigns of Andrew Jackson and Abraham Lincoln. Analyzing the first legislative attempts of campaign finance during the administration of Theodore Roosevelt and the passage of the Tillman Act of 1907, this chapter shows how campaign finance emerged from a larger outcry against corporate money in politics.[3] From that beginning, the evolution of campaign finance law is presented showing that campaign finance regulations began as a means to limit corruption in American politics but also served to curtail the larger corporate and union donations that would influence politics in the early- to mid-twentieth century.

Particular attention is paid to the legal history surrounding the Watergate scandal during the Nixon administration and how campaign finance regulations, including the formation of the FEC, resulted from the reform climate in the mid-1970s. The impact of these laws is analyzed showing the impact on campaign fundraising and how until the early twenty-first century campaign finance cases, more or less, resulted in greater restrictions on fundraising. However, with the changes to the membership of the U.S. Supreme Court in the 2000s began a new trend of campaign finance analysis, which ultimately resulted in the watershed case *Citizens United v. FEC*.[4] That case, along with some other lesser-known holdings, resulted in a new reality of campaign finance that allowed for millions of dollars into the political system, for example, the rise of the super-PAC, multibillion-dollar campaigns, and the decline of the public funding was the direct result of this new legal reality.

Chapter 2 shows how campaign finance laws affected fundraising from the administrations of Theodore Roosevelt through the 2016 presidential election. The chapter shows that until the 1970s campaign finance regulations, particularly the establishment of the FEC, the process of fundraising did not have the established norms that they have today. However, during this pre-FEC era, it is clear that many of the conventions of political fundraising were being established. Moreover, in the 1960s with an increase in televised political advertising and debates, the level of sophistication of campaign fundraising increased with the campaigns of Goldwater, Humphrey, and

Nixon teaching valuable lessons to campaigns in the late twentieth and early twenty-first century.

This history of campaign fundraising also shows certain themes that have endured in American politics for over a century: big donors are equated to corruption, small donors are portrayed as giving candidates grassroots support, and, perhaps most importantly, campaigns need cash. This history of campaign fundraising also shows that from the 1970s until the late 2000s the public finance system did quiet the issues in campaign finance, but that system did not endure because candidates realized they could get competitive advantages by opting out of the system. This also demonstrates a larger political issue that campaign finance reform is supported and not supported on a bipartisan basis. Democrats and Republicans have both taken paths that allow more money in politics, and history shows that the need for cash in a campaign is bipartisan as well. At certain points in history Republicans or Democrats may have been better at raising funds (Republicans in the 1980s, Democrats in the 2010s), but both are in a race to keep up with each other's progress. In sum, being competitive as a candidate means playing by the rules but also taking advantage of all of the opportunities the rules provide.

Chapter 3 begins this book's analysis of the 2020 presidential campaign by exploring the Democratic primary from 2019 through 2020. The analysis shows that in a crowded field of Democrats, candidates needed money to keep their campaigns going through a prolonged primary season. This chapter also shows that early fundraising does not equal electoral success. Democrat candidates Bernie Sanders (D-VT) and Elizabeth Warren (D-MA) raised millions, only to be beaten by Joe Biden by March of 2020. This chapter also shows the importance political space has as candidates vying for the same voters are likely vying for the same donors. As a result, candidates have to take every opportunity to use free media to position themselves competitively for fundraising.

The Democratic primary in 2020 also showed another important aspect of Democratic fundraising. As a political issue, Democrats have made corporate contributions and super-PACs a talking point that distinguishes them from Republicans. Many candidates, particularly progressive Democrats, tie their view of the importance of the judiciary (made all the more important because of Justice Ruth Bader Ginsberg's death in September 2020) as related to campaign finance reform. Chief among these concerns is the power of the precedent of *Citizens United v. FEC*, decided in 2010 by a conservative majority on the U.S. Supreme Court.[5] However, at the same time, Democrats utilize the avenues, for example, super-PACs created by *Citizens United v. FEC*, and outraise Republicans.[6] This became an issue in the Democratic primary in 2020 and showed the fracture lines between ideological progressives and more pragmatic moderate candidates. Neither approach lends itself to an elegant solution because the progressive Democratic base dislikes and distrusts corporate contributions and super-PACs in campaigns, but competitively Democrats can outraise and outspend Republicans because of it.

Chapter 4 is related to the role of personal money in presidential elections, specifically the role of self-funding by wealthy candidates. Early in the Democratic primary there was a thought that if Michael Bloomberg, the New York–based media mogul billionaire, entered the race, Democrats would not be able to compete with his self-financed campaign. In fact, it was believed by many that his self-financing would provide him with a political advantage in that he would not be beholden to the special interests that other candidates who had to fundraise would. This would position him as a type of anti-Trump, a pragmatic New York billionaire who could appeal to both Democrats and Republicans disenchanted with the incumbent president.

However, Bloomberg found himself in the center of a political identity firestorm within the Democratic Party. The progressives and moderates were continually at odds with him during the campaign. For progressive candidates, Bloomberg became emblematic of what was wrong with politics and how money harmed the political system. Ridiculed by candidates on both sides in the party, Bloomberg's self-financing became a liability, rather than an asset. The chapter shows that despite the over $1 billion spent by Bloomberg in the primary, he was ultimately unsuccessful.[7]

Chapter 5 examines President Donald Trump's primary campaign. An incumbent president usually does not have to face a strong primary challenge, and those who do face usually end up having a difficult time in the General Election (e.g., Ford in 1976 and Carter in 1980). However, Trump's primary season saw a unique set of circumstances. His fundraising was strong, and he was able to build a war chest going into the General Election. However, Trump also faced certain political realities, including impeachment and the beginnings of the COVID-19 pandemic, which should have created a difficult time for him to raise money. However, using financial disclosures from the FEC, this chapter shows that Trump actually had a strong primary season. The chapter also examines the never-Trump movement in the Republican Party, and how it may have affected Trump going into the General Election.

Chapter 6 focuses on then candidate Joe Biden's fundraising and PAC support from the Democratic National Convention in August through the General Election. Biden's campaign fundraising also illustrates the differences between the Democratic Party position on campaign finance reform and the reality of running a modern presidential election. In his campaign platform, Biden called for a return to public funding and greater reforms to campaign finance, including an end to the massive amounts of money raised by super-PACs. In an apparent acknowledgment of the reality of a conservative majority on the U.S. Supreme Court, Biden even called for an Amendment to the U.S. Constitution that will, in effect, overturn the decision in *Citizens United v. FEC*.[8] However, Biden benefited from the tremendous amount of money raised by super-PACs on his behalf. He also established in his own campaign a highly successful fundraising approach that got him over $1 billion in donations.[9] The chapter explores Biden's campaign fundraising efforts and then compares the amounts of joint fundraising committee, the DNC, and PAC money that benefited Democrats and Biden in the General Election.

Chapter 7 examines Trump's post-convention fundraising, looking at both his campaign fundraising along with the Republican National Committee (RNC) and pro-Trump and Republican PACs. This chapter also analyzes Trump's view of campaign finance and how he has used the donations of opponents, both in the 2016 and 2020 election, as political talking points to distinguish his campaign. Trump frequently casts himself as a political outside, and part of that narrative is that his opponents are beholden to the special interests that are actively trying to keep him and the America First agenda out of power. Trump's fundraising in 2020 shows that he was not as successful as Biden or the Democrats. However, his fundraising also shows that his amount raised dramatically increased from 2016. He was about to outperform both what he and Hillary Clinton raised in 2016, and, even though he came up short compared with Biden, his campaign had a massive fundraising effort going into the General Election. Trump's campaign also demonstrates some unique issues that are emerging in both super-PACs and within the Republican Party. However, the most important takeaway from Trump's 2020 fundraising is how it will impact elections in 2022 and 2024. In the post-election fundraising, Trump indicated that he will have a politically active post-presidency, and perhaps will seek the presidency and the Republican nomination in 2024. He has already established himself through his fundraising as a figure who can help Republicans retake the House and Senate in 2022. Moreover, given that some Members of Congress supported his second impeachment and removal from office, there are groups emerging to fundraise for those members against likely primary challengers.

This book concludes in chapter 8 with some observations about campaign finance and its role within the American political system. Specifically, the chapter examines trends in campaign finance, the main takeaways about campaign fundraising in 2020, the impact of finances on the 2020 election, and the future of campaign finance as a political issue in the United States. Presidential campaign fundraising shows that as an issue campaign finance likely will continue to be a political issue that is actively talked about, especially in progressive Democratic circles. However, it is unlikely that anything substantively will change in campaign finance law in the near future. While Biden's campaign pledge included creating a constitutional amendment undoing the super-PAC reality created by *Citizens United v. FEC*, the likelihood of that happening is remote, especially given the very razor-thin Democratic majorities in the U.S. House and Senate.[10]

If things remain unchanged, campaign fundraising in the 2020s will be an escalating amount of campaign dollars, donors, and spending. The presidential elections in the United States have now reached a new norm of the multibillion-dollar campaign, and 2020 serves as a snapshot of the power and importance that fundraising plays in candidate viability. However, the analysis of 2020 also shows that money is not always everything in American politics. Candidate quality, issues, and sometimes events beyond any candidate's control can shape elections. However, what is true is that money provides access to the race itself, and as history has shown fundraising and donations are the necessary ingredients to enter the political fray—especially in America in the 2020s.

NOTES

1. Presidential Campaign Map, Federal Election Commission, accessed July 25, 2021, https://www.fec.gov/data/candidates/president/presidential-map/.

2. Buckley v. Valeo, 242 U.S. 1, 48–49 (1976).

3. Tillman Act of 1907, Pub L No 59-36, 34 Stat. 864, chap. 420 (1907).

4. Citizens United v. FEC, 558 U.S.310 (2010).

5. Ibid.

6. Ibid.

7. Michael Bloomberg, Financial Summary, Federal Election Commission, accessed July 25, 2021, https://www.fec.gov/data/candidate/P00014530/?cycle=2020&election_full=true.

8. Biden Harris, "The Biden Plan to Guarantee Government Works for the People," accessed July 25, 2021, https://joebiden.com/governmentreform/.

9. Joseph R. Biden, Jr., Financial Summary, Federal Elections Commission, accessed July 25, 2021, https://www.fec.gov/data/candidate/P80000722/?cycle=2020&election_full=true.

10. Ibid. At the time of this writing the Democratic majority exists only because Kamala Harris is Vice President, the Senate is split 50-50 between Republicans and Democrats (forty-eight Democrats and two Independents that caucus with the Democrats). The Democratic majority in the House of Representatives is 220–212 with 3 vacancies which the slimmest majority in the House since World War II. As a result, big legislative bills, especially constitutional amendments, are unlikely to pass.

Chapter 1

Money as Communication

History of Campaign Finance and Regulation

The role of money in politics is directly related to the laws that govern campaign finance. Those laws, largely developed in the twentieth century, set the standard for campaign finance today. Because of that, understanding those laws is important to understand how and why campaign finance operates the way it does. The creation of PACs, super-PACs, 527s, joint fundraising committees, contribution caps, and mandatory reporting of campaign contributions all came into existence because of campaign finance statutes or case law created by appellate courts.

However, as the following chapter will show, campaign finance law is not static. It has evolved over the past century as the issue of campaign finance has ebbed and flowed as a political issue. Born out of the concern of government graft and the pressures of civil service employees, campaign finance laws have grown into a complex system of regulations targeted at individuals, corporations, and unions. However, the purpose behind these laws has not changed. They are all rooted in the concept that regulation of campaign contributions results in more honest politicians and better government. Regardless of the law, there is a view that underlies all of the campaign finance regulations since the nineteenth century. That is, money can be a corrupting influence in politics, and politicians are potentially worse because of the temptations of fundraising.

Certain themes have also emerged over the past century in campaign finance laws that seem to be clearly established norms. First is that reporting donations and their sources is a bulwark against corrupt influences in politics. Although controversial and not absolute, campaign finance reporting is something that emerged as an issue over fifty years ago, and has, more or less, remained in place in some form (despite the existence of dark and now so-called gray money). Second, caps of campaign donations are something to level the playing field politically. However, caps do not apply across all types of campaign organizations; for example, super-PACs do not have donation caps. Third, there are attempts at work-arounds for all restrictive campaign finance laws. The creations of PACs, super-PACs, and 527s are all institutional responses to more restrictive campaign finance laws affecting individual campaigns. Fourth, campaign finance law is the result of politics, and there is a political aspect to the impetus for these changes. Born out of the concern that companies may have too much influence in politics, campaign finance laws are something that are politicized. Issues such as corporate donations, union donations, and super-PACs are absorbed into the political debates of the time.

This chapter examines campaign finance laws in the United States over the past 150 years. Specific attention is given to federal campaign finance laws, U.S. Supreme Court jurisprudence on campaign finance, the rise of the so-called super-PAC that has dominated modern politics, and an overview of current campaign finance law in the 2020s. This chapter serves not only as a foundation for understanding contemporary issues in campaign finance but also as a guide for how political parties and candidates raised money during the 2020 Election. These laws show that over the past century and a half campaign finance regulation has largely failed to control the costs of political campaigns in the United States, and, if anything they have led to the increase in expense in modern U.S. elections.

EARLY FEDERAL CAMPAIGN FINANCE LAWS

Prior to the mid-1800s, campaign finance was not strictly regulated. In part this can be attributed to the nature of early U.S. presidential elections, which did not require campaigns for the popular vote. However, that is not to say that money did not influence elections. George Washington in his quest to become a member of the Virginia House of Burgesses in 1757 gave away £39 and 6 shillings, approximately $195, worth of hard cider, punch, and wine to voters. The legislature would later ban politicians from giving away alcohol and other consumables to win the election.[1] In fact, this type of ban was in existence in the British system in the 1830s. Barrister John David Chambers compiled the election laws of England, Scotland, and Ireland in 1837, which, detailed how Members of Parliament were banned from rewarding voters with gifts in exchange for votes. The law stated that "no person hereafter to be elected . . . to make any promise, &c. to give or allow any money, meat, drink, provision, present, reward, or entertainment to any person having voice or vote in any election."[2] Of course, these laws were more about the uses of funds to entice voters rather than voter donations.

Cash in elections was important in the U.S. elections in the early nineteenth century but not as essential as today. In what could be considered the first modern presidential election, Andrew Jackson created the spoils system to reward campaign loyalists who helped him win the presidential election of 1828.[3] Abraham Lincoln paid some of his own campaign expenses in his presidential election in 1860. Taking leave from his law office to run for president, Lincoln had little personal revenue coming in. In 1859 Lincoln, through his friend Jacob Bunn, purchased *Illinois Staats-Anzeiger*, a German-speaking newspaper, for $400. After the sale, the paper promptly endorsed the Republican Party. Because of the lack of revenue for his presidential campaign, Lincoln's law partner, Stephen Logan, raised $5,000 in $500 increments from Republican Party members who later became known as the Sangamon County Finance Committee.[4] Later the committee would pay for hotels, meals, and a rally in Springfield, Illinois that totaled $12,500.[5]

By 1867, the federal government attempted its first law directly related to campaign finance with the Naval Appropriations Bill. This law banned the solicitation of Navy Yard workers for donations.[6] By 1883, the spoils system came under attack and was replaced by a civil service exam with the passage of the Pendleton Civil Service Reform Act.[7] This law ended the long-standing expectation that political contributions could be made in exchange for political appointments within the civil service of the U.S. federal government.

The environment of reform in elections was an issue during the late nineteenth century. Campaign finance during this era was intertwined with the concern over government corruption, graft, bribes, and the increased power of corporations. As the laws and political issues during the late nineteenth century demonstrate, there was a real concern that money was a corrupting influence on the political process. It was during this time that there was an exponential growth of corporations, and, as a result, corporate influence in politics. In 1875, the U.S. Supreme Court heard its first case stating that contingency contracts were not allowed in federal lobbying because of the concern that such contracts would invite fraud within the political system.[8] The concern over the role of lobbying within the government was so much a concern that the Georgia legislative banned lobbying state legislators outright, and declared the act of lobbying a crime in its state constitution in 1877.[9]

The issue of the relationship with spoils and campaign contributions continued in the 1880s and 1890s. States began passing their own campaign disclosure laws for candidates, but these laws had little effect on campaign finance disclosures.[10] New York politician Elihu Root, who would later go on to be the U.S. Secretary of State under President Theodore Roosevelt, called for campaign finance reforms in regard to corporate contribution as early as 1894.[11] In fact, it was Roosevelt, a pro-civil service and anti-spoils Republican, who was appointed to the Civil Service Commission under the administrations of Benjamin Harrison, a Republican, and Grover Cleveland, a Democrat. Roosevelt's experience on the Commission demonstrates the nexus between spoils and political campaign contributions. Under the 1883 Pendleton Act there were limits to the new Commission. The Civil Service Commission rules applied to only one-fourth of federal jobs; the other three-fourths were still governed under the spoils system.[12]

Men like Philadelphia department store magnate John Wanamaker was an obstacle to these changes. Wanamaker, who was appointed as Postmaster General by President Benjamin Harrison, was a large Republican fundraiser raising a record $200,000 for Harrison in 1888.[13] Later he continued as a huge contributor to William McKinley's campaigns in 1896 and 1900, contributing $50,000 to a fund to stop election fraud.[14] Roosevelt was generally uncomfortable with the spoils system of appointments in exchange for contributions. His time on the Civil Service Commission from 1889 until 1895 was noted for clashes over spoils, and his stance created some political backlash.[15]

Campaign finance as a political issue emerged as a major topic in U.S. politics during the 1904 presidential election. With the assassination of William McKinley in 1901, Theodore Roosevelt became president in the United States, so it was in his reelection campaign 1904 he would face his first Democratic opponent, Alton Parker, a well-financed New York judge. A New York judge on the Court of Appeals, Parker had support from insurance companies. Roosevelt's campaign was also well financed, and conflated the role of politics with his appointment of a former secretary of commerce and labor, George Cortelyou, to the role of the chairman of the RNC.[16] Backlash over the role of money in politics prompted Roosevelt to address this issue. The *New York Times* heavily criticized Roosevelt and Cortelyou, saying that trusts were "buying" the president with their campaign contributions.[17] Roosevelt addressed the issue in his message to Congress in December 1905 stating that the federal government was best equipped to address the issue of regulating corporations' role within society. He said:

> Experience has shown conclusively that it is useless to try to get any adequate regulation and supervision of these great corporations by State action. Such regulation and supervision can only be effectively exercised by a sovereign whose jurisdiction is coextensive with the field of work of the corporations—that is, by the National Government.[18]

In his address to Congress in 1907 Roosevelt again addressed the issue of corporations and political campaigns stating:

> Under our form of government voting is not merely a right but a duty, and, moreover, a fundamental and necessary duty if a man is to be a good citizen. It is

well to provide that corporations shall not contribute to Presidential or National campaigns, and furthermore to provide for the publication of both contributions and expenditures. There is, however, always danger in laws of this kind, which from their very nature are difficult of enforcement; the danger being lest they be obeyed only by the honest, and disobeyed by the unscrupulous, so as to act only as a penalty upon honest men. Moreover, no such law would hamper an unscrupulous man of unlimited means from buying his own way into office.[19]

The result of this criticism of campaign funding resulted in the Tillman Act, passed in 1907 with the sponsorship of Democratic South Carolina Senator Ben "Pitchfork" Tillman. The Act had strong Republican opposition, but ultimately passed both houses and was signed by President Roosevelt.[20] It had many restrictions on corporations, and it would not be until 1947 with the Taft-Hartley Act that it would apply equally to labor unions.[21] The Tillman Act specifically banned corporations or national banks from making contributions to any campaign, including to state representative electors of U.S. Senators (in 1907 Senators were not popularly elected). A corporation that violated the Act could be fined up to $5,000, and any corporate officer who violated the Act could be fined up to $1,000 and be imprisoned for up to a year.[22]

The Tillman Act was a change in campaign finance law, but it had serious limitations. First, it only applied to the General Election, and was only applicable to federal elections, not state. Corporate executives could donate from their personal funds without limits. Corporations could donate to state elections without limits. Primary elections were also exempt under the Tillman Act. This was particularly important in an era where Democratic Party dominated the elections in former-Confederate states to the point where the Democratic primary was tantamount to a General Election. There was no enforcement mechanism implemented under the Act, and politicians were not subject to any penalties for accepting these contributions. However, by 1911 the Federal Corrupt Practices Act (FCPA) was amended to extend the Tillman Act regulations to primary elections. The FCPA also placed caps on election expenses in the House ($5,000) and Senate ($10,000) and mandated disclosure of campaign contributions.[23]

These restrictions of the FCPA were met with opposition and challenged in court. In 1921 the U.S. Supreme Court struck down some of the provisions in the FCPA that addressed campaign spending caps. That case, *Newberry v. U.S.*, addressed the constitutionality of a Michigan state law that limited campaign contributions to U.S. Senate campaigns.[24] That state law allowed candidates to use only 25 percent of their expected federal salary for the primary and 25 percent of their expected federal salary for the General Election. This amounted to a total cap of $3,750 on a Senate campaign in 1918. However,

Truman H. Newberry, a Michigan Republican who had a strong primary challenge from automobile magnate Henry Ford, spent $175,000 on his campaign.[25] Newberry won the Republican primary and the General Election, but was indicted, along with 134 other conspirators, for violating the campaign expenditure cap imposed by Michigan law. He appealed and the U.S. Supreme Court held that such laws were unconstitutional, and his conviction was overturned. Writing for the majority, Justice James McReynolds pointed out the enumerated powers of Congress in Article I, section 4 of the U.S. Constitution did not permit any limits on campaign contributions, and that the recent 17th Amendment, which allowed direct election of U.S. Senators, did not provide power to limit campaign expenditures.[26] Newberry would continue to have issues with the Senate, and his campaign expenditures were "severely condemned" by the Senate even though the Senate voted 46 to 41, largely on party lines, that he was the duly elected Senator from Michigan.[27]

Despite the U.S. Supreme Court ruling in *Newberry v. U.S.*, campaign finance regulation continued.[28] In 1925, in the wake of President Warren Harding's Teapot Dome scandal, the FCPA was amended to require mandatory disclosure of campaign contributions over $100 and required quarterly reporting of campaign contributions.[29] Those regulations were challenged, but the U.S. Supreme Court upheld the new FCPA reporting requirements in *Burroughs v. U.S.*[30] In that case two political fundraisers, James Cannon Jr. and Ada Burroughs, were indicted for violating campaign finance law when they attempted to influence the presidential election in two states and challenged the law's constitutionality. Writing for the majority, Justice Sutherland wrote that Congress created this reporting requirement for a good reason. The decision said, "Congress reached the conclusion that public disclosure of political contributions, together with the names of contributors and other details, would tend to prevent the corrupt use of money to affect elections. The verity of this conclusion reasonably cannot be denied."[31]

Legislation in the 1930s and 1940s continued to limit campaign finance. In 1935 President Franklin Roosevelt signed the Public Utility Holding Company Act (PUHCA), which, among other things, banned public utilities from making political donations to campaigns for candidates or parties at both the federal and state levels.[32] That law was the result of what was viewed as widespread abuses by public utilities, which resulted in a Federal Trade Commission (FTC) report that detailed political pressures done on behalf of public utilities. Despite legal challenges to the PUHCA, it remained law until 2005.[33]

In 1939, the Hatch Act was passed to curtail the use of civil service employees in the political process.[34] In 1940, Congress amended the Hatch Act to include state and local government workers who were funded through federal grants.[35] During World War II several acts related to campaign finance were passed. The Smith-Connelly Act, known as the National War Labor Board Administration Act, was passed to prevent workers at wartime industries to strike.[36] Passed over President Roosevelt's veto, Smith-Connelly permitted federal seizure of industries to compel manufacturing of war materials. It also forbade union contribution to political campaigns. That provision led the CIO-PAC to create the first political action committee, which was legally distinct organization that could fundraise for candidates.[37]

The CIO-PAC was pro-Democrat and sought to repeal the restrictions on unions that were instituted by Republicans and conservative Democrats.[38] However, the 1946 midterm elections were a Republican victory, the GOP taking both houses of Congress for the first time since 1931. Within six months after the end World War II, Smith-Connelly's restrictions expired. Because of that, the union restrictions were extended through a new piece of legislation known as the Taft-Hartley Act, known officially as the Labor Management Relations Act of 1947.[39] Enacted through a veto override in the Republican-controlled Congress, the Taft-Hartley Act was born out of criticism of union strikes in the years following World War II. Taft-Hartley had multiple sections that regulated union strikes and unfair labor practices. Part of these new prohibitions included a ban on union contributions to political campaigns. Part of the rationale for this prohibition was that union dues paying members should not be made to pay dues, which then could be used to support political parties and candidates that they personally opposed. In 1936, for instance, unions contributed approximately $770,000 to the DNC.[40] Taft-Hartley gave rise to a second union PAC, the Labor's League for Political Education, which was the PAC for the American Federation of Labor.[41]

Federal regulations of elections were more established by the end of the 1940s. These regulations included both the general and primary elections.[42] Union challenges to election laws came before the U.S. Supreme Court twice. In 1947, the CIO published the *CIO-News*, which was a union newsletter that advocated for the election of Ed Garmatz in a Maryland congressional race. The CIO was indicted for violating the FCPA under the provision that unions could not become connected with federal elections. The U.S. Supreme Court held that an endorsement of candidate by the CIO was protected under the First Amendment and that FCPA could not be used to prosecute the CIO for the newsletter content.[43] However, endorsement in a union newspaper is not the same as a television ad. In 1957, the U.S. Supreme Court held that union dues being used for a television advertisement to influence the public to support specific congressional candidates would be violative of the Corrupt Practices Act.[44]

Other challenges emerged from using union dues for campaign donations. In 1961, the U.S. Supreme Court in *International Association of Machinists v. Street* held that a union using railroad employees union dues for campaign contributions was constitutional because of the union shop agreement.[45] Similarly in 1963, employees of a railroad challenged their union when union dues were used to support a political candidate over employee objections.[46] In 1977, union shop dues given to political candidates were challenged by a teacher's union, the first such case with a public sector union's challenge. Again, the U.S. Supreme Court held that union dues used for political purposes were permissible under the U.S. Constitution and did not violate the First Amendment.[47] Union contributions toward political campaigns were taken up again by the U.S. Supreme Court in 1971 when the PAC of the Pipefitters Union was indicted for violating Taft-Hartley. For over a decade, the union had set up the PAC using voluntary union dues contributions, but used regular union dues to run the PAC and employed union officers. That case was affected by the passage of the Federal Election Campaign Act (FECA) of 1971, which ultimately approved this type of structure in a union PAC.[48]

MID-CENTURY REFORMS TO
CAMPAIGN FINANCE LAWS

Campaign finance laws continued to develop during the 1960s and 1970s. In 1966, the Presidential Election Campaign Fund Act was enacted which allowed public funding for presidential elections through an income tax checkoff box.[49] This resulted in an increased pressure to have transparency in government. What occurred was a watershed moment in campaign finance reform—the creation of the FEC in 1974.

The FECA of 1971, and its subsequent amendments passed in 1974 and 1976 made major reforms to campaign finance law.[50] The new law incorporated many of the types of regulations first proposed by Theodore Roosevelt and the campaign reformers of the early 1900s. FECA's 1974 amendments mandated (1) limits on political contributions to $1,000 per individual or $5,000 by political committee while also limiting an individual's aggregate amount of donations to all candidates at $25,000; and (2) capped campaign spending by individual candidates, mandated record keeping of all individuals who made political contributions in excess of $10, established the FEC, and established for public funding in the IRS code for major political party candidates for President of the United States.[51] These regulations were challenged by several individuals and groups including New York Senator James Buckley who was a member of the New York Conservative Party, the New York Civil Liberties Union, Democrat Eugene McCarthy, and the Libertarian Party, among others. This challenge ended up in the U.S. Supreme Court in 1976, *Buckley v. Valeo*.[52] The appellants challenged the FECA laws on First and Fifth Amendment grounds. The court's opinion upheld and stuck down various aspects to the FECA law, but, on the whole, the campaign finance regulations in FECA remained. The court did find the method FEC Commissioners were appointed to be unconstitutional, and they also stuck down caps on individual expenditures of campaigns.[53]

In its per curium opinion the Court provided its rationale for why campaign finance was so regulated:

> These limitations [on campaign contributions], along with the disclosure provisions, constitute the Act's primary weapons against the reality or appearance of improper influence stemming from the dependence of candidates on large campaign contributions. The contribution ceilings thus serve the basic governmental interest in safeguarding the integrity of the electoral process without directly impinging upon the rights of individual citizens and candidates to engage in political debate and discussion.[54]

The court made a note of the connection between money and modern campaigning in a society with mass media:

> Restriction on the amount of money a person or group can spend on political communication during a campaign necessarily reduces the quantity of expression by restricting the number of issues discussed, the depth of their exploration, and the size of the audience reached. This is because virtually every means of communicating ideas in today's mass society requires the expenditure of money. The distribution of the humblest handbill or leaflet entails printing, paper, and circulation costs. Speeches and rallies generally necessitate hiring a hall and publicizing the event. The electorate's increasing dependence on television, radio, and other mass media for news and information has made these expensive modes of communication indispensable instruments of effective political speech.[55]

The U.S. Supreme Court also delineated what it believed to be express advocacy for purposes of applying federal campaign finance rules. In what is now known as the "eight magic words," the U.S. Supreme Court, in footnote 52, delineated what is express advocacy for campaign laws. They are "vote for," "elect," "support," "cast your ballot for," "Smith for Congress," "vote against," "defeat," and "reject."[56]

Going forward, the next thirty years would be a discussion of how election laws were applied to various types of political committees and groups. FECA was amended in 1979 to allow parties to raise money for parties, but those fundraising efforts were still governed under federal law. However, the way FECA was written made it apply only to federal officeholders. Candidates for state offices were not subject to FECA, and party fundraising at the state level was subject only to state law. Because of that, fundraising at the state level was able to get around FECA creating the category of "soft money," which is money that is raised under the regulation of state law and outside of FECA. Used by both Republicans and Democrats, soft money fundraising gained traction with the 1980 presidential campaign of Ronald Reagan. It allowed federal candidates to indirectly benefit from the state party fundraising.[57]

Corporate PACs also began emerging in the 1970s as a byproduct of FECA. These corporate PACs were in response to post-Watergate criticism of corporate money in finance. It is thought that these corporate PACs were merely legally establishing what had been going on for years in campaign finance.[58] PACs even became a political issue in 1984 with President Reagan accepting PAC money during his primary, while his Democratic challenger Walter Mondale refused PAC money from unions. This became a political issue for Democrats, including Bill Clinton and Barack Obama, who stated they did not want to receive PAC money for their elections.[59]

The U.S. Supreme Court heard several cases affecting campaign finance in the late 1970s starting with the *First National Bank of Boston v. Bellotti* in 1978.[60] That case involved a challenge to a Massachusetts law that banned corporate involvement in ballot initiatives unless the initiative has the impact of "materially affecting" the corporation's interests.[61] In 1976, Massachusetts had a ballot initiative to gradually raise income tax on individuals, and the First National Bank of Boston wanted to speak out against the initiative, but the Massachusetts Attorney General informed the bank that he would enforce the Massachusetts law. The U.S. Supreme Court held that this prohibition was unconstitutional. Although the law was not a federal restriction, the decision stated that a corporation's ability to speak was protected. Writing for the majority, Justice Lewis Powell defended a right of a corporation to speak on political issues:

> If the speakers here were not corporations, no one would suggest that the State could silence their proposed speech. It is the type of speech indispensable to decision making in a democracy, and this is no less true because the speech comes from a corporation rather than an individual. The inherent worth of the speech in terms of its capacity for informing the public does not depend upon the identity of its source, whether corporation, association, union, or individual.[62]

Other campaign finance issues came to the U.S. Supreme Court following the *Bellotti* decision in 1978. The U.S. Supreme Court upheld FECA solicitation requirements for PACs in 1982.[63] In 1986, the court in *FEC v. Massachusetts Citizens for Life* decided whether a 501(c)(4) nonprofit corporation would be required to make independent expenditures without using a PAC. Massachusetts Citizens for Life published pro-life campaign material encouraging voters to elect pro-life candidates in an upcoming primary election.

The U.S. Supreme Court held that FECA regulations barring this type of direct expenditure restriction were not intended to be applied to this type of political nonprofit corporation that did not receive money from for-profit corporations.[64] In 1990 the U.S. Supreme Court held that Michigan state laws that banned corporations from using money for independent expenditures were constitutional.[65] In that case, Justice Thurgood Marshall wrote for the majority that the First Amendment was not violated in placing restrictions on independent expenditures, even for nonprofit corporations.[66] It was this decision that would later become the basis for the challenge in the landmark decision *Citizens United v. FEC* in 2010.[67]

THE RISE OF CAMPAIGN REFORM AND ITS LIMITATIONS: 2000s TO PRESENT

While the 1970s through the 1990s was a time that placed restrictions on campaign finance, the 2000s were an era where restrictions were loosened. The issues centered around the amount of money in campaigns, and the role corporate dollars played in elections. There was criticism in the 1990s over the expenses in campaigns, particularly by Republican Arizona Senator John McCain, who along with Democratic Senator Russ Feingold of Wisconsin called for campaign finance reform. In an op-ed in *The Washington Post* in 1996, both Senators sounded the alarm about fundraising in campaigns and the corrupting influence that money had in campaigns where cash was more important than issues.[68] The result of this campaign finance issue resulted in the McCain-Feingold Act, which ultimately became the Bipartisan Campaign Reform Act of 2002 (BCRA).[69]

The BCRA was a major reform to campaign finance law. Its intention was to address soft money and issue advocacy advertising. It banned the national parties and candidates from accessing or fundraising non-federal money. It placed limits on the level of non-federal money state parties could use for party building. There were also new limits on campaign advertising under the "electioneering communication" section of the BCRA. Those requirements mandated identifying information of the source of the ad, which was an attempt to hold candidates accountable for election advertising. The BCRA also provided for higher contribution levels, $2000 per individual.[70]

Legal challenges to the BCRA quickly followed with the U.S. Supreme Court hearing *McConnell v. FEC* in 2003. In that case, Republican Senator Mitch McConnell from Kentucky challenged the soft money provisions in the BCRA under the First Amendment and Fifth Amendment equal protection clause.[71] What resulted from this ban of soft money was the rise of the 527, called that because it is established under Title 26 U.S.C. §527 of the

IRS code. However, it is inaccurate to say that 527s were exactly in place of soft money, because soft money was directly raised by a state party and 527s were groups unaffiliated with a political party.[72] Their rise proliferated after the BCRA and included groups across the political spectrum, but Democratic leaning groups were more prevalent in 527s.[73] However, 527s declined because of increased regulation by the FEC, which required 527s to register as PACs and provide campaign disclosures.[74]

The U.S. Supreme Court's decision in McConnell would mark the last time the court upheld campaign finance regulations. Starting in 2007 with the case *FEC v. Wisconsin Right to Life*, the court struck down many campaign finance provisions as violating speakers' constitutional rights. For instance, the court held that Wisconsin Right to Life qualified for an exemption under the BCRA for using treasury funds for advertisements.[75] A year later, the U.S. Supreme Court struck down a FECA amendment, commonly referred to as the "Millionaires Amendment," that allowed opponents of self-funded candidates triple the amount of normal limit for individuals.[76]

The change of the U.S. Supreme Court's treatment of campaign finance law coincided with new Supreme Court Justices being appointed during the Presidency of George W. Bush, Chief Justice John Roberts, confirmed in 2005, and Justice Samuel Alito, confirmed in 2006. By 2010, the U.S. Supreme Court would hear the most consequential campaign finance case since *Buckley v. Valeo—Citizens United v. FEC*.[77] The *Citizens United v. FEC* case involved a 501(c)(4) corporation, Citizens United, that made a video-on-demand about Democrat Hillary Clinton, entitled *Hillary: The Movie*, which was highly critical of her. The film was released in January 2008 during Clinton's Democratic primary campaign for president of the United States. Citizens United claimed that the BCRA section 441(b), which banned corporations or unions from using general treasury funds for independent expenditures for "electioneering communication," or speech that calls for the election or defeat of a specific candidate.[78] Writing for the majority, Justice Anthony Kennedy said the provisions of 441(b) were unconstitutional under the First Amendment and overruled the 1990 opinion of *Austin v. Michigan Chamber of Commerce*.[79] Commenting on the evolving nature of media and politics, Justice Kennedy wrote:

Our Nation's speech dynamic is changing, and informative voices should not have to circumvent onerous restrictions to exercise their First Amendment rights. Speakers have become adept at presenting citizens with sound bites, talking points, and scripted messages that dominate the 24–hour news cycle. Corporations, like individuals, do not have monolithic views. On certain topics corporations may possess valuable expertise, leaving them the best equipped to point out errors or fallacies in speech of all sorts, including the speech of candidates and elected officials. Rapid changes in technology—and the creative dynamic inherent in the concept of free expression—counsel against upholding a law that restricts political speech in certain media or by certain speakers.[80]

The impact of the *Citizens United v. FEC* decision, and a D.C. Circuit Court of Appeals case *SpeechNow.org v. FEC*, laid the foundation for the creation of the super-PAC, or independent expenditure committees that can take unlimited donations from individuals, corporations, and unions.[81] *Speechnow .org v. FEC* involved a 527 organization that challenged the FECA restriction on individual contribution caps of $5,000 to PACs. In light of *Citizens United v. FEC* decision, the U.S. Court of Appeals for the District of Columbia Circuit struck down the provision.[82] This permitted the raising of large sums of money, which led to the increase in costs for elections. Donors also were no longer limited in the amounts they could donate in aggregate under FECA after the U.S. Supreme Court's decision in *McCutcheon v. FEC* in 2014.[83] Writing for the majority, Chief Justice Roberts held that caps on aggregate limits on campaign finance donations to individual candidates, parties, and PACs violated the First Amendment[84] The aggregate limits under FECA at the time of the case were $48,600 to federal candidates and $74,600 to other political committees for a total cap of $123,200.[85] Chief Justice Roberts wrote:

It is no answer to say that the individual can simply contribute less money to more people. To require one person to contribute at lower levels than others because he wants to support more candidates or causes is to impose a special burden on broader participation in the democratic process. And as we have recently admonished, the Government may not penalize an individual for "robustly exercis[ing]" his First Amendment rights.[86]

During the same time as campaign finance laws were challenged, the public financing of elections was also diminishing. The presidential election in 2008 saw the advantage of opting out of public financing. Barack Obama opted out of public financing during the General Election allowing him to raise millions of dollars. By 2012, both President Obama and his Republican challenger Mitt Romney opted out of public financing. The U.S. Supreme Court dealt a blow to state public funding in 2011, striking down an Arizona law that gave increased public funding to candidates facing wealthy self-financed challengers.[87] Public funding for party conventions ultimately ended in 2014, ending a public funding program for party conventions that had been in place since 1976.[88]

CONCLUSION

What the legal history of campaign finance shows is that money in campaigns has long been thought to be a problem, but few workable solutions are available. Statutory attempts to regulate campaign finance have largely been challenged, especially in the twenty-first century, under First Amendment grounds. However, the challenge of money in politics is that political speech is tied to the ability to spend money, especially in an era with mass media. It is easy to think of money in politics as a tainted system that is set up only to provide access for the privileged few. Of course, that was the real concern in the late nineteenth century when the rules of donation were less codified. However, the changes to campaign finance have taken a new form now that there are individual groups speaking about a specific issue, such as abortion, that have the ability to create their own content and pay for their own media messages.

However, the bigger legal issue for campaign finance is the perception of the darkness of campaign contributions. Mandatory reporting for campaign expenditures provides the type of transparency needed to make the public feel better about how money is influencing elections. However, this issue has never been fully satisfied by the law. The narrative of campaign finance is one that is a push and pull between reform and free speech, and rules and caveats. The regulation of campaigns only seems to create new entities and new strategies for raising and spending money. The concern over union and corporate influence over elections dates back to the early twentieth century, but again the reality of campaign finance in 2020 is much the same as it was in 1910. Corporate and union contributions during elections are large, and statutory attempts to curtail this influence have largely given way to new campaign finance structures and organizations that operate as work-arounds to federal law. The net result of more than a century of attempts of regulating campaign finance is that elections, especially at the presidential level, are increasingly expensive. The 2020 presidential election would prove that being the most expensive in U.S. history.

NOTES

1. Jaime Fuller, From George Washington to Shaun McCutcheon: A Brief History of Campaign Finance Reform, *Washington Post*, April 2, 2014. https ://www.washingtonpost.com/news/the-fix/wp/2014/04/03/a-history-of-campaign-finance-reform-from-george-washington-to-shaun-mccutcheon/; https://www.aarp .org/politics-society/government-elections/info-04-2012/campaign-cash-key-issues .html.

2. John Chambers, *A Complete Dictionary of The Law and Practice of Elections of Members of Parliament and of Election Petitions and Committees for England, Scotland, and Ireland* (London: Saunders and Benning, Law Booksellers, 1837), 514–515, http://books.google.com.

3. "Did You Know . . . Samuel Swartwout Skimmed Staggering Sums?," U.S. Customs and Border Protection, December 20, 2019, https://www.cbp.gov/about/hist ory/did-you-know/samuel-swartwout. This spoils system led to abuse of office by some government officials. Scandals such as that of Samuel Swartwout, a New York Customs collector under President Jackson. Swartwout caused a scandal when he used his position to embezzle more than $1.2 million in customs payments and fled to London. The spoils system would legislatively end in 1883 with the passage of Pendleton Civil Service Reform Act, which replaced spoils with a competitive exam for government positions and established the U.S. Civil Service Commission. That commission was later replaced in 1978 with the Office of Personnel Management and Merit Promotions Board.

4. Henry Pratt, *Personal Finances of Abraham Lincoln* (Chicago: Lakeside Press, 1943), 110. https://quod.lib.umich.edu/l/lincoln2/5250244.0001.001/1:17.2?rgn=div2 ;view=fulltext.

5. Ibid, 112. It is interesting to note that Lincoln's own contributions to Republicans and Whigs sometime took the form of legal representation.

6. "The Federal Election Campaign Laws: A Short History," Federal Election Commission, accessed January 31, 2021, https://transition.fec.gov/info/appfour.htm.

7. Pendleton Civil Service Reform Act, 22 Stat. 403 (1883).

8. Trist v. Child, 88. U.S. 441 (1875).

9. Ga. Const. art. I, §2, pt V.

10. U.S. v. UAW-CIO, 352 U.S. 567, 570–571 (1957). This history of campaign finance was written by U.S. Supreme Court Justice Felix Frankfurter.

11. Ibid.

12. Richard White, "The Bullmoose and the Bear: Theodore Roosevelt and John Wannamaker Struggled Over the Spoils," *Pennsylvania History: A Journal of Mid-Atlantic Studies* 71 (2004): 1–24, 4.

13. Ibid., 8; "John Wanamaker Portrait," Smithsonian National Portrait Museum, https://postalmuseum.si.edu/collections/object-spotlight/john-wanamaker-portrait.

14. White, "The Bullmoose and the Bear," 19.

15. Ibid.

16. Robert Sitkoff, "Political Speech, Political Extortion, and the Competition for Corporate Charters," *The University of Chicago Law Review* 69 (2002): 1103–1166.

17. "Buying the President," *New York Times*, October 1, 1904, 8.

18. Theodore Roosevelt, Fifth Annual Message, December 5, 1905, The Miller Center, University of Virginia, accessed January 15, 2021, https://millercenter.org/ the-presidency/presidential-speeches/december-5-1905-fifth-annual-message.

19. Theodore Roosevelt, "Seventh Annual Message," December 3, 1907, The Miller Center, University of Virginia, accessed January 15, 2021, https://millerc enter.org/the-presidency/presidential-speeches/december-3-1907-seventh-annual-me ssage.

20. Sitkoff, "Political Speech, Political Extortion, and the Competition for Corporate Charters,"1130. Senator William Chandler, a New Hampshire Republican had tried to pass campaign finance law as early as 1901 with no success.

21. Ibid., Labor Management Relations Act of 1947 ("Taft-Hartley Act"), Pub L No 100, 61 Stat. 136, 159, codified at 29 USC §§ 151–166 (1947).

22. Tillman Act of 1907, Pub L No 59-36, 34 Stat. 864, chap. 420 (1907).

23. Federal Corrupt Practices Act, Pub L No 61-274, 36 Stat. 822, codified at 2 USC §§241–248 (1910).

24. Newberry v. U.S., 256 U.S. 232 (1921).

25. U.S. Senate Historical Office, *United States Senate Election, Expulsion and Censure Cases: 1793–1990* (Washington: Government Printing Office, 1995), 302–305, accessed https://www.senate.gov/about/powers-procedures/expulsion /102TrumanNewberry_expulsion.htm. Newberry would go on to resign his Senate seat on November 18, 1922, rather than to face another well-funded challenge from Ford.

26. Newberry v. U.S., 256 U.S. 232 (1921).

27. U.S. Senate Historical Office, United States Senate Election, Expulsion and Censure Cases, 302–305.

28. Ibid.

29. Federal Corrupt Practices Act of 1925, 43 Stat. 1053, codified in 2 U.S.C. §241 (1925). Teapot Dome scandal was a major event that tarnished Harding's presidency. Albert Bacon Fall, the Secretary of the Interior, leased naval petroleum reserves to private companies resulting in Fall's conviction for bribery in 1929.

30. Burroughs v. U.S., 290 U.S. 534 (1934).

31. Ibid., 548.

32. Public Utility Holding Act of 1935, Pub L No 74-333, codified in 15 UCC §79 (1935).

33. The PUHCA was repealed by the Energy Policy Act of 2005, Pub L No 109-58, 119 Stat. 594, codified in 42 U.S.C. §1501 et seq., 16 USC §2601 et seq., 42 USC §13201 et seq.

34. The Hatch Act of 1939, Pub L 76-252, 53 Stat. 1147, codified in 5 USC §§7321–7326 (1939).

35. Shannon Azzaro, "The Hatch Act Modernization Act: Putting the Government Back in Politics," *Fordham Urban Law Journal* 42 (2016): 781–839, 783.

36. National War Labor Relations Act, 57 Stat. 163, codified in 50 USC §1501 et seq. (1943).

37. Political action committees today are officially organized under federal statute 26 USC §527, which was created in 1975.

38. Robert Mutch, *Campaign Finance: What Everyone Needs to Know* (New York: Oxford University Press, 2016), 61–62. Mutch details the rise of the CIO and its political activities in the 1936 presidential election of Franklin Roosevelt. The CIO was formed when several unions broke from the AFL to become actively involved in the campaign for Roosevelt.

39. Labor Management Relations Act of 1947, Pub L No 80-101, 61 Stat. 136, codified in 29 USC §§ 141–197 (1947). Part of the reason Taft-Hartley was able to be

passed is that the U.S. House and Senate had Republican majorities for the first time since 1931.

40. Joseph Kallenbach, "The Taft-Hartley Act and Union Political Contributions and Expenditures," *Minnesota Law Review* 33 (1948): 1–27, 2. Kallenback cited a 1937 Senate report. Sen Rep. No. 151, 75th Cong., 1st Sess. 127–133 (1937). He noted that this Senate Special Committee, chaired by Democratic Senator Lonergan of Connecticut, called for an expansion of the FCPA of 1925 to include a provision banning union involvement in election campaign contributions. That request was not taken up by Congress at that time.

41. Mutch, *Campaign Finance*, 62–63. The AFL had largely been out of politics since the death of Samuel Gompers in 1924. These campaign restrictions on unions were the result of initiatives by Republicans and conservative southern Democrats.

42. The U.S. Supreme Court held that primary elections could be regulated under federal law in 1944. Smith v. Allwright, 321 U.S. 649 (1944). That case involved a larger discussion about racial discrimination and voting surrounding all white primaries.

43. U.S. v. Congress of Industrial Organizations, 335 U.S. 106 (1948).

44. U.S. v. UAW-CIO, 352 U.S. 567 (1957).

45. International Association of Machinists v. Street, 367 U.S. 740 (1961).

46. Railway Clerks v. Allen, 373 U.S. 113 (1963).

47. Abood v. Detroit Board of Education, 431 U.S. 209 (1977). This precedent was challenged again in 2016 in the case Freidrichs v., California Teachers Association, 578 U.S. ___(2016). The court affirmed the decision by the U.S. Court of Appeals for the 9th Circuit in a split 4-4 decision. There were nine justices at the time because of a vacancy caused by the death of Justice Antonin Scalia.

48. Pipefitters Local Union No. 562 v. U.S., 407 U.S. 385 (1972). The PAC had used this practice from 1949 through 1962.

49. Presidential Election Campaign Fund Act of 1966, 80 Stat 1553, Pub. L. 89-809 (1966). This checkoff has dramatically decreased in participants since the 1970s. Jaime Fuller, "From George Washington to Shaun McCutcheon: A Brief-ish History of Campaign Finance Reform," *Washington Post*, April 3, 2014, https:// www.washingtonpost.com/news/the-fix/wp/2014/04/03/a-history-of-campaign-finan ce-reform-from-george-washington-to-shaun-mccutcheon/. Although laws existed mandating disclosure of campaign contributions in 1925, it was not until 1967 that Pat Jennings, the Clerk of the House of Representatives, actually collected campaign finance reports.

50. Federal Election Campaign Act of 1971, Pub L 92-225 (1971); Federal Election Campaign Act Amendments of 1974, Pub L 93-443 (1974); Federal Election Campaign Act Amendments of 1976, Pub L 94-283 (1976).

51. Buckley v. Valeo, 424 U.S 1, 7 (1976).

52. Ibid.

53. Ibid., 50, 127–128.

54. Ibid., 58. A per curiam opinion is one issued in the name of the court rather than by a specific Justice or group of Justices.

55. Ibid., 19.

56. Ibid., 44, n. 52.

57. Robert Mutch, *Campaign Finance: What Everyone Needs to Know* (New York: Oxford University Press, 2016), 103–105.

58. Ibid., 64.

59. Ibid., 66. Mutch notes that declining PAC contributions is not the same as declining contributions from executives who fund PACs. Those contributions from individuals associated with PACs was accepted by some candidates.

60. First National Bank of Boston v. Bellotti, 435 U.S. 765 (1978).

61. Mass. Gen. Laws Ann. ch 5 § 8 (West Supp. 1977). This law went further stating that initiatives that materially affected corporations did not occur when the initiative was about taxation.

62. First National Bank of Boston v. Bellotti, 777.

63. FEC v. National Right to Work Committee, 459 U.S. 197 (1982).

64. FEC v. Massachusetts Citizens for Life, 479 U.S. 238 (1986).

65. Austin v. Michigan Chamber of Commerce, 494 U.S. 652 (1990).

66. Ibid. The nonprofit corporation in Austin differed from that in Massachusetts Citizens for Life. In Austin the Michigan Chamber of Commerce had many members that were for-profit corporations, and the purpose of the Chamber was not exclusively political.

67. Citizens United v. FEC, 558 U.S. 310 (2010).

68. John McCain and Russ Feingold, "A Better Way to Fix Campaign Financing," Washington Post, February 20, 1996, https://www.washingtonpost.com/opinions/a-better-way-to-fix-campaign-financing/2018/08/26/b45ede68-a935-11e8-a8d7-0f63ab8b1370_story.html.

69. Bipartisan Campaign Reform Act of 2002, 116 Stat 81, Pub L 107-155 (2002). McCain-Feingold was a popular name for this legislation; however, it was the House version, the Shays-Meehan Act, of the bill that ultimately became law.

70. Ibid.

71. McConnell v. FEC, 540 U.S. 93 (2003).

72. Mutch, *Campaign Finance*, 111.

73. Ibid. Mutch notes that part of the reason for 527s being more tied to Democrats is the Democratic Party's reliance on soft money. When that became more restricted under the BCRA the Democrats used 527s at a higher rate.

74. Ibid.

75. FEC v. Wisconsin Right to Life, 551 U.S. 449 (2007).

76. Davis v. FEC, 554 U.S. 724 (2008). The "Millionaire's Amendment" was used to deter self-financed candidates that had a large net worth from using their wealth to fund an election. The amount that triggered self-funding status was $350,000. Bipartisan Campaign Reform Act of 2002, 2 USC §441(a)-1(a) (2002). The candidate in this case was millionaire Jack Davis who ran in the New York 26th District as a Democrat and then later as an independent.

77. Citizens United v. FEC, 558 U.S. 310 (2010).

78. Ibid.

79. Ibid., 365.

80. Ibid., 364.

81. Speechnow.org v. FEC, 599 F.3d 686 (DC Cir. 2010). This case involved a 527 organization that challenged the FECA restriction on individual contribution caps of $5,000 to PACs. In light of Citizens United v. FEC decision, the U.S. Court of Appeals for the District of Columbia Circuit struck down the provision.

82. Ibid.

83. McCutcheon v. FEC, 572 U.S. 185 (2014).

84. Ibid., 193–194.

85. Ibid., 194. Of the $74,600 capped on political committees, only $48,600 could go to state or local committees.

86. Ibid., 204–205.

87. Arizona Free Enterprise Club's Freedom Club PAC v. Bennett, 564 U.S. 721 (2011).

88. Gabriella Miller Kids First Research Act, 128 Stat. 1086, Pub L 113-94, codified in 26 USC §9008 (2014). This law also established the transfer of any funds raised for party conventions to the 10-Year Pediatric Research Initiative Fund.

Chapter 2

Politicization of Campaign Fundraising

*An Overview of Presidential Fundraising
as a Political Issue from Theodore
Roosevelt to Donald Trump*

Campaign finance as a political issue has had a long history in the United States. Starting in the early twentieth century, campaign cash and its effects on access to politicians have been a mainstay of American discourse. However, amid the legal reforms to campaign contributions, there is the political issue of campaign finance. While the jurisprudence of the U.S. Supreme Court follows a certain logic under the First Amendment, the campaign communication of campaign finance uses the a political rhetoric that argues donations corrupt politicians and provides unfair access for wealthy individuals, corporations, or unions.

The politicization of campaign finance is usually couched in terms of criticism of opponents. Since the twentieth century, the donations received by candidates have been fodder for political attacks. Certain names are used in attack advertising and debates that symbolize the money in politics, for example, unions, big corporations, and large donors such as George Soros and the Koch brothers.[1] In modern political discourse there is the emergence of the issue of not only how much a candidate raises but where their money actually comes from. This has particularly become an issue in the Democratic Party where progressive candidates eschew donations from corporations, and routinely criticize the laws and court decisions, namely the 2010 U.S. Supreme Court case *Citizens United v. FEC*, that provide the legal mechanisms for these corporate donations. The rise of the so-called small donor, which has been part of presidential politics since the 1920s, has been a political talking point, especially for progressive candidates. The use of the small donor is used as an indicator that the candidate has a large groundswell of grassroots support. Candidates turn these small donations into talking points about how opponents with large donors are subject to the interests and control of big business and wealthy donors. However, fundraising is the lifeblood of political campaigns, and it has been that way for some time in American politics. It is essential to keep a campaign afloat, and the lack of campaign contributions means that a campaign likely will not continue.

This chapter looks at campaign finance as a political issue from Theodore Roosevelt's 1904 reelection through the 2016 election of Donald Trump. Specifically, this chapter looks at the politics behind fundraising at the presidential level, and how different campaigns handled fundraising and the changing political landscape the required ever more cash. The chapter examines this in three eras, Theodore Roosevelt through World War II; Truman's 1948 campaign through Nixon's Watergate scandal, and Post-Watergate reform through the rise of Donald Trump. This shows that an increased politicization of campaign finance was frequently coupled with a greater strategic awareness of its importance. Fundraising techniques in presidential campaigns became increasingly sophisticated, and by the time campaign finance reform gained political traction in the 1970s the public finance model of campaign finance led to a long-term stabilization of campaign finance issues. However, the growth of technology in the twenty-first century coupled with the limitations that came with public funding ultimately led to a resurgence of campaign finance as a political issue. With candidates opting out of public financing, innovations in the field of campaign finance flourished, especially with the growth of the internet. Technology coupled with U.S. Supreme Court decisions including *Citizens United v. FEC* and *McCutcheon v. FEC*, created new norms for campaign finance in the 2010s and into the 2020 election.[2] Each section shows that the issue of campaign finance revolves around various political issues such as the role of small donors, pay for play returns, issues of campaign transparency, and how political campaigns' fundraising provides momentum to victory.

CAMPAIGN REFORM AND CAMPAIGN EXCESS: PRESIDENTIAL FUNDRAISING FROM THEODORE ROOSEVELT THROUGH FRANKLIN ROOSEVELT

At beginning of the twentieth century political fundraising became an actual political issue with the increased role of corporate donations. Much like the political fundraising today, political fundraising from the 1900s through World War II was highly debated. Looking at political fundraising in the first thirty years of the twentieth century there are a series of themes that emerge that were prescient of the issues facing political fundraising today: the role of corporate donations, the role of wealthy donors, and the actual impact money has on politics. Looking at the presidential elections in this era it is clear that laws were trying to catch up, with limited success, with the perceived excesses of money in politics.

Theodore Roosevelt is the first politician to make a national political issue out of campaign finance reform. His 1904 reelection had mixed campaign finance success. It was reported in 1905 that the Republican National Committee had only $1.9 million, which was not much compared with the $4.1 million Grover Cleveland had in 1892.[3] The Republican presidential 1904 campaign, had large expenditures with *The Washington Post* reporting that of the $1.9 million raised by the Republic National Committee, $700,000 went to state committees, $550,000 went to campaign literature, $175,000 to a speaker's bureau, and $150,000 to lithographs and advertising, and $150,000 for staff salaries.[4] However, this election had criticism because of the donations made to Roosevelt, and the progressive campaign finance reforms that were developing at the state level, notably in New York, and in Congress by South Carolina Senator "Pitchfork" Ben Tillman.[5] Roosevelt's fundraising was contradictory to his later push for reform. Because of that, by 1905 Roosevelt was asking Congress for campaign finance reform, making campaign finance a major issue. In his address to Congress in 1905 he said:

In political campaigns in a country as large and populous as ours it is inevitable that there should be much expense of an entirely legitimate kind. This, of course, means that many contributions, and some of them of large size, must be made, and, as a matter of fact, in any big political contest such contributions are always made to both sides. It is entirely proper both to give and receive them, unless there is an improper motive connected with either gift or reception. If they are extorted by any kind of pressure or promise, express or implied, direct or indirect, in the way of favor or immunity, then the giving or receiving becomes not only improper but criminal. It will undoubtedly be difficult, as a matter of practical detail, to shape an act which shall guard with reasonable certainty against such misconduct; but if it is possible to secure by law the full and verified publication in detail of all the sums contributed to and expended by the candidates or committees of any political parties, the result cannot but be wholesome. All contributions by corporations to any political committee or for any political purpose should be forbidden by law; directors should not be permitted to use stockholders' money for such purposes; and, moreover, a prohibition of this kind would be, as far as it went, an effective method of stopping the evils aimed at in corrupt practices acts.[6]

Later Roosevelt's criticism of corporate influence in campaigns continued. In December 3, 1906, President Theodore Roosevelt in an address to Congress said, "Let individuals contribute as they desire; but let us prohibit in effective fashion all corporations from making contributions for any political purpose, directly or indirectly."[7] His advocacy for campaign finance reform continued during his administration, although Roosevelt knew of the technical and logistical difficulties in implementing such a plan. In his 1907 address to Congress he said:

It is well to provide that corporations shall not contribute to Presidential or National campaigns, and furthermore to provide for the publication of both contributions and expenditures. There is, however, always danger in laws of this kind, which from their very nature are difficult of enforcement; the danger being lest they be obeyed only by the honest, and disobeyed by the unscrupulous, so as to act only as a penalty upon honest men. Moreover, no such law would hamper an unscrupulous man of unlimited means from buying his own way into office. There is a very radical measure which would, I believe, work a substantial improvement in our system of conducting a campaign, although I am well aware that it will take some time for people so to familiarize themselves with such a proposal as to be willing to consider its adoption.[8]

By 1912 during his third race for president as a Bull Moose candidate, Roosevelt's use of Wall Street donations was known, with the *San Francisco Call* reporting that a $ 2.2 million fund existed in which corporations made up 73 percent of the donors.[9] Woodrow Wilson's 1912 presidential campaign also made an issue from campaign finance. In August 1912, Wilson's publicity director, Josephus Daniels, made a commitment to publish every donor who gave $1 and up to the campaign.[10] However, Wilson's contributions presented some issues. In 1916 Wilson came under attack by Republicans that large campaign donors received special appointments by Wilson. They included Charles Crane ($15,000), the secretary to the secretary of state, Francis Harrison ($7,000), the governor of the Philippines, James Gerard ($5,000) the ambassador to Germany, and David Francis ($5,000), the ambassador to Russia.[11] Republicans took advantage of this information using it in a formal statement by the Western Republican spokesman.[12]

An emerging theme in money in politics is the concern over political corruption that comes with political donors. One of biggest campaign finance issues in the early twentieth century was Warren G. Harding, whose presidency would become embroiled by the Teapot Dome scandal from 1921 until 1923. Harding, however, ran a very low-key front porch campaign in 1920, similar to that of another Ohioan candidate, William McKinley, in 1896.[13] Newspaper accounts of his early campaign showed Harding happy with small donations, with one account saying that he was "delighted" with a $5 campaign contribution from an eleven-year-old boy.[14] Harding also used the campaign finance reform rhetoric as Roosevelt did in 1905. At the time this was thought to be problematic for the Republicans who had a long-standing association with Wall Street contributors, he wanted to use reform rhetoric to appear to be more aligned with regular voters.[15] Harding's election would ultimately cost Republicans over $3.4 million according to Fred Upham, the Republican Party treasurer (Democrats spent $878,831 for James Cox).[16] Once in office, Harding's presidency would be damaged by the Teapot Dome scandal, in which Secretary of the Interior Albert Ball leased oil reserves to private companies in exchange for bribes (Ball later became the first Cabinet member to go to prison). In the Teapot Dome Inquiry Committee, Jake Hamon, an Oklahoma oil tycoon admitted that he paid for $18,700 hotel bill for Harding in 1920 during the Republican Convention and also paid for $25,000 worth of miscellaneous items the Harding boosters bought on credit. All told Hamon spent $525,000 during the 1920 Harding campaign, in which $400,000 went for carrying Oklahoma for Harding.[17]

However, fallout from the scandal resulted in an increased interest in contributions to campaigns, a theme that would stay in presidential politics for decades. Congress would pass the Federal Corrupt Practices Act in 1925, and issues surrounding campaign finance became a larger political issue.[18] In 1924, Senator Kenneth McKellar (D-TN) published an op ed in the *New York Times* stating that campaign contributions were an "evil," which needed to be "eliminated if we are to have honest government."[19] He wrote, "The system is bad. It is fraught with evil for this republic. A large contributor to a campaign fund expects to receive attention and consideration after the election is over."[20] By the late 1920s, campaign finance as a political issue focused on cleaning up politics. In 1927 Senator William Borah (R-ID) was calling for the nationalization of elections and treating parties as "quasi-governmental institutions" so that political contributions could not be a corrupting influence on politics.[21]

As with any political scandal, especially in terms of political financing, the law attempted to respond to the excess of political fundraising. By the time Herbert Hoover ran for president in 1928, there was an established law on campaign contributions disclosures, but in October 1928 Hoover still enjoyed large cash donations from California and large donations from wealthy businessmen.[22] Hoover, however, ran a very low-profile campaign, using seven radio speeches to communicate with voters. He also benefited from a controversial opponent Democrat Al Smith from New York, whose Catholicism was a political liability in traditionally Democratic voting states in the South.[23] Smith's campaign would end in a deficit, and in 1930 Democratic National Committee Chair, John Raskob, held a New York fundraiser to pay off $1 million in Smith campaign debts. The strategy was to raise $1.5 million so the DNC could have $500,000 going into the 1932 election, and then raise an additional $4.5 million for the presidential race. Part of the strategy was to have 12-15 men contribute $50,000 to create a base for the funds.[24]

By the time Franklin Roosevelt ran for president in 1932, the radio would become an important part of campaigning, and his campaign used radio to raise donations. Roosevelt was the first president to make direct national appeal for campaign donations after receiving the Democratic nomination.[25] Roosevelt needed $1.5 million, which was 25 percent of what Smith had in 1928, to run his campaign. Campaign strategists thought he would only reach $1.2 million at best. In his speech, Roosevelt detailed the travel costs of presidential campaigning, and noted that unlike Republicans, Democrats had no preferential donora to generate money and that he believed small contributions combined were more impactful than large donations[26] He also criticized what he saw as waste in campaigns and vowed that his use of campaign contributions would be spent more reasonably.[27]

Roosevelt would do well in campaign fundraising in 1936, with the *Chicago Daily Tribune* stating that Roosevelt was making use of direct mail, dances, Jackson dinners, and political rallies. By August 1936 he had raised $1 million and was expected to raise another $1.5 million using these campaign techniques.[28] Roosevelt would benefit from campaign contributions during his subsequent three elections for president. However, he would be criticized for large contributions from unions including the United Mine Workers who gave Roosevelt $500,000 for his 1936 presidential campaign.[29] The Hatch Act of 1939, which banned both public service employees from fundraising for political candidates and the use of spoils in exchange for political support among civil servants, changed the political landscape in the United States.[30] Its passage was said to harm the fundraising of both Republicans and Democrats, with the U.S. Senate investigating whether campaign donation advertisements for Republican nominee for President Wendell Willkie in 1940 violated the law.[31]

By the 1940s, there was greater attention paid to campaign finance. The press covered high-profile donors, such as Eugene DuPont, Jr., Franklin Delano Roosevelt Jr.'s father-in-law's, contribution to the Republican nominee Willkie in 1940.[32] However, the Smith-Connally Act created the new phenomenon of the PAC. What resulted was the CIO's National Political Action Committee that sought $3 million in donations from nonlabor contributors across the United States in 1944.[33] That same year League of Women Voters sought to raise $50,000 for a get-out-the-vote drive in New York City.[34]

The first half of the twentieth century saw many of the same themes that would emerge later on in campaign finance reform. However, two themes remained dominant, even in the 2020s. First is while large donations are necessary to fund a presidential campaign those donations are a political liability.

Tying a campaign to big business and big donors has an effect of portraying a candidate as being controlled by those interests. Second is that organizations want to be part of the campaign fundraising efforts. The fight for those rights would continue well into the 2000s.

GROWING COSTS IN PRESIDENTIAL CAMPAIGNS: CAMPAIGN FUNDRAISING FROM TRUMAN TO NIXON

In post–World War II America, campaign finance reform was focused on the role of reining in the power of unions and donations by civil servants. However, the 1950s and 1960s saw the emergence of new communication technology, namely television, which created new opportunities for fundraising and more expenses for national campaigns. What this era in campaign fundraising history shows is how fundraising and technology are inextricably intertwined and how as communication technology, especially television advertising, grew, presidential candidates needed more money to be competitive. This trend continues today with the growth of internet and social media both being a source of paid advertisement and political fundraising sources.

By the 1948 election, the importance of campaign donations was no longer something that had to be explained to the public, like Roosevelt did in 1932. Harry Truman's first $1,000 donation was profiled in the *Atlanta Daily World*, an African-American newspaper based in Atlanta.[35] The donation came from Sherman Hibbitt, the unofficial Mayor of Harlem. Coverage of this donation focused on the small donor aspect of Truman's campaign. A woman being evicted from her Chicago apartment, Emma B. Johnson, was reported as giving $5 to the president.[36] Despite these donations, Truman did not enjoy robust fundraising in 1948, because of lack of voter enthusiasm. Democratic donors Joseph Kennedy and Bernard Baruch did not contribute anything to Truman in 1948 because they saw his defeat as inevitable and they did not want to waste their money.[37] In addition, Truman's civil rights stances, particularly his integration of the military resulted in some fundraising problems with southern donors.[38] The Georgia Democratic Party even said that it was considering not donating to Truman's campaign in 1948 over his civil rights stances.[39] Still allegations of Hatch Act violations continued with Republicans accusing Democrats of coercing civil servants to donate to Truman in 1948.[40] Campaign contribution reporting also became a political issue for Republicans with the *Wall Street Journal* noting that Republicans were reporting contributions of $1 to illustrate that they were not just recipients of large corporate donations, but also received small donations from individual donors.[41]

This coverage shows that organized fundraising was developed going into the 1950s. Eisenhower had a strong fundraising system with one Illinois group limiting individual contributions to Eisenhower to $3,000 per person. Eisenhower's Republican challenger Robert Taft had similar groups, one known as Bob Taft Clubs that had a $1 contribution limit.[42] The moderate and conservative wings of the Republican Party united with Taft endorsing Eisenhower after first-round voting at the Republican National Convention. However, it was Eisenhower's running mate Richard Nixon who caused the biggest campaign issue in 1952.[43]

Nixon received campaign contributions of $18,000, known as the Fund, during the early 1950s, which paid for various political activities after he won his Senate seat in 1950. The press covered this issue in the latter months of the 1952 election, and speculation grew that Nixon would be dropped from the Republican ticket. Nixon, in response, gave his famous Checkers speech, unrehearsed on a yellow legal pad to a 60-million-person television audience, the largest at that time.[44] In the speech, which ultimately saved Nixon's career, he noted how his personal finances were quite meager as a career politician. Nixon used the speech to turn the argument toward the Democratic National Committee Chairman, Stephen Mitchell, saying that Mitchell was insisting only the rich could run for national office. He concluded with a story about a gift of a cocker spaniel that his daughter named Checkers, and concluded with criticisms of the Democratic nominee Adai Stephenson.[45] Eisenhower watched the speech delaying his own speech in Cleveland that night. After watching the speech, Eisenhower's former opponent Taft said he thought Nixon would stay on the ticket, which he did ultimately becoming vice president for two terms.[46]

John F. Kennedy was a highly successful campaign fundraiser, but that ability had brought him criticism. He had been involved in a contentious Senate reelection in 1958 in which his opponent Vincent Celeste accused him of "immoral financial steam rolling tactics" (Kennedy denied the allegations and won handily).[47] In his presidential campaign in 1960, Kennedy received the AFL-CIO's endorsement, and the union called on its members to back Kennedy in the election and asked them to contribute to his campaign.[48] The 1960 presidential election was expensive with the campaigns costing $20 million, and both parties ending the campaign in debt (Republicans $700,000 and Democrats $3.82 million).[49] However, Kennedy continued fundraising after his election. From 1961 through 1962 Kennedy attended twenty-one fundraising dinners, including two $1,000 per plate dinners and one $1,000 per person cocktail event.[50] Republicans also racked in money during this time from dinners making $7.7 million during the same timeframe. Kennedy set up the Bipartisan Commission on Campaign Costs in 1961, which was headed by Alexander Heard, the chancellor of Vanderbilt University.[51] Heard noted that despite the call for small campaign donations, two-thirds of all campaign donations were $500 or more, which made large donors essential for campaign success. At the suggestion from the Commission, Kennedy supported tax incentives for campaign contributions. In 1962 Kennedy supported a tax credit for small- and medium-sized donors of $10 to $20, and a larger $750 tax credit for large donors.[52]

By the mid-1960s, campaign fundraising was entering into a new phase of sophistication with the growth of television advertising. Alexander Heard estimated that in 1964 the election costs were around $200 million in the United States and that television advertising was a major cost associated with campaigns.[53] According to Heard, fundraising changed in 1964 with Republicans looking more to aggregate small donors, and Democrats looking to large donors to fill campaign coffers. Democrats began using President's Clubs, whose membership required a $1,000 donation.[54] Part of the reason for this change in campaign strategy was that more liberal, so-called Rockefeller Republicans, did not support Republican Barry Goldwater. Many of these Republicans came from the business community, which constituted wealthy donors. Goldwater turned to new strategies in raising donations that included direct mail and televised appeals. While Goldwater was an innovator in generating donations, his lack of campaign coordination was a massive problem. This mainly reflected Goldwater's fiscal decisions and attitude toward debt. When the campaign received enough donations by October to repurchase the air time, it was gone.[55] However, Goldwater insisted that his campaign would not engage in deficit spending on the campaign, and his campaign did not borrow any money even though contributions were not to the level they needed to be. Because of that, his television advertising for the last ten days of the campaign was canceled because the campaign account was empty by September. Had Goldwater taken a loan prior to September he could have kept his air time and not lost that valuable space.[56]

By the late 1960s there was a recognition that small donors were important as a source of campaign fundraising. Similar to the election in 2020, politicians worked to grow small donors in aggregate to gain competitive advantages in the presidential election. Richard Nixon learned from Goldwater's campaign the value of aggregate small donors and went after them in 1968. Nixon, however, benefited from his opponent's campaign finance problems both in terms of donations and coordination. Humphrey's loss to Nixon was thought by some to be the result of campaign finance problems.[57] One problem for Humphrey was the fractured Democratic Party, and its infamous 1968 convention in Chicago. Also at issue was Humphrey's association with the Johnson administration's decisions on Vietnam, which alienated supporters of Eugene McCarthy, who had considerable support in the party. Strategically, Humphrey also had some fundraising problems. Humphrey had called for a campaign fundraising moratorium after the assassination of Robert Kennedy in June 1968.[58] However, Humphrey's donation problems were much deeper than that caused by a self-imposed fundraising hiatus. By June 1968 he had to lay off 25 percent of his campaign staff in order to save $8,000 a week.[59] He also lacked funds to run ads in competitive states like California. Humphrey was able to raise money, but most of that came in the last few weeks of the campaign. His campaign manager, Larry O'Brien later opined that if Humphrey had $10 million he could have beat Nixon in the election.[60] Nixon would raise $21 million for his campaign against Humphrey, with record-setting expenditures for television ads. In fact, by 1968 television spending was double what it was in 1964, and in aggregate both parties spent $7.4 million in TV ads in 1968.[61]

Nixon's presidency and his use of money would prove to be a watershed moment in campaign finance. His actions in Watergate led to many of the 1970s reforms to campaign finance, and ushered in an era in the late twentieth century where campaign finance reform was supported. However, in 1972 Nixon and the Republican Party were thought to be highly successful in fundraising. Maurice Stans, who was Nixon's Secretary of Commerce who was later convicted of violated campaign laws, was profiled in 1972 in *The Washington Post* as a master fundraiser for Republicans.[62] He was the finance chairman of the Committee to Re-Elect the President (CREEP), which would later become a source of focus during the Watergate investigation because it paid for legal expenses of the Watergate burglars. A big game hunter, Stans was portrayed as being able to get big donors as well. Having raised considerable sums for Richard Nixon's reelection in 1972, Stans had some difficulty in getting toward his $45 million goal because Nixon's opposition, George McGovern, was considered weak opposition.[63]

McGovern was a weak candidate in part because the Democratic Party was in disarray in 1972. Their convention did not reach a nomination until late with McGovern giving his televised acceptance speech at 2:48 a.m. Outraising McGovern, Nixon was a clear favorite to win. For example, in Maryland McGovern raised $11,000 in one day after twenty-eight events, Nixon came two days later and raised $200,000 in a single day.[64] However, Nixon's fundraising became the focus of investigations. Prior to his termination as Watergate Special Prosecutor in the Saturday Night Massacre, Archibald Cox investigated campaign fundraising irregularities.[65] Nixon fundraising became a focus of the Watergate scandal with an inquiry into the creation of a campaign "slush fund" that was given out at the direction of Nixon, and Senate investigators were looking into Rebozo's role in dispensing campaign money.[66] Investigators said Nixon used campaign contributions to purchase gifts for his wife, make improvements to his Florida home, and provide personal loans for his brother.[67]

AGE OF REFORM TO AGE OF EXEMPTION: FUNDRAISING FROM FORD TO TRUMP

The 1970s served as a watershed moment in American campaign finance history. In many ways the reforms in the 1970s set the debate that continues today about the excesses of money in politics. With the Watergate scandal there was series of reform-minded politicians, including then senator Joe Biden, who wanted to reform the political campaign finance laws to ensure equity and more transparency. The reforms of the 1970s ultimately gave way to the loosening of campaign finance regulations in the 2000s. This tension between the reforms of the 1970s and the changes in the 2000s represents the general issue of campaign finance debates in the 2020s. Understanding that past is important to contextualizing the modern debates. However, as the following analysis of the 2020 presidential election shows, the positions staked out during contemporary campaign finance debates do not necessarily reflect the way politicians finance their campaigns.

Nixon's resignation on August 9, 1974, placed Gerald Ford into a tumultuous time for the American presidency. Nixon's actions as president led to a reform movement in campaign finance, which resulted in the 1974 Amendment to the FECA.[68] Originally passed in 1971 and ironically signed into law by President Nixon, FECA did not go into effect until after the 1972 election. In his signing statement, Nixon said that the passage of such an act was "laudable" and said "this legislation will guard against campaign abuses and will work to build public confidence in the integrity of the electoral process."[69] Post Watergate there were extensive calls for reform, which resulted in amendments that included campaign contribution caps and the creation of the FEC. Ford signed the 1974 amendment into law stating:

> I can assure you from what I have heard, from the American people in writing and other communications, they want this legislation. So, it will soon be law. I think we do recognize that this legislation seeks to eliminate to a maximum degree some of the influences that have created some of the problems in recent years.[70]

Public funding would change the nature of presidential campaign contributions, and as a system it would continue until 2012 when candidates began opting out of public funding in order to raise higher totals of donations.[71] Public funding was an old idea in Washington with the first calls for public funding of presidential elections dating back to 1904 when U.S. Representative William Bourke Cockran (D-NY) called for public funding. In 1966 this funding concept was passed in a statute, but was quickly repealed.[72] The 1968 presidential campaign of Hubert Humphrey made the

Democratic Party go into debt $9 million, which renewed many Democrats' interest in creating a public funding option. The original 1971 FECA did not include public funding, but the 1974 amendments did.[73] With the decision in *Buckley v. Valeo* affirming the constitutionality of FECA the public funding in presidential campaigns.[74] As a system the public financing option provided more restrictions on presidential candidates in financing in an attempt to provide equity in the election process while also providing greater transparency. Public funding is a system that still exists today, although its use by presidential candidates began to wane in the 2000s with the last presidential candidate accepting public financing being John McCain in 2008. At its inception the public financing of presidential elections had three components: (1) matching funds for presidential primary candidates, (2) funds for presidential party nominating conventions, and (3) funding for major party nominees with funding for minor party nominees who met certain requirements.[75] Essentially public funding of elections provides eligible presidential candidates public funding for "qualified expenses," which has a precise definition set forth by the FEC under 11 CFR 9002.11.[76] The FEC defines "qualified expense" as requiring three core criteria:

1. It is incurred by or on behalf of a candidate or the candidate's authorized committees from the date the individual becomes a candidate through the last day of the candidate's eligibility as determined under 11 CFR 9033.5
2. It is made in connection with his or her campaign for nomination; and
3. Neither the incurrence nor payment of which constitutes a violation of any law of the United States or of any law of any state in which the expense is incurred or paid, or of any regulation prescribed under such law of the United States or of any state.[77]

This public funding had a provision from 1976 until 2012 that would allow the public funding of party conventions, but that has since been removed.[78] Additionally, the public funding of presidential elections provided for primary matching funds if the candidate was seeking nomination of a political party by establishing that candidacy had "broad-based public support."[79] Currently this means that the candidate had to raise at least $5,000 in at least twenty states, from a maximum of $250 in contributions per donor. There are also primary spending limits of $10 million plus a cost-of-living adjustment (COLA), which was $48.07 million in 2016. There are also requirements to limit spending in each state during a primary based on the number of voting-age individuals that also includes a COLA. This has serious implications for campaign expenditures in competitive primary states, especially with large populations. For instance, the FEC reported that under this formulae a candidate in 2016 could only spend a bit over $23 million in California and only

$961,400 in Wyoming. Self-financing is also limited under these rules to only $50,000 in personal donations for primaries.[80]

Similar rules also apply for the General Election, with COLA being a major factor in the amount of money that can be raised and spent in the campaign. The main condition of accepting public funding is that a party nominee may not accept private contributions and can only spend $50,000 of their own money that does not count toward the grant. The fixed rate of public funding is $20 million plus COLA, which varies depending upon the year of the campaign. In 1976 this amount was $21.8 million, but by 2020 the amount would have been $103.7 million (far lower than the actual amounts raised by Trump and Biden).[81] It is important to note that one of the realities of public funding is it does tend to support a two-party political system, because minor party candidates can only receive funding if the candidate receives between 5 and 25 percent of the total popular vote in the preceding election, and the amount a minor party nominee receives is based on the ratio.

Part of the appeal of public funding is the equalization of resources of the candidates, and the sense that the public is invested in the process. By the time Reagan challenged Carter in 1980, public funding was an established norm, and both candidates took public funding for the primaries and the General Election. That was a norm that continued in Reagan's 1984 election, George H.W. Bush's election in 1988, and Clinton's elections in 1992 and 1996. The way this public funding worked was through federal taxpayer checkoff boxes for $1, which was raised to $3 in 1993. Qualifications for public funds meant that candidates had to raise funds of at least $5,000 in each of twenty states in contribution of less than $250, which was used because the low number encouraged small donations. These funds had to come from individuals and not parties or PACs.[82]

In his quest to be elected as president in his own right, Ford's fundraising in 1976 was hampered by Watergate and Nixon's legacy. Ford had trouble getting staffers, because he could not heavily recruit from those who worked for Nixon in 1972. In October 1975, Ford had campaign offices in thirty-five states and had taken in only $700,000.[83] Ford's fundraising, however, included many of the time-honored traditions in politics mixed with new technology. In 1975, he used a computer-generated letter to appeal for small donations for Republican candidates for the House of Representatives.[84] Ford would also be harmed by an intra-party challenge by then governor Ronald Reagan, which also caused issues for Ford's campaign. In 1975 Reagan had more campaign funding than Ford, with Reagan boasting $2 million raised to Ford's $1.7 million.[85]

Jimmy Carter, however, did well in fundraising in 1976, in one case doubling his expected totals to $3 million from a $1,000 a plate dinner between the end of the primaries and the Democratic Convention.[86] His campaign at that time was so flush with cash that there was speculation that Carter was returning $250,000 in matching funds. Carter's potential return of the funds was characterized as a campaign strategy that would play well with voters post Watergate. However, both Ford and Carter were in an unusual position being the first candidates to receive the public funding for elections, which was then $22 million.[87]

Because of public funding, the issue of campaign finance became less of an issue in the 1980s and 1990s. However, the system was problematic. Few people contributed to the checkoff box, and most donors who made contributions in excess of $200 were older Republicans. This led to an increase of public funding checkoff to $3 in 1993, but again the fund did not grow.[88] However, fundraising did continue in PACs and party committees. For example, in 1980 *The Washington Post* reported that corporate PACs Republicans during 1980 and 1984 were more adept at developing soft-money contributions. However, by 1988 both parties were using soft money contributions at a similar rate.[89]

Cash matching under the public funding model did not mean that candidates only focused on minimum for fundraising. In 1988, George H. W. Bush took advantage of computer lists to generate maximum fundraising, then $1,000 per individual, for his presidential campaign. In May 1988 he used this system to create a campaign fund of $29 million; part of his success was his personal thank you cards to donors who gave more than $500.[90] Bush's campaign fundraising strategy was also included raising $27 million for the Republican Party at the national and state level.[91] In fact, Bush's fundraising started early, and his campaign manager, Lee Atwater, predicted in May 1987 that by December a successful Republican candidate needed $8 to $10 million in the bank to be competitive in the Republican primary.[92] The General Election of 1988 proved to be very expensive with all candidates in aggregate raising $213.8 million and spending $210 million.[93]

The 1992 presidential election brought a new dynamic into federal campaign fundraising with the introduction of Ross Perot as a third major candidate. Perot, a billionaire, self-financed his campaign pouring more than $68 million of his own money into the campaign, and receiving 18.9 percent of the popular vote (though receiving no Electoral votes). Creating the Reform Party in 1996, Perot received public funding under FECA, and declined to self-fund. During this same time soft money began to play a much larger role in presidential elections. Raised outside of the regulations of the FECA, soft money was money raised for state party development that would then be used to build party strength during elections that would benefit both federal and state candidates.[94]

Public funding continued in 1996, but in 2000 the first challenge occurred to the norm. This grew out of the restrictions of publicly funded elections.

Congress' public funding model did not index campaign contributions limits for individual donors or matching funds to inflation. Campaign finance scholar Robert Mutch argues this led to a problem for the fund because by 1996 $1,000 was worth about $300 in 1976.[95]

By 2000, the public funding model had its first defector when George W. Bush opted out of public funding during the primaries and caucuses.[96] He did this because he felt that he could raise more money without the public funding limits. While Democrats Al Gore and Bill Bradley were neck-and-neck in fundraising in 1999, Bush already had $30 million in his campaign because of his ability to raise money unencumbered by public funds regulations.[97] Bush was criticized for his decision to opt out of public funding, receiving criticism from his primary opponent John McCain who thought Bush's decision would lead to greater critical view of American politics.[98] Bush, however, couched his reason for opting out in terms of access and ability to engage in the election. Specifically, he argued that self-funded Steve Forbes, who had raised the second largest amount of money at that time due to self-financing, created a situation where Republicans were at a competitive disadvantage.[99]

By 2008, public funding would continue to break down as a system when Barack Obama declined public funding for the general election. Obama's decision was based on the fact that he could raise far more money without the limitations of public funding. In his announcement opting pointed out that public financing model of elections was not workable in the modern era, and that 527s, PACs that raise and spend non-FECA-regulated money, created a need for him to not accept public funding.[100] This stance was made into a political issue with McCain declaring that Obama had gone back on his word of promising to accept public funding.[101] However, Obama's campaign said that there was never an agreement between the candidates about public funding. There was a discussion of a potential meeting to discuss how the campaigns would finance going forward. However, Obama had been a high-performing fundraiser during the primaries, and his campaign would have made an agreement with McCain only if the Republicans agreed to limit spending by the RNC and special interest groups. In reality, Obama's campaign knew that they could outraise the limit of the public funding, which was $84.1 million in 2008. In fact, Obama's campaign thought in June 2008 that he could raise $200 to $300 million in donations by Election Day, not including DNC fundraising, given his strong fundraising abilities.[102] Obama would end up raising around $300 million alone and had so much money that he ended the General Election with a surplus of $30 million.[103]

Obama's record fundraising showed the public financing of elections produced a major disadvantage for candidates. In 2012, both Obama and his Republican opponent Mitt Romney declined public financing and raised over $1 billion each.[104] *Citizens United v. FEC* decided in 2010, paved the way for super-PACs to be heavily involved in the election for the first time in 2012.[105] Large contributions to Romney and Obama came in pro-Republican and Democrat PACs, but small donors also were made for both candidates. Obama would receive $42 million in donations that were $200 or less.[106]

The presidential election 2016 reflected the new norms of super-PACs and opting out of public financing. In the Democratic Primary Bernie Sanders made use of small donors, and actually outraised Hillary Clinton in individual contributions during the early stages of 2016.[107] However, Clinton's campaign had a large cash advantage over Donald Trump, who utilized earned media well through his televised interviews and campaign rallies. Ultimately Trump was outraised by Clinton, but the end result showed that presidential elections were going to continue to grow in terms of cash needed. If anything, 2016 signaled that the reforms of the 1970s and public financing had been replaced with the new norms of super-PACs and large campaign expenditures.[108]

THE POLITICIZATION OF MONEY:
CAMPAIGN FINANCE IN THE 2020s

The arc of the history of presidential campaign finance is almost circular. Campaign restrictions gave way to greater transparency and funding, but ultimately the reform of campaign finance collapsed on itself. The loopholes and opt-out options allowed for 2016's expensive election, and it seems that the U.S. system has almost returned to a pre-Theodore Roosevelt reality. Elections have grown more expensive, and the need for donors continues. However, what is interesting is that there are three main issues that cycle back through campaign finance: small donors, the horse race of raising money, and that acting like a campaign finance reformer never wins an election.

Small donations are both a political strategy and a talking point. The history of presidential campaign finance shows that candidates use the discussion about small donors to prove a political point. Not only is their candidate not beholden to big-money interest, but they have a groundswell of support. However, even during the time of Theodore Roosevelt it is clear that small donors are never enough to fund a campaign. Large donors are needed, and regardless of party, these donors provide the type of support that provides legitimacy and popularity to candidates.

Fundraising is competitive, and media accounts of fundraising point to the cash in accounts as a level of security. Campaigns that do not meet expectations go into a type of downward spiral, where lack of money yields even less money. That is because throughout history it is clear that donors want candidates that appear to be viable. Similar to Humphrey in 1968, if a candidate appears to be weak and unelectable donors will leave, which leaves the candidate in a more vulnerable position.

Last, campaign finance reform may be popular, but it is not a winning issue if a candidate lives it out. Humphrey in 1968 and McCain in 2008 put themselves at a political disadvantage by not making the most of their fundraising abilities. Humphrey's suspension of fundraising in 1968 caused him to lose money he needed. Goldwater's insistence on a balanced campaign budget with no deficit spending causes him to lose any advantage he could have had with October advertising. McCain, who had led the campaign reform movement in the 1990s and 2000s, was hindered by accepting public financing in the General Election. Obama's decision to turn it down, despite his promises to accept it, made no political difference. In fact, it signaled a new norm in presidential campaigns. What presidential fundraising shows is, like the quest for votes, the quest for cash is strong. Without it, a campaign will not win.

NOTES

1. George Soros is a billionaire who regularly donates to progressive political causes. His Open Society Foundations is one charitable organization used by Soros to promote causes such as civil rights and justice. The Koch brothers refer to Charles and David Koch, who are members of the Koch family who established the Charles Koch Foundation and the David H. Koch Charitable Foundation, which funds conservative and libertarian think tanks. Among the issues include political issues, education, free speech, and criminal justice. The David H. Koch Charitable Foundation also provides funding for medical research. David Koch died in 2019.

2. Citizens United v. FEC, 558 U.S. 310 (2010); McCutcheon v. FEC, 572 U.S. 185 (2015).

3. "Roosevelt's Campaign Fund," *Washington Post*, December 3, 1905, 1. There was some discussion that 1896 was also a very expensive campaign year with over $16 million used to secure a Republican victory. However,

4. Ibid. The budget also accounted for $50,000 in miscellaneous and ran a $100,000 balance at the end of the election cycle.

5. Tillman was a populist Democrat who wanted campaign finance reform because he believed it would help Democrats. Known for his anti-Reconstruction politics, Tillman was also a major advocate for the disenfranchisement of African-American voters, and was a proponent of violating African Americans' civil rights.

6. "Message of the President, December 5, 1905," U.S. Department of State, Office of the Historian, accessed March 2, 2021, https://history.state.gov/historicaldocuments/frus1905/message-of-the-president.

7. "Annual Message of the President Transmitted to Congress, December 3, 1906," U.S. Department of State, Office of the Historian, accessed March 2, 2021, https://history.state.gov/historicaldocuments/frus1906p1/annual.

8. "Message of the President, Annual, December 3, 1907, U.S. Department of State, accessed March 2, 2021, https://history.state.gov/historicaldocuments/frus 1907p1/message-of-the-president.

9. Ira Bennett, "Hard Facts are Dodged by Colonel," *San Francisco Call*, October 5, 1912, 1.

10. "Wilson in New York," *Washington Post*, August 25, 1912, 6.

11. "Officeholders' Gifts to Wilson Fund Assailed," *Chicago Daily Tribune*, October 13, 1916, 3.

12. Ibid.

13. So-called front porch campaigns are when a candidate stays at home, and has people come visit them on the "front porch." It is thought to be a highly effective way for a candidate to gain publicity without travel.

14. "Harding Confers on the Campaign with General Wood," *New York Times,* July 11 1920, 1.

15. "Bars Big Donations," *Washington Post*, June 26, 1920, 1.

16. "Republicans Spending $3,442,932.22 to Put Over Harding," *The Atlanta Constitution,* October 29, 1920, 1.

17. Hamon's $18,700 Harding's 1920 Hotel Bill," *Chicago Daily Tribune*, April 8, 1924. The testimony came from J.B. French who was a partner with the deceased Hamon.

18. Federal Corrupt Practices Act of 1925, 43 Stat. 1053, codified in 2 U.S.C. §241 (1925).

19. Kenneth McKellar, "Campaign Fund Evils Beset Both Parties," *New York Times*, March 30, 1924, XX1.

20. Ibid.

21. "Borah Denounces Corrupt Politics," *New York Times*, January 7, 1927, 1.

22. "Angelino Cash Aiding Hoover," *Los Angeles Times*, October 27, 1928, 5.

23. David Hamilton, "Herbert Hoover: Campaigns and Elections," The Miller Center, accessed March 1, 2021, https://millercenter.org/president/hoover/campaigns-and-elections.

24. "Raskob Opens Drive to Lift Party Debts," *New York Times*, October 6, 1931, 1.

25. "Gov. Roosevelt Asks Many Small Gifts to Run His Campaign," *New York Times*, August 26, 1932, 1.

26. Ibid., 1.

27. Ibid., 1.

28. "Donations to Roosevelt Fund Total Million," *Chicago Daily Tribune,* August 12, 1936, 5.

29. "Bill Would Bar Gifts to Campaign Funds," *Chicago Daily Tribune*, January 26, 1943, 2.

30. The Hatch Act of 1939, Pub L 76-252, 53 Stat. 1147, codified in 5 USC §§7321–7326 (1939).

31. "Political Arena: Senate Probing Ads for Willkie," *Washington Post*, September 13, 1940, 3.

32. "Republicans Get $529,551 in Month," *New York Times*, October 29, 1940, 16.

33. Louis Stark, "CIO Sets Up Group on Election Funds," *New York Times*, June 18, 1944, 29.

34. "First Lady Pleads for Alert Women," *New York Times*, April 19, 1944, 20.

35. "Large and Small Donations to President Truman's Campaign," *Atlanta Daily World*, August 18, 1948, 1.

36. Ibid.

37. Bernard Lemelin, "The U.S. Presidential Election in 1948: The Causes of Truman's 'Astonishing' Victory," *Revue française d'études américaines* 97 (2001): 38–61, 41.

38. Truman established the President's Committee on Civil Rights in 1946, and issued Executive Orders 9980 desegregating federal employment and 9981 desegregating the U.S. military. President Wilson actually segregated federal employment beginning in 1913 with the U.S. Postal Service and Department of Treasury. See, "Woodrow Wilson Federal Segregation," The Smithsonian, accessed March 3, 2021, https://postalmuseum.si.edu/research-articles/the-history-and-experience-of-african-a mericans-in-america%E2%80%99s-postal-service-3.

39. "Incensed Party May Skip Donations," *The Atlanta Constitution*, February 26, 1948, 1.

40. Jeffrey Kluttz, "The Federal Diary," *Washington Post*, October 20, 1948, B1.

41. "Washington Wire," *Wall Street Journal*, September 24, 1948, 1.

42. "Wyman Heads State Bakers of Eisenhower," *Chicago Daily Tribune*, February 8, 1952, 14.

43. Richard Amper, "Kefauver Lashes Rivals Over Gift," *New York Times*, October 11, 1956, 35. Eisenhower did come under attack for campaign contributions by Democrats, notably Senator Estes Kefauver of Tennessee, for 1952 campaign contributions from oil businessmen H.B. Keck of California. Keck had given Eisenhower $5,000 in 1952, which Kefauver compared to Harding's Teapot Dome scandal of the 1920s.

44. Richard Bergholz, "Two Decades Ago," *Los Angeles Times*, May 1, 1973, A3; Lee Huebner, "The Checkers Speech After 60 Years, *The Atlantic*, September 22, 2012, https://www.theatlantic.com/politics/archive/2012/09/the-checkers-speech -after-60-years/262172/.

45. "Nixon's Checkers Speech, September 23, 1952," PBS, accessed March 1, 2021, https://www.pbs.org/wgbh/americanexperience/features/eisenhower-checkers/. Checkers became famous after Nixon's speech so much so that when the dog died in September 8, 1964, at twelve years old the Associated Press ran a story detailing the dog's death and impact on American politics. "Famous Nixon Dog, Checkers, Is Dead," *Washington Post*, September 9, 1964, p. A2.

46. Edward Folliard, "Ike Delays Cleveland Speech to Hear Nixon on Television," *Washington Post*, September 24, 1952, 1.

47. "Kennedy Reports No Donations or Spending in Race," *New York Times*, October 29, 1958, 11.

48. "AFL-CIO Backs Kennedy," *Chicago Daily Tribune*, August 27, 1960, 4. Interestingly the AFL-CIO backed Stephenson in 1952 and 1956, but its rank-and-file members voted overwhelmingly for Eisenhower.

49. Alexander Heard, "A New Approach to Campaign Finances," *New York Times*, October 6, 1963, 244.

50. Ibid. It is worth noting that campaign dinners were not Kennedy's invention. They had become a mainstay of campaign fundraising in the 1930s.

51. Ibid.

52. E.W. Kenworthy, "Kennedy Asks Tax Break for Campaign Donors," *The Atlanta Constitution*, May 30, 1962, 2.

53. Earl Mazo, "Politics Cost Put $200 Million," *New York Times*, October 27, 1963, 31.

54. Ibid.

55. Dan Nimmo, *Political Persuaders: The Techniques of Modern Election Campaign* (New Brunswick, NJ: Transaction Publishers, 2001), 90–91.

56. Ibid.

57. Ibid., 91.

58. Roy Reed, "Humphrey Donations have Dropped Since Kennedy's Death," *New York Times*, June 20, 1968, 41.

59. Ibid.

60. Nimmo, *Political Persuaders*, 90–91.

61. Walter Pincus, "21 Million Raised for Nixon Bid," *Washington Post*, January 3, 1969, A1.

62. Lou Cannon, "GOP's Big Game Hunter," *Washington Post*, September 17, 1972, A1.

63. Ibid.

64. "Maryland Money Flows to Nixon," *Washington Post*, September 30, 1972, D1.

65. "Cox Aimed at Nixon Fundraising," *New York Times*, October 25, 1973, 43. The Saturday Night Massacre occurred on October 20, 1973. Nixon ordered his Attorney General Elliot Richardson to fire Cox. Richardson resigned refusing to fire Cox. William Ruckelshaus the Deputy Attorney General also refused to fire Cox and resigned. Finally, Robert Bork, who was third in command at the Department of Justice, fired Cox.

66. John Crewdson, "Nixon's Taped Remark on Apparent Slush Fund Called Key Evidence in Rebozo Inquiry," *New York Times*, December 9, 1974, 27.

67. Ibid.

68. Federal Election Campaign Act Amendments of 1974, Pub L 93-443 (1974).

69. Richard Nixon, "Statement on Signing the Federal Election Campaign Act of 1971," The American Presidency Project, accessed March 2, 2021, https://www.presidency.ucsb.edu/documents/statement-signing-the-federal-election-campaign-act-1971.

70. Gerald Ford, "Remarks on Signing the Federal Election Campaign Act Amendments of 1974," The American Presidency Project, accessed March 2, 2021,

https://www.presidency.ucsb.edu/documents/remarks-signing-the-federal-election-c ampaign-act-amendments-1974.

71. Mutch, Campaign Finance 25–26.

72. Ibid., 28–29. Mutch describes the biggest issue in the 1966 public funding law was interparty fighting among Democrats, and the concern over how public funding would be financed. Public funding was not part of the original 1971 FECA bill, but was later added in an amendment signed into law by President Nixon.

73. U.S. Federal Election Commission. The Presidential Funding Program, Federal Election Commission, 1993, https://transition.fec.gov/info/pfund.htm.

74. Buckley v. Valeo, 424 U.S. 1 (1976).

75. Ibid.

76. FEC Qualified Election Expense, 11 C.F.R. §9002.11 (2020).

77. "Public Funding of Presidential Elections," Federal Election Commission, accessed July 24, 2021, https://www.fec.gov/introduction-campaign-finance/under standing-ways-support-federal-candidates/presidential-elections/public-funding-p residential-elections/.

78. Raising and spending funds for the national party's nominating convention, Federal Election Commission, accessed July 25, 2021, https://www.fec.gov/ help-candidates-and-committees/taking-receipts-political-party/national-nominating -convention/.

79. Ibid.

80. Ibid.

81. Ibid.

82. Mutch, *Campaign Finance*, 26. Public funds are somewhat criticized because it benefits major parties, or those parties that receive up to 25 percent of the vote in a General Election. Small parties can receive funds if they receive between 5 and 25 percent of the vote. New parties running the first time have to fund themselves.

83. Robert Shogan, "Ford's Campaign Hurt By Watergate," *Los Angeles Times*, October 9, 1975, B22.

84. Don Oberdorfer, "Ford Fund Appeal Nets $1 Million," *Washington Post,* December 13, 1975, A3.

85. "Reagan Leading Ford in Donations," *New York Times*, January 7, 1976, 30.

86. Kenneth Reich, "Carter Campaign Doubles Its Fundraising Projection," *Los Angeles Times*, June 29, 1976, B8.

87. Ibid.; Mutch, *Campaign Finance*, 25.

88. Ibid., 35.

89. Ibid., 105–106.

90. Charles Babcock and Richard Morin, "Bush's Money Machine," *Washington Post*, May 15, 1988, 1.

91. Ibid.

92. Ronald Brownstein, "Raising Bucks for Bush," *New York Times*, May 17, 1987, 311.

93. Richard Berkes, "'88 Presidential Candidates Spent $210 Million, *New York Times*, August 27, 1989, 23.

94. Mutch, *Campaign Finance*, 34,

95. Ibid., 44.

96. Ibid.

97. Ceci Connally and Susan Glasser, "Bradley's Campaign Bankroll Nearly Equals Gore's," *Washington Post*, July 16, 1999, A1.

98. Ibid.

99. Ibid.

100. Adam Nagourney and Jeff Zeleny, "Obama Forgoes Public Funding in a First for Major Candidate," *New York Times*, June 20, 2008, https://www.nytimes.com/2008/06/20/us/politics/20obamacnd.html.

101. John Whitesides and Caren Bohan, "Obama Rejects Public Financing Against McCain," *Reuters*, June 19, 2008, https://www.reuters.com/article/us-usa-politics/obama-rejects-public-financing-against-mccain-idUSN1828132020080619.

102. Michael Luo and Zelensky, "Obama, in Shift, Says He'll Reject Public Financing," *New York Times*, June 20, 2008, https://www.nytimes.com/2008/06/20/us/politics/20obama.html.

103. Michael Luo, "Obama Hauls in Record $750 Million for Campaign," *New York Times*, December 4, 2008, https://www.nytimes.com/2008/12/05/us/politics/05donate.html.

104. Kenneth Vogel and David Levinthal, "Obama, Romney Both Top $1B," *Politico*, December 7, 2012, https://www.politico.com/story/2012/12/barack-obama-mitt-romney-both-topped-1-billion-in-2012-084737.

105. Citizens United v. FEC, 558 U.S. 310 (2010).

106. Ibid.

107. Cayce Myers, "Campaign Finance and Its Impact in the 2016 Presidential Campaign," in *The 2016 U.S. Presidential Campaign*, ed. Robert Denton (London: Palgrave MacMillan, 2017), 259–283, 270.

108. Ibid., 276–278.

Chapter 3

Democratic Fundraising during 2020 Presidential Primary

The 2020 Democratic primary was filled with candidates and campaign funds. The primary was typical in many ways in that a candidate's ability to raise money had a large impact on the longevity of their campaign. However, it differs in two major ways. First, the Democratic primary contained a self-financed campaign from billionaire, and former New York City mayor, Michael Bloomberg. Second, the field was so large that the nomination was a more protracted process that ultimately ended up being a competition between progressive independent Senator Bernie Sanders and the more moderate former Vice President Joe Biden. Sanders and Biden's campaigns in the primary also demonstrated the depth of their fundraising abilities, with both candidates outlasting their rivals into March 2020. This not only showed that both progressive and moderate wings of the Democratic Party have the ability to raise cash, but it also showed protracted primary battles do not necessarily weaken the eventual nominee. Like Trump in 2016, Biden won in 2020 after a long nomination fight and avoided the anticipated convention fight over delegates.

Perhaps what was the most interesting aspect of the Democratic primaries is how campaign financing was used as a political issue. Unlike the days of campaign finance reform, like that of John McCain in the Republican primary in 2000, the Democratic candidates challenged each other on where their campaign dollars came from. The issues of PACs, super-PACs, and the wealth of donors created was a political issue itself. The Democrats in 2020, especially those from the more progressive wing of the party, expressed criticisms of the billionaire class in the United States. Using campaign donations from these people has not yet become a political liability but has become a talking point.

As a political issue, campaign finance was linked to a larger Democratic talking point about the role of corporations within the United States. For progressive Democrats the idea that corporations would be involved in the campaign process served as a warning about their power and the perceived undemocratic influence money has within campaigns. Warren and Sanders both made political talking points about the level of donations their campaigns received from small donors. However, campaign platforms and debate talking points included discussions about campaign finance.

Sanders' criticism of campaign fundraising has been long-standing. His platform in 2016 and 2020 was a large criticism of corporations and billionaires' role within politics. In his 2016 book, *Our Revolution*, Sanders details in the introduction a list of reforms to corporations that include dismantling large banks and closing tax loopholes for corporations.[1] He called the *Citizens United v. FEC* decision "disastrous" and stated that high dollar donations by wealthy individuals, who he refers to as oligarchs, was damaging democracy in the United States.[2]

This chapter looks at the fundraising during the Democratic primary. This chapter looks at preconvention fundraising of Top-Tier Democratic Candidates, the fundraising of Lower-Tier Democratic Candidates, the issue of campaign finance and donations as political talking points, and concludes with how money affected the Democratic primary in 2020.

LEADING UP TO 2020: EARLY PRIMARY FUNDRAISING 2019

The 2020 Democratic primary season was large, consisting of twenty-nine major candidates, which eclipsed the sixteen Republican primary candidates in 2016. It was the largest Democratic primary since 1972 when primaries at the presidential level began.[3] The top-tier candidates (candidates that won delegates at the Democratic convention in August 2020) included: Vice President Joe Biden, Senator Bernie Sanders (I-VT), Senator Elizabeth Warren (D-MA), and former New York City mayor Mike Bloomberg. However, other candidates rose and fell from top-tier status staying through the Democratic primaries including South Bend, Indiana Mayor Pete Buttigieg, businessman Andrew Yang, Representative Tulsi Gabbard (D-HI), Senator Amy Klobuchar (D-MN), Governor Deval Patrick (D-MA), Senator Michael Bennet (D-CO), and hedge fund manager Tom Steyer. Still, the majority of Democratic primary candidates dropped out before the primaries began. These candidates included some well-known figures including Senator Corey Booker (D-NJ), Senator Kamala Harris (D-CA), former representative

Beto O'Rourke (D-TX), and former U.S. secretary for housing and urban development Julián Castro.

Historically, defeating an incumbent president is difficult, with only three incumbents presidents since World War II losing an election: 1976 Jimmy Carter defeating Gerald Ford, 1980, with Ronald Reagan defeating Jimmy Carter, and 1992, with Bill Clinton defeating George H.W. Bush. Both of those races had anomalies that cause damage to the incumbent as well. In the Democratic primary for 1980, Carter had a strong primary challenge from Senator Ted Kennedy (D-MA), which was thought to have weakened Carter in the national election.[4] In 1992, third party candidate Ross Perot split the vote from Clinton and Bush. Nothing like this occurred in 2020, so the match-up between Trump and Biden was similar to elections where incumbent presidents won reelection.

In the Democratic primary, media coverage portrayed the race as a struggle between progressives, led by Sanders and Warren, and the moderate Joe Biden. Initial fundraising for Biden, Warren, and Sanders was strong, as the media touted the money raised on their first day as Democratic candidates for president. It is important to note that during 2019 the frontrunners of the campaign, Biden and Sanders, did not announce early. The earliest announcements were Representative Tulsi Gabbard, Secretary Julián Castro, Senator Kirsten Gillibrand, and Senator Kamala Harris. In fact, in her April Quarterly, Harris' campaign, Kamala Harris for the People, raised over $12 million in individual donations.[5] Gillibrand, whose campaign would be suspended in August 2019 because of now qualifying for the Democratic primary debates, had raised just under $3 million in the first quarter.[6]

In the early days of the Democratic primary perhaps no candidate received more attention than Robert Francis "Beto" O'Rourke. His fundraising early in campaign was impressive. Having come to national attention for running the most competitive Senate race in forty years against incumbent Senator Ted Cruz in the very Republican state of Texas, O'Rourke had been considered by many to be a good national-level candidate.[7] The same month that O'Rourke announced his candidacy for the Democratic nomination for president, he was featured in a flattering feature story in *Vanity Fair* complete with photos by famed photographer Annie Leibovitz.[8] The article even touched on his campaign finance philosophy. He pointed out that in his 2016 campaign against Cruz, that he followed the Sanders philosophy of no PAC money or corporate donors. In the first twenty-four hours of his campaign, he raised $6.1 million, and his first quarter of fundraising was $9.4 million.[9] Small donors were a large part of his success, and the media pointed out that his average donor during the second quarter of 2019 gave around $30.[10] His fundraising declined significantly by the summer, and he suspended his campaign by November, nine months into his campaign.[11]

Harris, who went on to be Democratic ticket in 2020, started strong in her fundraising in 2019. She announced her candidacy early on January 21, 2019. Her announcement came on *ABC*'s Good Morning America. Harris, who was a first-term senator from California, had gained a national spotlight from her questioning of then-nominee for Attorney General Jeff Sessions and her position on the Senate Judiciary Committee during the confirmation of Brett Kavanaugh. Within twenty-four hours of her announcement, Harris raised $1.5 million.[12] Her early campaign was successful, especially after she challenged Joe Biden during a June Democratic primary debate over school desegregation and busing. Harris was best known for the comment "that girl was me," when referring to her being a child who experienced busing in California during the 1970s. Harris raised $2 million within twenty-four hours of that debate, using the tagline "that girl was me" on campaign t-shirts that sold for $29.99 to $32.99.[13] Her campaign fundraising was strong. Her April Quarterly showed $12 million in individual donations, and July and October quarterly were still strong with just under $12 million each.[14]

Bernie Sanders announced his campaign for president on February 19, 2019, raising $5.9 million within the first twenty-four hours of his campaign, boasting an average campaign donation amount of $27.[15] He had come a long way from his insurgent campaign against Hillary Clinton in 2016. His 2020 campaign focused on progressive issues and talking points that focused on economic inequality and corporations. His strength in fundraising was his use of small donations and the ability to harness the aggregate small donations to equal those candidates, such as Pete Buttigieg, who fundraised among wealthy donors. This was nearly four times what he raised in 2015 during the primary, when during the first twenty-four hours of his campaign Sanders raised $1.5 million.[16] The amounts candidates raised during the first twenty-four hours of announcing their candidacies became a news story and signaled the strength of the candidacy. Sanders's strong showing within the first twenty-four hours of his campaign became a talking point demonstrating his position as a front-runner for the Democratic nominations. When Joe Biden eventually entered the race, his initial twenty-four-hour fundraising signaled his front-runner by the media. On the date he announced his candidacy, April 25, 2019, his campaign raised $6.8 million within twenty-four hours.[17]

Looking at campaign contributions only in Table 3.1, the early Democratic primary race in 2019 showed a very competitive race between Warren, Sanders, and Harris. Biden declared his candidacy relatively late, which accounts for his lack of an April Quarterly report. However, his campaign outperformed Sanders, Warren, and Harris in the July Quarter, which was from April 1 until June 30. However, Biden's campaign lost some momentum in fundraising between July 1 and September 30. Part of the reason behind this competitive fundraising was that no clear presumptive nominee had emerged. Biden was thought to provide the best chance of defeating Donald Trump. However, the enthusiasm of progressive voters centered on Sanders and Warren (although some Sander's supporters had heavy criticism of Warren).[18]

By the summer of 2019 the Democratic primary debates provided the best opportunity for candidates to distinguish themselves from the large pool of candidates. The candidate list was so large that debates were broken into two rounds, each appearing in consecutive nights. Democratic primary debates had a fundraising component to its debate qualifications. Candidates had to secure donations from at least 65,000 donors and have at least 200 donors from at least 20 states (the candidate also had to receive at least 1 percent from three DNC-approved polls).[19] The DNC had a two-part debate during June 26 and June 27 in Miami sponsored by NBC, which the crowded field of candidates tried to distinguish themselves from each other.

The first night debate featured ten candidates including Warren, Booker, Castro, and O'Rourke. A standout performance by Castro was noted the following day by the *New York Times*, and Warren was the only candidate who had achieved double-digit polling to that point.[20] However, it was the second Democratic debate that held the high-profile candidacies of Joe Biden, Bernie Sanders, Kamala Harris, and Pete Buttigieg. It was during this debate that the memorable exchange between Biden and Harris where Harris said "that girl was me" in response to Biden's former position on busing.[21]

After the second debate the landscape of the Democratic primary changed somewhat. Eric Swalwell suspended his campaign on July 8, having a little over $2.6 million in total receipts,[22] and billionaire Tom Steyer announced his candidacy the same month (he would drop out February 2020 contributing more than $202 million to his own campaign in 2019).[23] The Democrats had a second debate in Michigan, which was again a two-part debate split between two nights on July 30 and 31. Like the first debate, the second debate had the top-tier candidates split with Warren, Sanders, and Buttigieg appearing in the first night and Biden, Harris, and Booker in the second night. It is important to note that even though these top-tier candidates of Biden, Sanders, Warren, and Harris, were split, candidates such as O'Rourke and Booker had made impressive gains in contributions. O'Rourke had hauled in over $17 million in total receipts during his primary campaign, and Booker had raised $22.3 million in individual contributions with total receipts of $25.4 million.[24]

Debates continued in 2019 with candidates dropping out citing the lack of fundraising, which sometimes coincided with them failing to qualify for debates. John Hickenlooper dropped out on August 15, 2019, raising only $221,875 in individual contributions, $335,671 in total receipts, from July to September.[25] Kristen Gillibrand shortly followed suspending her campaign on August 28 in total receipts 2019. She was once thought to be a strong

Table 3.1 Individual Contributions to Democratic Primary Candidates January–December 2019*

Month	Biden ($, million)	Sanders ($, million)	Warren ($, million)	Harris ($, million)
April Quarter	--	18. 1	6	12
July Quarter	21.9	18	19.1	11.7
October Quarter	15.6	25.2	24.6	11.6
End-of-Year	23.2	34.4	21.2	3.7

"Report of Receipts and Disbursements, Biden for President, July Quarterly Amended," Federal Election Commission, accessed March 4, 2021, https://docquery.fec.gov/cgi-bin/forms/C00703975/1360571/; "Report of Receipts and Disbursements, Biden for President, October Quarterly Amended," Federal Election Commission, accessed March 4, 2021, https://docquery.fec.gov/cgi-bin/forms/C00703975/1366660 5/; "Report of Receipts and Disbursements, Biden for President, Year-End," Federal Election Commission, accessed March 4, 2021, https://docquery.fec.gov/cgi-bin/forms/C00703975/1390990/; "Report of Receipts and Disbursements, Bernie 2020, April Quarterly," Federal Election Commission, accessed March 4, 2021, https://docquery.fec.gov/cgi-bin/forms/C00696948/1326070/; Sanders: "Report of Receipts and Disbursements, Bernie 2020, July Quarterly Amended," Federal Election Commission, accessed March 4, 2021, https://docquery.fec.gov/cgi-bin/forms/C00696948/1354560/; Sanders: "Report of Receipts and Disbursements, Bernie 2020, October Quarterly Amended," Federal Election Commission, accessed March 4, 2021, https://docquery.fec.gov/cgi-bin/forms/C00696948/1367132/; "Report of Receipts and Disbursements, Bernie 2020, Year-End Amended," https://docquery.fec.gov/cgi-bin/forms/C00696948 /1392261/; Warren: "Reports of Receipts and Disbursements, Warren for President, Year End," Federal Election Commission, accessed March 4, 2021, https://docquery.fec.gov/cgi-bin/forms/C00693234/1 378669/; "Reports of Receipts and Disbursements, Warren for President, October Quarterly Amended," Federal Election Commission, accessed March 4, 2021, https://docquery.fec.gov/cgi-bin/forms/C006932 34/1366132/; "Reports of Receipts and Disbursements, Warren for President, July Quarterly Amended," Federal Election Commission, accessed March 4, 2021, https://docquery.fec.gov/cgi-bin/forms/C006932 34/1350879/; "Reports of Receipts and Disbursements, Warren for President, April Quarterly Amended," Federal Election Commission, accessed March 4, 2021, https://docquery.fec.gov/cgi-bin/forms/C00693 234/1343914/. "Report of Receipts and Disbursements, Kamala Harris for the People, April Quarterly Amended, Federal Election Commission, accessed March 4, 2020, https://docquery.fec.gov/cgi-bin/forms /C00694455/1391946/; Kamala Harris for the People, July Quarterly Amended, Federal Election Commission, accessed March 4, 2020, https://docquery.fec.gov/cgi-bin/forms/C00694455/1391947/; Kamala Harris for the People, October Quarterly Amended, Federal Election Commission, accessed March 4, 2020, https://docquery.fec.gov/cgi-bin/forms/C00694455/1391948/; Kamala Harris for the People, Year-End Amended, Federal Election Commission, accessed March 4, 2020, https://docquery.fec.gov/cgi-bin/ forms/C00694455/1391949/.

*These figures include itemized and unitemized total contributions from persons/individuals other than political committees. These figures do not include party committee, other committees, or candidate contributions.

**Note that Biden has no number for April 2019 Quarterly because he did not declare his candidacy until April 25, 2019. Quarterly amounts include the following dates: April (January 1–March 31), July (April 1–June 30), October (July 1–September 30), and End-of-Year (October 1–December 31).

contender raising over $2.2 million in the previous quarter, and over $6.2 million in total individual contributions in 2019.[26] Other candidates also suspended their campaigns after the second debate including Mike Gravel, Jay Inslee, and Seth Moulton.

By September, the Democratic primary field was winnowed down to the point there was only a single debate. The qualifications became more stringent as candidates had to meet the DNC's polling and fundraising requirements, whereas candidates only had to meet one of the criteria in the earlier debates. This resulted in billionaire Tom Steyer, Michael Bennet, and Marianne Williamson being excluded. Steyer had raised just over $2 million in his 2019 October Quarterly, and had $47.5 million candidate contributions during the same time.[27] Bennet had also raised a little over $2.1 during the October quarter, and Williamson, best invoking love as a cornerstone of her campaign, raised over $3 million in individual contributions during the October 2019 quarter.[28]

Campaign finance became an issue during the September Democratic primary debates with businessman Andrew Yang announcing that he would give away $1,000 per month to ten families from his own campaign funds to highlight his universal basic income provision.[29] This caused a stir with some people alleging this program could violate campaign finance laws. Yang declared that was not an issue because his lawyers had looked into how campaign dollars could be given away in a lottery. One critic, Larry Noble, who worked as General Counsel for the FEC, saw this as potentially a fundraising strategy by Yang. Interestingly, Yang's fundraising from $ 2.8 million in his July Quarterly to $9.9 million by his October Quarterly filing.[30] From October through December Yang's fundraising continued to rise taking in over $16.5 million in individual contributions for a total of over $31.6 million in individual contributions for 2019.[31]

The debates for the Democratic primary continued to include fewer candidates as fundraising and polling tightened between a few candidates. By September, New York Mayor Bill DeBlasio, whose campaign committee raised just over $330,000 in total contributions in the October quarter of 2019, dropped out of the race.[32] By November, O'Rourke dropped out of the race never having a strong showing in the primary polls, despite raising over $17 million from individual contributions.[33] A November debate sponsored by *MSNBC* and *The Washington Post* featured ten candidates, and the December debate featured only seven candidates. Kamala Harris dropped out on December 3, 2019 citing a lack of funds. She said that she could not continue in the race and said she could not afford to fund her own campaign because she was not a billionaire.[34]

The billionaire Harris was referring to was former New York City mayor Mike Bloomberg, who got into the primary race very late in 2019. He set up his exploratory committee on November 21 and launched his campaign on November 24, 2019. Bloomberg came in the race with high expectations because his wealth made his fundraising not as important because he was going to self-finance his campaign. He also was thought to appeal to moderate voters. The former Republican turned independent turned Democrat, was the former mayor of New York City for three terms as a moderate mayor. His financing of his campaign committee, Mike Bloomberg 2020, raised only $245,569 in individual contributions in the last part of 2019, but received over $200 million in donations from the candidate contributions.[35] Media reports of Bloomberg's candidacy focused on his wealth as a major advantage in the race. However, his late entry into the race was the cause of some concern. With a large field of Democratic candidates in 2019, and given that at the end of 2019 no clear front-runner had emerged, Bloomberg's candidate served to further complicate the race. Some believed that his name recognition and serious money to purchase ads nationally made him a fierce competitor for 2019.[36] Moreover his status as a billionaire was thought to be a negative factor in the increasingly left-leaning Democratic Party. In fact, Bloomberg's stances on the issue served as a contrast to the progressive stances of Warren and Sanders, and he criticized the leftward tilt of Democrats. The *New York Times* reported that in his quest for the presidency Bloomberg did not want to accept campaign contributions, and instead use his own personal fortune to fund his presidential campaign. The paper pointed out that this itself presented some logistical issues because of the fundraising requirements to be included in Democratic primary debates.[37] Bloomberg's individual contributions would remain low for the entirety of his campaign, totaling only $914,487, most of which were small donations of $200 or less.[38] His personal contributions to his campaign would be over $1 billion.[39]

For progressive candidates, the criticism of wealthy donors and corporate influence in campaigns was a major issue that came up during the December Democratic primary debate in Los Angeles. One of the most heated exchange during the debates came when Elizabeth Warren called out Mayor Pete Buttigieg over holding a fundraiser in a California wine cave with wealthy donors. She used the event to criticize the role the wealthy played within the campaign process and declared that super-wealthy fundraisers allowed special access to political candidates. The issue turned into a multipronged attack on Buttigieg in which Sanders and Yang criticized the use of such events. The event served as a flashpoint in the Democratic primary, and the hashtag #winecave trended on Twitter.[40] However, criticism went both ways. Buttigieg pointed out that Warren used big donors to help her get into the presidential race, despite criticizing them during the primary. NBC reported that Warren in 2018 even held a wine fundraiser where souvenir bottles of wine were given to donors who gave at least $1,000 and VIP photo session and premium seating for donors who gave the maximum per individual and couple.[41] Buttigieg couched his response in terms of realities of presidential campaigns arguing that large campaign contributions were necessary for candidates to defeat Donald Trump. Democrats also defended Buttigieg's fundraising, with Rufus Gifford stating that attacks on campaign fundraising could be by Republicans in the election.[42]

DEMOCRATIC PRIMARY FUNDRAISING DURING 2020

The 2020 Democratic primary still had no clear front-runner before the Iowa Caucuses. There was a sense that the battle in the election would consist of the electability of candidates, and the progressive enthusiasm of Sanders and Warren. However, there was an unusual contest emerging. Moderate Joe Biden was the standard-bearer of the centrist wing of the party and was viewed by many as making his case for the presidency based on electability. Bloomberg similarly was basing his campaign on electability and that he served as a sort of anti-Trump being a Democratic New York businessman who was a multibillionaire. Pete Buttigieg, a mayor of South Bend, Indiana, brought enthusiasm as a millennial candidate who was an openly gay married man. Still, Sanders and Warren represented the progressive wing of the party, which had grassroots enthusiasm. The field began significantly winnowing with Booker, Castro, Delaney, and Williamson dropping out of the race in January 2020. The stage was set for a more concentrated campaign fight between moderate and progressive candidates. As with any primary season, the issue was staying power of the candidates, which is indicated by fund-raising efforts. Joe Biden was thought to be the standard-bearer for moderate Democrats would not emerge as the inevitable nominee until March, and even then, there was speculation that there could be a brokered convention because of the progressive wing of the party.

The Iowa Caucuses were the first test of the strength of Democratic candidates. The results proved controversial with DNC chairman Tom Perez calling for a recanvass of voters. The results were Sanders and Buttigieg emerged as victors, and Biden coming in third.[43] As table 3.2 shows, Sanders outperformed Biden during this time. The New Hampshire primary, which occurred a few days after Iowa Caucuses, was another Sanders and Buttigieg victory with Biden coming in fifth after Klobuchar and Warren.[44] In fact this strong showing of Klobuchar coincided with her raising over $18.7 million in individual contributions in February 2020.[45] The results of the New Hampshire primary led several candidates to exit the race. Yang, DeBlasio, and Steyer all left the race during February. The South Carolina primary resulted in a Biden victory, and his endorsement of South Carolina Congressman James Clyburn, who was also the U.S. Majority Whip, proved to be a consequential endorsement that may have affected the results in the South Carolina Democratic primary.[46]

The fundraising of the candidates reflected these Sanders victories and the later Biden victories after the New Hampshire primary. Sanders and Warren outraised Biden in the early months of 2020 for several potential reasons. Table 3.2 shows that the individual contributions to Sanders and Warren were strong in 2019. There was media chatter that Biden, despite high expectations, would not be the Democratic nominee for president.[47] Sanders had the edge in fundraising and enthusiasm of Democratic voters and as table 3.2 shows, the individual contributions to Democratic primary candidates in January 2020 favored the progressives over Biden. In fact, both Warren and

Chapter 3

Table 3.2   Individual Contributions to Democratic Primary Candidates January–June 2020*,i

Month	Biden ($)	Sanders ($)	Warren ($)	Bloomberg ($)
January	8.88 million	25 million	10.4 million	130,919
February	18 million	47.5 million	29.4 million	474,915
March	46.6 million	32. 7 million	4.9 million*	61,187*
April	43.5 million	1.2 million*	–	0
May	36.9 million	0	–	288
June	63.2 million	0	–	1,245
July	48.2 million	14	25,298**	143

Biden
"Presidential Committee Reports Biden for President," Federal Election Commission, accessed January 2, 2021, https://www.fec.gov/data/reports/presidential/?is_amended=false&data_type=processed&committee_id=C00703975&cycle=2020
"Reports of Receipts and Disbursements Biden for President, February Monthly," Federal Election Commission, accessed July 26, 2021, https://docquery.fec.gov/cgi-bin/forms/C00703975/1400463/.
"Reports of Receipts and Disbursements Biden for President, March Monthly," Federal Election Commission, accessed July 26, 2021, https://docquery.fec.gov/cgi-bin/forms/C00703975/1391701/.
"Reports of Receipts and Disbursements Biden for President, April Monthly," Federal Election Commission, accessed July 26, 2021, https://docquery.fec.gov/cgi-bin/forms/C00703975/1402986/.
"Reports of Receipts and Disbursements Biden for President, May Monthly," Federal Election Commission, accessed July 26, 2021, https://docquery.fec.gov/cgi-bin/forms/C00703975/1407726/.
"Reports of Receipts and Disbursements Biden for President, June Monthly," Federal Election Commission, accessed July 26, 2021, https://docquery.fec.gov/cgi-bin/forms/C00703975/1414186/.
"Reports of Receipts and Disbursements Biden for President, July Monthly," Federal Election Commission, accessed July 26, 2021, https://docquery.fec.gov/cgi-bin/forms/C00703975/1427451/.
"Reports of Receipts and Disbursements Biden for President, August Monthly," Federal Election Commission, accessed July 26, 2021, https://docquery.fec.gov/cgi-bin/forms/C00703975/1434676/.
Sanders
"Presidential Committee Reports Bernie 2020," Federal Election Commission," accessed January 2, 2021, https://www.fec.gov/data/reports/presidential/?is_amended=false&data_type=processed&committee_id=C00577130&committee_id=C00696948&cycle=2020
"Reports of Receipts and Disbursements Sanders 2020, Februrary Monthly," Federal Election Commission, accessed July 26, 2021, https://docquery.fec.gov/cgi-bin/forms/C00696948/1384482/.
"Reports of Receipts and Disbursements Sanders 2020, March Monthly," Federal Election Commission, accessed July 26, 2021, https://docquery.fec.gov/cgi-bin/forms/C00696948/1391404/.
"Reports of Receipts and Disbursements Sanders 2020, April Monthly," Federal Election Commission, accessed July 26, 2021, https://docquery.fec.gov/cgi-bin/forms/C00696948/1402435/.
"Reports of Receipts and Disbursements Sanders 2020, May Monthly," Federal Election Commission, accessed July 26, 2021, https://docquery.fec.gov/cgi-bin/forms/C00696948/1407412/.
"Reports of Receipts and Disbursements Sanders 2020, June Monthly," Federal Election Commission, accessed July 26, 2021, https://docquery.fec.gov/cgi-bin/forms/C00696948/1414055/.
"Reports of Receipts and Disbursements Sanders 2020, July Monthly," Federal Election Commission, accessed July 26, 2021, https://docquery.fec.gov/cgi-bin/forms/C00577130/1423238/.
"Reports of Receipts and Disbursements Sanders 2020, August Monthly," Federal Election Commission, accessed July 26, 2021, https://docquery.fec.gov/cgi-bin/forms/C00696948/1434336/.
Warren
"Presidential Committee Reports Warren for President, Inc.," Federal Election Commission, accessed January 2, 2021, https://www.fec.gov/data/reports/presidential/?is_amended=false&data_type=processed&committee_id=C00693234&cycle=2020
"Reports of Receipts and Disbursements Warren for President, Inc., February Monthly," Federal Election Commission, accessed July 26, 2021, https://docquery.fec.gov/cgi-bin/forms/C00693234/1385191/.
"Reports of Receipts and Disbursements Warren for President, Inc., March Monthly," Federal Election Commission, accessed July 26, 2021, https://docquery.fec.gov/cgi-bin/forms/C00693234/1391678/.
"Reports of Receipts and Disbursements Warren for President, Inc., April Monthly Amended," Federal Election Commission, accessed July 26, 2021, https://docquery.fec.gov/cgi-bin/forms/C00693234/1466617/.
"Reports of Receipts and Disbursements Warren for President, Inc., July Quarterly," Federal Election Commission, accessed July 26, 2021, https://docquery.fec.gov/cgi-bin/forms/C00693234/1511820/.
Bloomberg
"Presidential Committee Reports Mike Bloomberg 2020, Inc.," Federal Election Commission, accessed January 2, 2021, https://www.fec.gov/data/reports/presidential/?is_amended=false&data_type=processed&committee_id=C00728154&cycle=2020

Sanders outraised Biden in individual contributions in January and February of 2020 with Biden receiving only $8.88 million in January compared to Sanders's $47.5 million and Warren's $10.4 million. February was no better for Biden with Sander's individual donations topping $25 million and Warren's $29.4 million.

One factor was that Sanders and Warren made use of smaller, more individualized campaign strategies that grew small donors. In fact, Sanders received $176.3 million from donors pledging $200 or less; Warren's figure of small donors was also large with $94.9 million from small donors.[48]

Both Sanders and Warren eschewed large donors during their primary campaigns and criticized campaigns that took money from large donors. On his campaign website, Sanders explicitly called for a ban on corporate contributions to the Democratic Party Convention, mandate for public financing of all elections, and proposed an amendment to the U.S. Constitution declaring that money is not considered speech and that corporations are not individual people (presumably this last request in part response to *Citizens United v. FEC*).[49] Warren similarly took a hard stand for campaign finance reform in her presidential campaign declaring she would not take any donations over $200 from "big tech companies, big banks, private equity firms, or hedge funds."[50]

Buttigieg dropped out of the race on March 1, leaving Biden, Warren, Bloomberg, and Sanders remaining as the four main contenders for the nomination.[51] However, Bloomberg loomed large as a candidate because of

---

Table 3.2 (*Continued*)

"Reports of Receipts and Disbursements Mike Bloomberg 2020 February Monthly," Federal Election Commission, accessed July 26, 2021, https://docquery.fec.gov/cgi-bin/forms/C00728154/1392150/.

"Reports of Receipts and Disbursements Mike Bloomberg 2020 March Monthly," Federal Election Commission, accessed July 26, 2021, https://docquery.fec.gov/cgi-bin/forms/C00728154/1407504/.

"Reports of Receipts and Disbursements Mike Bloomberg 2020 April Monthly," Federal Election Commission, accessed July 26, 2021, https://docquery.fec.gov/cgi-bin/forms/C00728154/1413718/.

"Reports of Receipts and Disbursements Mike Bloomberg 2020 May Monthly," Federal Election Commission, accessed July 26, 2021, https://docquery.fec.gov/cgi-bin/forms/C00728154/1413716/.

"Reports of Receipts and Disbursements Mike Bloomberg 2020 June Monthly," Federal Election Commission, accessed July 26, 2021, https://docquery.fec.gov/cgi-bin/forms/C00728154/1413697/.

"Reports of Receipts and Disbursements Mike Bloomberg 2020 July Monthly," Federal Election Commission, accessed July 26, 2021, https://docquery.fec.gov/cgi-bin/forms/C00728154/1427097/.

"Reports of Receipts and Disbursements Mike Bloomberg 2020 August Monthly," Federal Election Commission, accessed July 26 2021, https://docquery.fec.gov/cgi-bin/forms/C00728154/1434715/.

Note that all of the data from these sites incorporates the candidate's February, March, April, May, June, July, and August 2020 Monthly Filings, or in the case of Warren July Quarterly filing.

¹This table appears in Cayce Myers, "Campaign Finance and its Impact on the 2020 Campaign," in *The 2020 Campaign: Political Communication and Practice*, ed. Robert Denton (Lanham, MD: Roman and Littlefield, 2021, 163).

*Indicates the Month Candidate Suspended Campaign.

**In April 2020–June 2020 Warren had no monthly reports as she switched to a quarterly report, which was filed in as her July Quarterly report covering 4/1/2020 through 6/30/2020.

***These figures include itemized and unitemized total contributions from persons/individuals other than political committees. These figures do not include party committee, other committee, or candidate contributions.

his ability to self-finance, and the thought that a moderate candidate, such as him, would be able to be more electable in a General Election. Michael Bloomberg's campaign began in November 2019, well after the top-tier candidates began. His perceived strategy was to enter the race late and win delegates during Super Tuesday. His campaign was largely self-financed, but his self-financing equaled the dollar amount of well-financed candidates such as Biden and Sanders. In fact, in his April 2020 FEC filing, Bloomberg showed he raised a total of $912,592 in individual contributions year-to-date, compared to donating over $1 billion to his own campaign.[52] His presence in the campaign served as a lightning rod of criticism from progressive candidates, particularly Warren, who chastised Bloomberg for his behavior and presence within the Democratic field.[53]

Biden would go on to win big in Super Tuesday held on March 3, 2020 winning the primaries in Alabama, Arkansas, Massachusetts, Maine, Minnesota, North Carolina, Oklahoma, Tennessee, Texas, and Virginia. Sanders would win California, Colorado, Utah, and, as expected, his home state of Vermont. Like many self-funded candidates before him, Bloomberg did not do well in the primaries. His campaign only won one primary contest, America Samoa. Warren would win no primary on Super Tuesday, not even her home state of Massachusetts (she would come second).[54] After Super Tuesday, Bloomberg and Warren dropped out of the race within a day of each other; he would endorse Biden she would not endorse anyone until April 5 when she endorsed Biden.[55] Sanders suspended his campaign on April 8, and endorsed Biden and on April 13.[56] Biden would go on to announce Kamala Harris, his fierce opponent early in the Democratic primary season, as his running mate on August 11, and they received the nomination at the convention later that month.[57]

HOW MONEY AFFECTED EVENTUAL
SELECTION OF DEMOCRATIC NOMINEE

Biden's victory as the Democratic nominee showed that candidate quality and message can outperform large amounts of campaign cash. He overcame well-financed opponents such as Sanders and Bloomberg. Sanders's early entry into the race and early victories normally would be indicators of campaign victory, and Bloomberg's seemingly endless supply of campaign cash should have made it difficult for other candidates to overcome Bloomberg are indicators of campaign victory, namely media exposure and name recognitions. What the Democratic primary campaign showed is that money is essential to success in the primaries, but it is not a guarantee to victory. Campaign finance reform has been predicated on the idea that money is a corrupting influence within democracy because it leads for the best financed candidate to win. If that were the case Michael Bloomberg would have won the primary decidedly, and without any real competition. After all, he was the only candidate rich enough to finance his own campaign, and the only candidate to have $1 billion on hand for primary campaign expenditures.

The other big takeaway from the Democratic primary season is that progressive candidates are competitive because they can be effective fundraisers. Sanders and Warren both showed that fundraising for progressive candidates can yield the same type of level as moderate Democrats. While electability of candidates like Sanders has not been tested in a General Election, what is clear is the Democratic Party has the fundraising abilities to have progressives be competitive within primaries. Even Joe Biden was outpaced by Warren and Sanders in early 2020, showing that even establishment candidates can struggle with financing even with high name recognition. In fact, the progressive candidates showed that small donations may be one way to offset larger donors within an election.

The 2020 Democratic primary was unusual also because of its large candidate pool. Conventional wisdom on campaigns suggests that this is, in fact, harmful to the party. Too many candidates, with campaigns dragging on too long make for difficult selection of candidates. That, in turn, harms later fundraising because of fractures within the party and because the eventual nominee has to spend far too much time and resources focused on primary fundraising and campaigning. However, this type of deep pool shows that less well-known candidates can turn this into a fundraising boost. Because of the lack of a clear front-runner candidates that suffer from lower identity recognition can emerge as top-tier candidates if their campaign fundraising organization is strong. For instance, Pete Buttigieg, a relative unknown, was able to mount a compelling campaign, which resulted in a cabinet position in the Biden Administration as U.S. Secretary of Transportation.

The Democratic primary was an expensive race, and the end result showed that the Democrats were highly successful fundraisers. Their ability to recruit donors and subsequently donor data allowed them to mount a successful General Election campaign, and ultimately win the White House. However, it is worth noting that President Trump with nominal opposition in the Republican Party was building his own war chest that would prove formidable.

NOTES

1. Bernie Sanders, *Our Revolution: A Future to Believe In* (New York: St. Martin's Press, 2016), 3.
2. Ibid., 189.

3. Louis Jacobson, "The Record-Setting 2020 Democratic Primary Field: What You Need to Know," *Politico*, last updated January 31, 2020, https://www.politifact .com/article/2019/may/02/big-democratic-primary-field-what-need/.

4. Ted Kennedy won twelve presidential primaries in 1980 in the west and New England. He refused to drop out of the race despite having no chance of the nomination, and challenged the party platform in a televised speech at the convention.

5. Report of Receipts and Reimbursements, Kamala Harris for the People, Federal Election Commission, accessed February 7, 2021, https://docquery.fec.gov/ cgi-bin/forms/C00694455/1326016/. This April quarterly began on January 21, 2019, the date Harris announced her candidacy, and ended on March 31, 2019.

6. Report of Receipts and Reimbursements, Gillibrand 2020, Federal Elections Commission, accessed February 7, 2021, https://docquery.fec.gov/cgi-bin/forms/C 00694018/1326061/.

7. Patrick Svitek and Abby Livingston, "How the Race Between Ted Cruz and Beto O'Rourke Became the Closest in Texas History in 40 Years," *The Texas Tribune*, last updated November 9, 2018, https://www.texastribune.org/2018/11/09/ ted-cruz-beto-orourke-closest-texas-race-40-years/

8. Joe Hagan, "Beto O'Rourke: "I'm Just Born to Be In It," *Vanity Fair*, April 2019, https://www.vanityfair.com/news/2019/03/beto-orourke-cover-story.

9. Jonathan Martin, "Beto O'Rourke Raised $6.1 Million Online in First 24 Hours, New York Times, last updated March 18, 2019, https://www.nytimes.com/2 019/03/18/us/politics/beto-o-rourke-fundraising.html; David Siders, "Beto O'Rourke Fundraising Fell to 3.6 million in Second Quarter," *Politico*, last updated July 15, 2019, https://www.politico.com/story/2019/07/15/beto-orourke-fundraising-second-q uarter-1416486

10. Max Greenwood, "O'Rourke Raises $3.6 Million in Second Quarter," *The Hill*, last updated July 15, 2019, https://thehill.com/homenews/campaign/453213- orourke-raises-36-million-in-second-quarter.

11. Alexander Burns, "Beto O'Rourke Drops Out of the Presidential Race," *New York Times*, November 1, 2019, https://www.nytimes.com/2019/11/01/us/politics/bet o-orourke-drops-out.html.

12. David Wright, "Kamala Harris Touts $1.5 million Haul in 24 hours after Campaign Announcement," *CNN* Online, January 22, 2019, https://www.cnn.com/ 2019/01/22/politics/kamala-harris-fundraising-announcement/index.html.

13. Evan Real, "Kamala Harris Campaign Selling T-Shirts Inspired by Viral Joe Biden Moment," *Hollywood Reporter*, June 28, 2019, https://www.hollywoodrepo rter.com/news/kamala-harris-selling-t-shirts-inspired-by-viral-biden-debate-moment -1221674.

14. July was $11.7 million and October $11.6 million in individual donations. "Report of Receipts and Disbursements, Kamala Harris for the People, October Quarterly 2019," Federal Election Commission, accessed March 1, 2021, https:/ /docquery.fec.gov/cgi-bin/forms/C00694455/1358880/; "Report of Receipts and Disbursements, Kamala Harris for the People, July Quarterly 2019," Federal Election Commission, accessed March 1, 2021, https://docquery.fec.gov/cgi-bin/forms/C 00694455/1341232/; "Report of Receipts and Disbursements, Kamala Harris for the

People, April Quarterly 2019," Federal Election Commission, accessed March 1, 2021, https://docquery.fec.gov/cgi-bin/forms/C00694455/1326016/

15. Lauren Gambino, "Bernie Sanders Raises $5.9m in 24 hours after Announcing 2020 Campaign" *The Guardian*, February 20, 2019, https://www.theguardian.com/us -news/2019/feb/20/bernie-sanders-2020-presidential-campaign-fundraising.

16. Dan Merica, "Windfall at Bernie's: Sanders raises $1.5 million in 24 hours," *CNN* Online, updated May 1, 2015, https://www.cnn.com/2015/05/01/politics/bernie -sanders-fundraising/index.html.

17. Marc Caputo and Scott Bland, "Biden Crushes It In First-Day Fundraising: 6.3 Million," updated April 26, 2019, *Politico*, https://www.politico.com/story/2019/04/2 6/biden-fundraising-numbers-2020-1291180.

18. This lack of support across the candidates is attributed by some to a gender gap issue. Giovanni Russonello, "Why Warren Supporters Aren't a Lock to Get Behind Sanders," *New York Times*, March 6, 2020, https://www.nytimes.com/2020/03/06/us /politics/elizabeth-warren-bernie-sanders-voters.html.

19. Alex D'Elia, "What Do Democratic Candidates Need to Make the First 2020 Debates?," *PBS NewsHour* Online April 3, 2019, https://www.pbs.org/newshour /politics/what-do-democratic-candidates-need-to-make-the-first-2020-debates. The three polls could be either national polls or polls in Iowa, New Hampshire, South Carolina, or Nevada, which are all primary or caucus states.

20. Reid J. Epstein, Sydney Ember, Shane Goldmacher and Katie Glueck, "7 Takeaways From the June 26 Democratic Debate: Castro's Big Night," *New York Times*, June 26, 2019, https://www.nytimes.com/2019/06/26/us/politics/2020-dem ocratic-debate-tonight.html.

21. Eileen Connelly, "Kamala Harris Raises $2M in 24 Hours with Help of 'That Little Girl Was Me' Shirts," *New York Post*, June 29, 2019, https://nypost.com/2019 /06/29/kamala-harris-raises-2m-in-24-hours-with-help-of-that-little-girl-was-me-sh irts/.

22. "Termination Report, Swalwell for America," Federal Election Commission, accessed March 3, 2021, https://docquery.fec.gov/cgi-bin/forms/C00701698/1 376364/.

23. "Reports of Receipts and Disbursements, Tom Steyer 2020, Year-End," Federal Election Commission, accessed March 3, 2021, https://docquery.fec.gov/cgi -bin/forms/C00711614/1379864/.

24. "Presidential Candidate Map, Beto O'Rourke," Federal Election Commission, accessed March 3, 2021, https://www.fec.gov/data/candidates/president/presidential -map/; Presidential Candidate Map, Cory Booker," Federal Election Commission, accessed March 3, 2021, https://www.fec.gov/data/candidates/president/president ial-map.

25. "Report of Receipts and Disbursements, Hickenlooper 2020, October Quarterly," Federal Election Commission, accessed March 3, 2021, https://docquery .fec.gov/cgi-bin/forms/C00698258/1367731/.

26. "Report of Receipts and Disbursements, Gillibrand 2020, July Quarterly," Federal Election Commission, accessed March 3, 2021, https://docquery.fec.gov/cgi -bin/forms/C00694018/1340492/; "Report of Receipts and Disbursements, Gillibrand

2020, Year-End," Federal Election Commission, accessed March 3, 2021, https://do cquery.fec.gov/cgi-bin/forms/C00694018/1378930/.

27. "Report of Receipts and Disbursements, Steyer 2020, October Quarterly," Federal Election Commission, accessed September 28, 2021, https://docquery.fec. gov/cgi-bin/forms/C00711614/1521517/.

28. "Report of Receipts and Disbursements, Bennet for America, October Quarterly," Federal Election Commission, accessed March 3, 2021, https://docquery.fec.gov/cgi-bin/forms/C00705186/1416743/; "Report of Receipts and Disbursements, Marianne Williamson for President, October Quarterly," Federal Election Commission, accessed March 3, 2021, https://docquery.fec.gov/cgi-bin/forms/C00696054/1379354/; Alex Thompson, "Oprah Pal and Spirituality Guru Plans 2020 Run," *Politico*, November 16, 2018, https://www.politico.com/story/2018/11/16/oprah-pal-williamson-2020-run-996174.

29. Alex Thompson, "Andrew Yang Announces $120,000 Giveaway During Debate," *Politico*, updated September 12, 2019, https://www.politico.com/story/2019/09/12/andrew-yang-120000-giveaway-for-ubi-pilot-program-1493622.

30. "Report of Receipts and Disbursements, Friends of Andrew Yang, October Quarterly," Federal Election Commission, accessed March 3, 2021, https://docquery.fec.gov/cgi-bin/forms/C00659938/1371212/; "Report of Receipts and Disbursements, Friends of Andrew Yang, July Quarterly," Federal Election Commission, accessed March 3, 2021, https://docquery.fec.gov/cgi-bin/forms/C00659938/1369581/.

31. "Report of Receipts and Disbursements, Friends of Andrew Yang, Year-End," Federal Election Commission, accessed March 3, 2021, https://docquery.fec.gov/cgi-bin/forms/C00659938/1391831/.

32. "Report of Receipts and Disbursements, de Blasio 2020, October Quarterly," Federal Election Commission, accessed March 3, 2021, https://docquery.fec.gov/cgi-bin/forms/C00706697/1414451/.

33. O'Rourke's $17 million was raised through June 20, 2016. He converted his campaign committee Beto for America to the People Powered Action committee, which helps Democratic candidates in Texas. "Presidential Candidate Map, Beto O'Rourke," Federal Election Commission, accessed March 3, 2021, https://www.fec.gov/data/candidates/president/presidential-map/; Patrick Svitek, "Beto O'Rourke Unveils PAC With Focus on Boosting Texas Democrats in 2020, *Texas Tribune*, December 20, 2019, https://www.texastribune.org/2019/12/20/beto-orourke-launches-pac-focused-texas-2020-elections/.

34. Shawn Langlois, "'I'm Not a Billionaire': Kamala Harris Receives Internet Consolation after Dropping Out of Presidential Race," *Market Watch*, December 3, 2019, https://www.marketwatch.com/story/non-billionaire-kamala-harris-feels-the-internet-love-after-dropping-out-of-race-2019-12-03.

35. The End-of-Year statement covers all donations from October 1, 2019 until December 31, 2019. "Reports of Receipts and Disbursements, Bloomberg 2020, Year-End," Federal Election Commission, accessed March 3, 2021, https://docquery.fec.gov/cgi-bin/forms/C00728154/1392145/.

36. Dam Merica, Cristina Alesci, and Jake Tapper, "Mike Bloomberg is the Latest 2020 Hopeful," *CNN* Online, updated November 24, 2019, https://www.cnn.com/2019/11/24/politics/michael-bloomberg-2020-election/index.html.

37. Alexander Burns, "Michael Bloomberg Joins 2020 Democratic Field for President," *New York Times*, updated March 4, 2020, https://www.nytimes.com/2019 /11/24/us/politics/michael-bloomberg-2020-presidency.html.

38. "Financial Summary, Michael Bloomberg 2020, Inc., Federal Election Commission, accessed March 3, 2021, https://www.fec.gov/data/candidate/P0001 4530/?cycle=2020&election_full=true.

39. Ibid.

40. Associated Press, "Warren's Souvenir Bottle Pops Up in Buttigieg Wine Cave Debate," *NBC* Online, December 21, 2019, https://www.nbcnews.com/politics/2020 -election/warren-s-souvenir-bottle-pops-buttigieg-wine-cave-debate-n1106186.

41. Ibid.

42. Ibid.

43. "2020 Iowa Democratic Caucuses Live Results," *Washington Post*, February 27, 2020, https://www.washingtonpost.com/elections/election-results/iowa/.

44. "New Hampshire Results," *NBC News* Online, February 14, 2020, https://ww w.nbcnews.com/politics/2020-primary-elections/new-hampshire-results.

45. "Report of Receipts and Disbursements, Amy for America, March Monthly," Federal Election Commission, accessed March 3, 2021, https://docquery.fec.gov/cgi -bin/forms/C00696419/1424472/.

46. Eric Bradner and Paul LeBlanc, "South Carolina Rep. Jim Clyburn endorses Joe Biden Ahead of Primary," *CNN* Online, February 26, 2020, https://www.cnn .com/2020/02/26/politics/jim-clyburn-endorses-joe-biden/index.html.

47. Ron Elving, "Joe Biden's Long and Rocky Road To The Democratic Nomination," *NPR* Online, August 16, 2020, https://www.npr.org/2020/08/16/9026 40265/joe-bidens-long-and-rocky-road-to-the-democratic-nomination.

48. "Presidential Candidate Map, Elizabeth Warren," Federal Election Commission, accessed March 3, 2021, https://www.fec.gov/data/candidates/president/presidential-m ap/; "Presidential Candidate Map, Bernie Sanders," Federal Election Commission, accessed March 3, 2021, https://www.fec.gov/data/candidates/president/presidential-map/.

49. "Issues: Get Corporate Money Out of Politics," Bernie, accessed March 3, 2021 https://berniesanders.com/issues/money-out-of-politics/.

50. "Getting Big Money Out of Politics," Warren Democrats, accessed March 3, 2021, https://elizabethwarren.com/plans/campaign-finance-reform.

51. Reid Epstein and Trip Gabriel, "Pete Buttigieg Drops Out of Democratic Presidential Race," *New York Times*, March 1, 2020, https://www.nytimes.com/2020 /03/01/us/politics/pete-buttigieg-drops-out.html.

52. "Reports of Receipts and Disbursements, Bloomberg 2020, April Monthly," Federal Election Commission, accessed March 3, 2021, https://docquery.fec.gov/cgi -bin/forms/C00728154/1413718/.

53. Reid Epstein and Lisa Lerner, "Warren Says Bloomberg Shouldn't Be Nominee, Citing Redlining Remarks," *New York Times*, February 13, 2020, https:// www.nytimes.com/2020/02/13/us/politics/elizabeth-warren-bloomberg.html.

54. "Live Results: Super Tuesday 2020," *Washington Post,* accessed March 3, 2021, https://www.washingtonpost.com/elections/election-results/super-tuesday/.

55. Douglas Mackinnon, "Bloomberg Made a Yuge Mistake Dropping Out," *The Hill*, March 7, 2020, https://thehill.com/opinion/white-house/486269-bloomberg-made-a-yuge-mistake-dropping-out; Maggie Astor and Katie Glueck, "Elizabeth Warren Endorses Joe Biden: 'When You Disagree, He'll Listen,'" *New York Times*, updated May 22, 2020, https://www.nytimes.com/2020/04/15/us/politics/elizabeth-warren-endorse-biden.html.

56. Marc Caputo and Holly Otterbein, "Bernie Makes it Official: It's Biden or Bust," *Politico,* updated April 13, 2020, https://www.politico.com/news/2020/04/13/sanders-endorses-biden-183961.

57. James Oliphant and Joseph Ax, "Democrat Joe Biden Chooses Kamala Harris for White House Running House," *Reuters*, August 11, 2020, https://www.reuters.com/article/us-usa-election-biden-harris/democrat-joe-biden-chooses-senator-kamala-harris-for-white-house-running-mate-idUSKCN2572MZ.

Chapter 4

Self-Funding in the 2020 Democratic Primary

Billionaire Candidates

Mike Bloomberg and Tom Steyer represented the type of corporate figure reviled by candidates such as Sanders and Warren. In fact, Sanders in his book, *Our Revolution*, devotes a chapter to billionaire influences on elections, entitled "Defeating Oligarchy."[1] In that chapter Sanders argues that billionaires are ruining American democracy by attempting to purchase seats in Congress and that court cases such as *Citizens United v. FEC* only serves to embolden oligarchy in the United States for right-wing causes.[2] The issue confronting Democrats in 2020 was Bloomberg and Tom Steyer, who made their fortunes in hedge fund management and were vying for the Democratic Party nomination alongside candidates like Sanders.

In 2020, the Democratic primary had many obstacles to overcome before victory in the General Election. First was the issue of the party split between progressive and moderate wings of the party. Bernie Sanders and Joe Biden's race in February and March 2020 epitomized that debate, and it was ultimately resolved in Biden's favor. Second was the issue of the sheer number of Democratic candidates in the primary race. A record number of twenty-nine candidates were seeking the nomination, although to be fair some were long shots. This created crowded fields for Democratic debates, and consequently long-shot candidates likely took votes, and money, from more viable candidates who needed it. Third, and most interestingly, was the fact that the Democrats, a party long known for representing the working class and unions, had two billionaire candidates seeking their party's nomination. Their candidacy represented a type of cognitive dissonance within the party. While Democrats, such as Sanders, have criticized the excesses of the corporate power within the United States, and the corporate power enshrined in campaign finance cases like *Citizens United v. FEC*, the Democratic Party has as part of its base extremely wealthy corporate figures.[3]

However, Bloomberg's presence in the race had more impact than just cognitive dissonance for progressive anti-billionaire Democrats. His candidacy signaled something very important about fundraising. As a candidate willing to invest his personal fortune into the Democratic primary, Bloomberg had an advantage that other candidates did not. He did not have to fundraise. He did not have to worry about having enough money to buy advertising space for name or platform recognition. He also served as mirror reflection of Trump. He was self-made billionaire, and, like Trump, was a New Yorker who had a reputation of being able to get things done. Moreover, unlike any candidate in the Democratic field, or the Republican, he had a media company, and his ability to understand media and use it to his benefit was thought to be a major competitive advantage.

As we now know, those advantages did not turn about to create victory. However, his candidacy and that of Tom Steyer represent the latest iteration of the unsuccessful self-financed candidate. This chapter explores the history of self-financed candidates in the United States, Bloomberg and Steyer's role in financing in the 2020 Democratic primary, and Bloomberg's contributions to Democrats in the General Election. From this analysis, this chapter concludes with assessing the impact, if any, of Bloomberg's contributions to the 2020 campaign and the future of self-funded candidates in the future.

SELF-FINANCE CANDIDATES: A HISTORY OF FAILURE

While *Buckley v. Valeo* provides the current legal structure for campaign finance, the exception of political candidate committees providing political contributions to party committee provides a loophole for caps on campaign contributions.[4] This presents an even greater campaign finance issue when the candidate is self-funded, because it allows an individual to spend a lot of money personally donated through a candidate campaign committee to a party committee.

Current campaign laws allow for self-funding of campaigns. However, unlike campaign contributions from other individuals, self-funding for a campaign has no limits. However, self-funding requires disclosure and must come from "personal funds" including salary, property, trusts, or dividends. However, if a candidate provides a loan to a campaign there are rules that apply for any loan over $250,000.[5] In fact, self-funding creates a peculiar campaign finance loophole that allows candidates to give unlimited amounts to parties. Known as the "Bloomberg loophole," this rule allows presidential candidates to give unlimited amounts to political parties. Critics note that this type of end-run around campaign finance laws for self-funded candidates raises certain issues about the fairness of self-funding and the purpose behind federal election law.[6]

While self-funding presents its own legal challenges, there are also the competitive challenges of self-funding elections. Democratic primary candidates in 2020, including Sanders, Klobuchar, and Biden, had harsh criticism of campaign self-funding, presumably because of the presence of Bloomberg and Steyer.[7] In fact, Klobuchar said that the self-funding of Bloomberg put her at a competitive disadvantage, because billionaires with seemingly limitless resources could make ad buys in the millions while she could not (Bloomberg had made approximately $500 million in ad buys by February 2020).[8]

However, self-funded campaigns are not new to American politics, and despite criticisms in 2020, most self-funded candidates have serious obstacles to victory. The reason is it compounds the issue of wealth in politics. While being a wealthy politician is a norm in American politics, it is not the norm for an individual to fund his or her own campaign. That is because self-funding has the obvious drawback of candidates having to use their own money to fund their elections, but also because candidates who self-fund typically do not win. Perhaps because self-funded candidates lack the grassroots support for their candidacy or because self-funding creates its own political issue of being out of touch with modern American voters, the end result is self-funded is rarely successful in American history.

The role of self-funding in modern American campaigns has roots in candidates from wealthy families using their connections and family members to donate to campaigns. Wealthy businessmen in American politics have been a norm for over a century. In 1918, industrialist Henry Ford sought the Senate seat in Michigan, and that primary campaign resulted in one of the first U.S. Supreme Court cases on campaign finance, *Newberry v. United States*.[9] However, the wealth of candidates is sometimes used to portray political independence. That was the case in the 1958 gubernatorial election in New York between Republican Nelson Rockefeller against Democrat Averell Harriman. Both candidates were wealthy scions of New York elite society, but Rockefeller was perceived by many voters to be not beholden to any special interest because of his family's immense wealth.[10] Harriman's own 1952 presidential campaign was largely under-funded, but his wealthy relatives and friends donated up to $5,000 each in support.[11] President John F. Kennedy benefited from his own family's wealth, even joking in 1958 in a speech at the Washington D.C. Gridiron Club that his father, millionaire Joseph P. Kennedy, sent him a telegram stating, "Dear Jack—Don't buy a single vote more than necessary—I'll be damned if I am going to pay for a landslide."[12]

Self-funding a political campaign became a focal point in the 1992 election when Ross Perot ran as a third-party candidate. Perot was a multibillionaire

Texan who made his fortune in information technology. His campaign in 1992 was largely self-funded, and he made that a key part of his presidential campaign. Even before he announced his candidacy, Perot said he would not accept donations for more than $5.[13] Part of his strategy on self-funding and speaking about people soliciting him to run was a political strategy used to draft him into running for president. Perot went on to spend $40 million in television advertising, including two 1-minute spots on Good Morning America that cost $1.5 million.[14] Perot did not win a single electoral vote in 1992, but his candidacy served as a watershed moment for the benefits and perils of self-funding in presidential elections. All told Perot would spend $65.6 million of his own money in 1992.[15]

Other wealthy candidates have self-funded since Perot. Steve Forbes spent $32 million of his own money in his quest for the Republican nomination in 2000. It was estimated that Forbes funded approximately 86 percent of his campaign, only to receive around 61,810 votes.[16] However, this did not deter others from self-funding campaigns for lower-level offices. Famously, eBay founder Meg Whitman self-funded her California governor's campaign with $143 million only to lose that race handily to Jerry Brown. Similarly, Linda McMahon and Carly Fiorina lost their respective Senate races in Connecticut and California.[17] However, self-funding is not a definite loss. New Jersey Senate candidate John Corzine, former Goldman Sachs CFO, spent $62 million to win his New Jersey Senate race in 2000.[18]

Self-funding also became a political issue in the 2016 presidential race in which Donald Trump donated over $66.1 million to his own campaign. Trump's self-funding was not the majority of his campaign, but he used the fact he provided funding as a political issue against Hillary Clinton. Trump's self-funding was also used, similar to other candidates, as an indication that he would not be beholden to special interest groups as president. However, media criticized Trump's self-funding narrative, stating that he did not completely self-fund his campaign, and was accepting donations like other candidates.[19] In the Second Presidential Debate, Trump even challenged Clinton on her presidential campaign donations asking why she did not, as a wealthy candidate, not contribute more to her campaign. He said:

Now, Hillary mentioned something about contributions just so you understand. So, I will have in my race more than $100 million put in—of my money, meaning I'm not taking all of this big money from all of these different corporations like she's doing. What I ask is this. So, I'm putting in more than—by the time it's finished, I'll have more than $100 million invested. Pretty much self-funding mine. We're raising money for the Republican Party, and we're doing tremendously on the small donations, $61 average or so. I ask Hillary, why doesn't—she made $250 million by being in office. She used the power of her office to make a lot of money. Why isn't she funding, not for $100 million, but why don't you put $10 million or $20 million or $25 million or $30 million into your own campaign?[20]

Clinton did provide $1.4 million in a candidate contribution to her campaign.[21] However, Trump's campaign donations may have been the result of lower fundraising totals than his opponent. By the end of the election Clinton raised $399 million in individual donations compared with $132 million for Trump.[22] However, the 2020 election would see the largest self-funded campaign in American history.

MIKE BLOOMBERG AND THE 2020
DEMOCRATIC PRESIDENTIAL PRIMARY

Michael Bloomberg's decision to self-fund his presidential campaign followed a pattern that had emerged since he was running for Mayor of New York City. In his mayoral races, Bloomberg, who had an estimated net worth in 2020 of $54.9 billion, used his self-funding as a political asset.[23] It showed how he was not beholden to the old political interests of the city, and he would act, more or less, independently because of that. His 2020 presidential campaign was hardly a long-shot campaign. He was the Mayor of New York City for twelve years and had a high popularity. He was also a moderate Democrat. Part of his strategy was to provide an alternative to the progressive Democratic candidates, such as Sanders and Warren, who were viewed by some as unelectable against Trump because of their progressive views. Bloomberg also positioned himself as a moderate in the race who had the electability to defeat Trump in the General Election.

Bloomberg's entry in the 2020 Democratic primary caused a stir because of his commitment to using his own money to finance his campaign. As he entered in the race in 2019, candidates began taking issue with his wealth and use of a self-funded campaign. Polling showed that Bloomberg was competitive, and his aggressive advertising strategy meant that his message and name recognition would be high compared to other candidates. However, his strategy of self-funding caused criticism from the Democrats who tried to equate Bloomberg's self-funding as an attempt to buy the election. In fact, Democrat candidate, and later Vice President, Kamala Harris even took a parting shot at Bloomberg when exited the race in December 2019 stating that she was not a billionaire and therefore could not afford to remain in the primary.[24]

However, Bloomberg's issue of self-funded campaign was only part of the issue. Other controversies emerged about *Bloomberg News* and his previous behavior and statements. His company *Bloomberg News* presented an interesting issue rarely seen before seen in an American election, except for Steve Forbes. Bloomberg owned a major news outlet, and there was a question of how this outlet would cover his campaign. A staff memo would emerge that stated that *Bloomberg News* would not be investigating any Democratic candidate for president because Mike Bloomberg was running for president. *Bloomberg News'* editorial writers would leave their posts at *Bloomberg News*, and joined Bloomberg's campaign. Part of the rationale was that it was the editorial writer who reflected most of Mike Bloomberg's views, and members of *Bloomberg News* David Shipley and Tim O'Brien were specifically mentioned as leaving Bloomberg to work on the Bloomberg campaign to limit editorial bias.[25] However, the most controversial aspect of the new *Bloomberg News* policy was to suspend any investigation into Democratic candidates and Bloomberg himself. The rationale was rooted in the fact that Bloomberg had a long-standing policy of not investigating Mike Bloomberg, Bloomberg's family, or his foundation, and now that he was a presidential candidate, they were going to extend that policy to his campaign, and, as a result, into all Democratic opponents. Conversely, *Bloomberg News* would continue to investigate Donald Trump, but left it open-ended as to if they would continue to investigate Trump if Bloomberg became the Democratic nominee.[26]

This led to backlash stating that this type of policy was actually harmful to journalism and to the Democratic process. Even Democratic candidate Elizabeth Warren criticized Bloomberg for how his company would handle the primary race saying that the limitation on covering Democratic candidates harmed reporters and free press.[27] However, *Bloomberg News* did continue its coverage of President Donald Trump during this time, making the news outlet criticized for its perceived biased reporting.[28] Interestingly, after Bloomberg withdrew from the primary *Bloomberg News* said it resumed its regular coverage of the presidential race.[29]

Bloomberg was also criticized for the perception that he represented a billionaire class that was too wealthy and too conservative. *The Atlantic Monthly* quoted a Biden supporter saying that "The answer to one Republican New York billionaire is not another slightly richer Republican New York billionaire."[30] However, strategically Bloomberg was hoping for a strategy that centered upon a Sanders surge, which would then allow Bloomberg to emerge as the nominee against a Democratic-Socialist that some perceived to be unelectable because he was too far left for the General Election. Another aspect of Bloomberg's strategy was that in a convention where the first round of voting would yield no nominee, the second-round voting would include more moderate and politically practical Democratic superdelegates who would be swayed to nominate Bloomberg.[31]

However, this scenario never materialized. Instead, Bloomberg's candidacy sparked backlash from many Democratic candidates, notably Elizabeth

Warren. Even back in November 2019, Warren stated that Bloomberg was trying to buy the presidency and that the General Election would be a contest between two billionaires. In Ankey, Iowa, she said that Bloomberg "doesn't need people, he only needs bags and bags of money."[32] However, it was at the Democratic primary debate in Nevada in February 2020 that Bloomberg was assailed by multiple Democratic candidates from the left and the center. Sanders began stating that Bloomberg's policies of stop and frisk while Mayor of New York City harmed Latinos and African Americans.[33] Elizabeth Warren took aim at Bloomberg describing him as an "arrogant billionaire" who had called women "fat broads and horse-faced lesbians."[34] She went on to say that he had hidden his tax returns, engaged in sexual harassment, supported redlining, and stop and frisk.[35] His wealth was also at issue with Senator Amy Klobuchar stating that Bloomberg wanted her and others to step aside so he could become the nominee for president of the United States. She called him out on his wealth saying, "I don't think you look at Donald Trump and say we need someone richer in the White House."[36]

Bloomberg responded to these criticisms stating that Sanders wanted to take away health insurance from 160 million people, which made him essentially unelectable compared with Donald Trump. Sparring with Sanders over the U.S. tax code, Bloomberg said that if Sanders had a problem with the tax code that he had only himself to blame because he along with ninety-nine members of the U.S. Senate wrote it. Sanders made more issues out of Bloomberg's wealth calling his billionaire status "immoral" because his wealth exceeded that of 125 million Americans. Bloomberg responded, "I can't speak for all billionaires. All I know is I've been very lucky, made a lot of money, and I'm giving it all away to make this country better. And a good chunk of it goes to the Democratic Party, as well."[37]

In fact, Bloomberg's wealth did benefit his campaign to become the Democratic nominee for president. Table 4.1 shows Bloomberg's campaign committee comparing the individual contributions with Bloomberg's candidate contributions. It shows that beginning in 2019, he declared his candidacy in November 21 and began aggressively contributing to his campaign with a candidate contribution of over $200 million between the months of October and December 2019. As his campaign progressed into January he contributed over $263 million to his campaign, and for the month of February 2020 contributed $471.8 million to his campaign. Most of Bloomberg's donations for the entirety of his campaign in 2020 were from small donors under $200. However, the total amount of candidate contributions for Bloomberg's 2020 primary campaign was over $1.08 billion.[38]

Bloomberg's strategy of self-funding made him formidable, but his strategy did not yield positive results. He famously skipped the Iowa Caucuses to campaign in California.[39] Because of the voting issues in Iowa and

Table 4.1 Independent Contributions versus Candidate Contributions to Mike Bloomberg 2020[i]

Month	Individual Contributions* ($)	Candidate Contributions ($, million)
Year End 2019**	245,569	200.1
January	130,919	263.6
February	474,915	471.8
March***	61,187	112.2

[i]Figures over $1 million are given to the out to the nearest $100,000. "Report of Receipts and Disbursements, Mike Bloomberg 2020, Year-End Amended," Federal Election Commission, accessed March 4, 2021, https://docquery.fec.gov/cgi-bin/forms/C00728154/1392145/; "Report of Receipts and Disbursements, Mike Bloomberg 2020, February Monthly Amended," Federal Election Commission, accessed March 4, 2021, https://docquery.fec.gov/cgi-bin/forms/C00728154/1392150/; "Report of Receipts and Disbursements, Mike Bloomberg 2020, March Monthly Amended," Federal Election Commission, accessed March 4, 2021, https://docquery.fec.gov/cgi-bin/forms/C00728154/1407504/; "Report of Receipts and Disbursements, Mike Bloomberg 2020, April Monthly Amended," Federal Election Commission, accessed March 4, 2021, https://docquery.fec.gov/cgi-bin/forms/C00728154/1413718/.
*Individual contributions include both itemized and unitemized contributions.
**Bloomberg filed a Year-End Statement in 2020 for the dates of October 1, 2019–December 31, 2019.
***Month Bloomberg dropped out of the primary race.

the subsequent fallout, *The Washington Post* in an editorial declared that Bloomberg was the real winner of the causes because he was not involved in the political infighting that the race produced.[40] In New Hampshire, Bloomberg was not on the ballot, but received 4,777 write-in ballots, beating two other Democrats, Governor Deval Patrick of Massachusetts and Colorado Senator Mike Bennett, both of whom had dropped out before the primary.[41] He even won though Bloomberg was not on the Nevada Caucus or the South Carolina primary ballot. However, even *Bloomberg News* reported Biden's win in South Carolina upset Bloomberg's strategy of forcing a brokered convention because of Sanders's perceived un-electability.[42]

Even though Bloomberg opted out of the first four Democratic primary races in 2020, he spent a massive amount of money on advertising. In February 2020, *The Washington Post* wrote that Bloomberg's purchases were garnering him 30,000 online ads a minute.[43] However, despite this massive expenditure on advertising Bloomberg's campaign did not do well in Super Tuesday, which contained primary races in fifteen states including California, Texas, and Virginia. Bloomberg only won one primary, American Samoa, failing to meet the 15 percent threshold needed in the primaries to qualify for delegates.[44] Bloomberg suspended his campaign March 4, 2020, and endorsed Joe Biden, who won ten of the fifteen Super Tuesday races.[45]

After he suspended his campaign, the media pointed to Bloomberg's use of self-funding as an example of how much money was spent on a campaign that yielded few victories. Bloomberg framed his endorsement of Joe Biden as necessary to defeat Donald Trump in the General Election. Controversially, he would also give the Democratic National Convention $18 million from his own campaign funds instead of starting a super-PAC to defeat Trump.[46] Later, Bloomberg would go on to spend $100 million to help defeat Trump in Florida, Texas, and Ohio only to see Trump win all three states in the General Election.[47]

TOM STEYER AND THE DEMOCRATIC PRESIDENTIAL PRIMARY

A lesser-known wealthy candidate in the 2020 Democratic primary was former hedge fund manager and philanthropist Tom Steyer. After running the hedge fund, Farallon Capital, Steyer focused his efforts in 2012 on liberal causes including environmentalism. Calling himself a "self-made billionaire," Steyer has promised to give away his fortune on a variety of causes related to climate change and racial justice.[48] Entering the presidential campaign in July 2019, Steyer remained in the race until February 2020. However, his campaign, like Bloomberg's, received millions in self-funding. His campaign tactic was to focus on later primaries instead of the first two races in Iowa and New Hampshire. The rationale for this was that this would give him a competitive advantage going into Super Tuesday, and he would outlast other candidates.

Interestingly Steyer's campaign agreed with many of the campaign finance reform initiatives advocated by progressive candidates like Bernie Sanders. Steyer advocated for a repeal of *Citizens United v. FEC's* holding in 2010, citing that the decision allowed corporations too much power within politics. He also advocated for a restructuring of the Federal Election Commission, stating that it needed different structures and more independence.[49]

However, despite these progressive views, Steyer did not garner the type of individual donations that other candidates like Sanders received. Looking at his campaign from July 2019 until February 2020, Steyer raised over $3.4 million from individual contributions, but candidate contributions exceeded $341 million.[50] Like many progressive candidates, Steyer's individual contributions were in small donations, less than $200, which amounted to over $2.6 million of the $3.4 million raised from individuals. Steyer's self-funded campaign late strategy did not work well. In the Iowa Causes he came in seventh after Buttigieg, Sanders, Warren, Biden, Klobuchar, and Yang.[51] In New Hampshire, Steyer did slightly better coming in sixth, but had a strategy to stay in South Carolina while other candidates focused on the New Hampshire primary.[52] Believing he could make serious inroads by focusing on support South Carolina's large African American population, Steyer had more South Carolina events than any other Democratic candidate at the time of the New Hampshire primary. Part of that included spending $672,000 on

statewide advertising.[53] Similarly, the Nevada primary was also a focus of
Steyer, but he struggled falling behind in the polling needed to participate in
the Democratic primary debate held on February 19, 2020.[54]

During the first two months of 2020 Steyer donated over $57.1 million in
January and over $56 million to his campaign in February.[55] This is com-
pared to individual donations that totaled over $638,000 in January and over
$163,000 in February.[56] Steyer would go on to place fifth in Nevada, and
his personal best at third in the South Carolina primary receiving just under
60,000 votes.[57] On February 29, 2020, Steyer suspended his presidential
campaign stating that he saw no path forward to winning the nomination.[58]

IMPLICATIONS OF SELF-FUNDING
AND THE 2020 CAMPAIGN

The narrative of self-funding in political campaigns has largely ended in
defeat. While there are obvious political issues that benefit self-funding, for
example, self-funding shows independence from special interests, there is
something that makes self-funded candidates weaker than their externally
funded counterparts. Perhaps this has something to do with candidate quality.
The reason a candidate has to self-fund is perhaps that they cannot generate
the type of donations needed to win at a national level. However, to be fair,
that is not always the case. For example, Trump's self-funding did not prevent him from winning in 2016 (nor did the fact that he raised far less than
his opponent).

Self-funding, however, is emblematic of a larger political issue that is
going to continue for some time in American politics. That is the role of the
ultra-wealthy individuals and their role within the campaign process. In the
1996 *Washington Post* op-ed by John McCain and Russ Feingold, one of their
biggest concerns was the role wealthy candidates played within the political
process.[59] At that time, they feared that American democracy could be eroded
by the wealthy elites who could afford to out-spend and therefore out-perform
their competition. That proved to be untrue largely. Ross Perot, Steve Forbes,
Meg Whitman, Linda McMahon, and Carly Fiorina all show that is not the
case. However, there are examples of other self-funded candidates at lower
offices that show that self-funding, to some extent, can be successful. Take,
for example, Florida Senator Rick Scott who spent $75 million of his own
money to win his seat in 2010 (he later said he did not need to self-fund in
2016).[60]

What was the impact of Bloomberg in 2020? To be fair, not a lot. His campaign fell flat, with him losing all of his primary races, save one American
Samoa, and his campaign coffers while full did not provide a groundswell

of support. His legacy in 2020 is likely going to center around the expense of his campaign, and perhaps his legacy will be that cash infused race for president will show the excesses of political campaigns and reignite the call for campaign finance reform. Certainly, his campaign created discomfort for progressive Democrats who wanted to show their party as one rejecting the moneyed Wall Street interests and billionaire class. Standing on the stage with Sanders and Warren, Bloomberg created a type of cognitive dissonance among some progressive Democrats who have wanted to push their party further left in the past four years. It is worth noting that Bloomberg's candidacy was different than Perot's in 1992 and 1996. Perot was an insurgent third-party candidate who, like Trump in 2016, was trying to appeal to an anti-establishment sentiment. His third-party status gave him a greater latitude to be outside the norm with self-funding. In fact, with no party infrastructure Perot needed to self-fund his campaign. Bloomberg, however, was a major party candidate, who was not running an insurgent campaign without an established party. The optics of that made Bloomberg's candidacy different, and the perception of self-funding, likely was perceived differently than Perot's.

However, his campaign and Steyer's also serves to show that campaign finances are not equal to electoral victory. Both candidates lost handily, and Bloomberg was shown to be a well-funded candidate who despite his wealth could not gain traction in the field. This proves the point that campaign donations do not mean electoral victory. This is a point made time and again, and, as the 2016 and 2020 presidential elections, showed candidate quality does matter in winning any election.

NOTES

1. Sanders, *Our Revolution*, 185.
2. Ibid.
3. Citizens United v. FEC, 558 U.S. 310 (2010).
4. Buckley v. Valeo, 424 U.S. 1 (1976); 11 C.F.R. § 113.2. However, it is important to note that in the public funding model of presidential campaigns self-donations are limited.
5. "Using the Personal Funds of a Candidate," Federal Election Commission, accessed February 9, 2021, https://www.fec.gov/help-candidates-and-committees/candidate-taking-receipts/using-personal-funds-candidate/.
6. John Martin, "Self-Funded Campaigns and the Current (Lack of?) Limits On Candidate Contributions to Political Parties," *Columbia Law Review Forum* 120 (2020): 178–197, 179.
7. Joshua Jamerson and Julie Bykowicz, "2020 Democrats Call for End to Self-Fundraising, Private Donors," *Wall Street Journal*, December 13, 2019, https://ww

w.wsj.com/articles/2020-democrats-split-on-whether-self-funding-should-be-legal-11576243674.

8. https://www.bloomberg.com/news/articles/2020-02-24/bloomberg-tops-half-a-billion-dollars-in-campaign-advertising

9. Newberry v. United States, 256 U.S. 232 (1921).

10. Marsha Barrett, "'Millionaires are More Democratic Now': Nelson Rockefeller and the Politics of Wealth in New York," *New York History*, http://www.nysm.nysed.gov/common/nysm/files/barrett_-_millionaires_are_more_democratic_now_a.pdf.

11. Ibid., 15, note 27.

12. John F. Kennedy, Remarks of Senator John F. Kennedy at the Gridiron Club, Washington, D.C., March 15, 1958, John F. Kennedy Library, accessed March 3, 2021, https://www.jfklibrary.org/archives/other-resources/john-f-kennedy-speeches/washington-dc-19580315.

13. Doron Levin, "Billionaire in Texas Is Attracting Calls to Run, and $5 Donation," *New York Times*, March 7, 1992, 11.

14. Richard Berke, "Perot Leads in $40 Million Ad Bliz," *New York Times*, October 27, 1992, 19.

15. "Reform Party," CNN, accessed March 3, 2021, https://www.cnn.com/ALLPOLITICS/1996/conventions/long.beach/perot/political.timeline.shtml.

16. Wayne Leslie, "Forbes Spends Millions, but for Little Gain," *New York Times*, February 10, 2000, A26.

17. Jeanne Cummings, "Self Funders Strike Out Big Time," *Politico*, last updated November 10, 2010, https://www.politico.com/story/2010/11/self-funders-strike-out-big-time-044677.

18. Bryan Burrough and Bethany McLean, "Jon Corzine's Riskiest Business," Vanity Fair, February 2012, https://www.vanityfair.com/news/business/2012/02/jon-corzine-201202.

19. David Graham, "The Lie of Trump's Self-Funding Campaign," *The Atlantic*, May 13, 2016, https://www.theatlantic.com/politics/archive/2016/05/trumps-self-funding-lie/482691/.

20. "Presidential Debate at Washington University in St. Louis Missouri," The Commission on Presidential Debates, October 9, 2016, https://www.debates.org/voter-education/debate-transcripts/october-9-2016-debate-transcript/. Trump did not put in $100 million of his own money into his 2016 presidential campaign. Instead, he put in approximately $66.1 million. In 2020 Trump's individual contributions to his campaign were $0.

21. "Candidate Map, Hillary Clinton, 2016," Federal Election Commission, accessed March 4, 2021, https://www.fec.gov/data/candidates/president/presidential-map/.

22. "Presidential Candidate Map, Clinton 2016," Federal Election Commission, accessed March 4, 2021, https://www.fec.gov/data/candidates/president/presidential-map/; "Presidential Candidate Map, Trump 2016," Federal Election Commission, accessed March 4, 2021, https://www.fec.gov/data/candidates/president/presidential-map/.

23. "#14 Michael Bloomberg," *Forbes*, March 4, 2021, https://www.forbes.com/profile/michael-bloomberg/?sh=727b8f871417.

24. Abagail Hess, "Kamala Harris Suspends Campaign, Says: 'I'm Not a Billionaire. I Can't Fund My Own Campaign,'" *CNBC* Online, updated December 3, 2019, https://www.cnbc.com/2019/12/03/kamala-harris-suspends-campaign-over-finances-im-not-a-billionaire.html.

25. Jon Allsop, "How Bloomberg Plans to Handle Its Owner's Run for President," *Columbia Journalism Review*, November 25, 2019, https://www.cjr.org/the_media_today/michael_bloomberg_news_president.php.

26. "Column: How Michael Bloomberg's Presidential Candidacy Harms Journalism," *Los Angeles Times* https://www.latimes.com/business/story/2019-11-24/bloomberg-news-coverage-presidential-race.

27. Sasha Pezenik and Will McDuffie, "Warren Slams Bloomberg for His News Organization not Covering Democrats," *ABC News* Online, January 23, 2020, https://abcnews.go.com/Politics/warren-slams-bloomberg-news-organization-covering-democrats/story?id=68464104.

28. https://www.cnbc.com/2019/11/24/bloomberg-news-will-not-investigate-mike-bloomberg-or-his-democratic-rivals-during-primary.html

29. Lauren Hirsch, "With Mike Bloomberg Out of Presidential Race, Bloomberg Journalists Resume Normal Political Coverage," *CNBC* online, updated March 4, 2020, https://www.cnbc.com/2020/03/04/bloomberg-journalists-free-to-resume-normal-political-coverage.html.

30. Edward-Issac Dovere, "Democrats Are Freaking Out Over Mike Bloomberg," *The Atlantic*, February 3, 2020, https://www.theatlantic.com/politics/archive/2020/02/mike-bloomberg-democratic-contested-convention/605956/.

31. Ibid.

32. Tim Reid and Michael Martina, "Democrat Warren Accuses Rival Bloomberg of Trying to Buy U.S. Presidential Election," *Reuters*, November 25, 2019, https://www.reuters.com/article/us-usa-election-warren/democrat-warren-accuses-rival-bloomberg-of-trying-to-buy-u-s-presidential-election-idUSKBN1XZ2G0.

33. Bobby Allyn, "'Throw Them Against The Wall and Frisk Them': Bloomberg's 2015 Race Talk Stirs Debate," *NPR* Online, February 11, 2020, https://www.npr.org/2020/02/11/804795405/throw-them-against-the-wall-and-frisk-them-bloomberg-s-2015-race-talk-stirs-deba. Stop and frisk was a policy in New York City that allowed police to temporarily stop and frisk citizens for weapons and contraband. The practice was based on the U.S. Supreme Court's holding in Terry v. Ohio, 392 U.S. 1 (1968). The policy became highly controversial in New York City because it was said to be disproportionately applied to African Americans and Latinos. Bloomberg was supportive of stop and frisk because he said it increased safety in the city. At issue in 2020 was a 2015 recording of Bloomberg at the Aspen Institute defending stop and frisk because crime disproportionately occurs in minority neighborhoods.

34. "Full transcript: Ninth Democratic Debate in Las Vegas," *NBC* News, February 20, 2020, https://www.nbcnews.com/politics/2020-election/full-transcript-ninth-democratic-debate-las-vegas-n1139546.

35. Dan Merica and Caroline Kenny, "Michael Bloomberg Said in 2008 that End of 'Redlining' Was to Blame for Financial Crisis," *CNN* Online, February 14, 2020, https://www.cnn.com/2020/02/13/politics/michael-bloomberg-redlining-housing-c risis/index.html. Redlining in New York City was the practice of not providing mortgages to certain low-income neighborhoods. In 2008 at a forum at Georgetown University, Bloomberg made a comment that the end of the practice of redlining coincided with the financial collapse and Great Recession of 2008. Although Bloomberg denied that he made equated the end of redlining with the financial crisis of 2008, he did make remarks that Congressional involvement with mortgages created a situation where low-income home owners qualified for mortgages that they had difficulty affording promoting the mortgage crisis in the late 2000s.

36. "Full transcript: Ninth Democratic Debate in Las Vegas," February 20, 2020.

37. Ibid.

38. "Presidential Campaign Map, Michael Bloomberg, 2020," Federal Election Commission, accessed March 4, 2021, https://www.fec.gov/data/candidates/president /presidential-map/

39. Michael Blood, "Snubbing the Iowa Caucuses, Michael Bloomberg Charts His Own Path in 2020 Contest," *Chicago Tribune*, February 3, 2020, https://www.chi cagotribune.com/election-2020/ct-michael-bloomberg-iowa-caucuses-2020-20200 203-5dab2kp455htxn555oi3tjkvmu-story.html.

40. Eugene Robinson, "Opinion: Mike Bloomberg Won the Iowa Caucuses," *Washington Post*, February 6, 2020, https://www.washingtonpost.com/opinions/ mike-bloomberg-won-the-iowa-caucuses/2020/02/06/aa110f1e-4928-11ea-b4d9-29c c419287eb_story.html.

41. Marc Fortier, "Bloomberg Beat 2 Well-Known Democrats in the NH Primary. He Wasn't Even on the Ballot," *NBC Boston* online, February 13, 2020, https://ww w.nbcboston.com/news/local/bloomberg-beat-2-well-known-democrats-in-the-nh-primary-he-wasnt-even-on-the-ballot/2076566/.

42. Mark Niquette, "Bloomberg's Path Clouded by Biden's South Carolina Win," *Bloomberg News* Online, March 1, 2020, https://www.bloomberg.com/ news/articles/2020-03-01/bloomberg-s-path-clouded-by-biden-s-decisive-south-car olina-win.

43. Kevin Schaul, Kevin Uhrmacher, and Anu Narayanswamy, "Bloomberg's immense spending gets him 30,000 online ads a minute, and a whole lot more," *Washington Post*, February 19, 2020, https://www.washingtonpost.com/graphics/ 2020/politics/bloomberg-ad-spending-scale/.

44. Eliza Relman and Sonam Sheth, "Mike Bloomberg Drops Out of the 2020 Presidential Race and Endorses Joe Biden," *Business Insider*, March 4, 2020, https:/ /www.businessinsider.com/mike-bloomberg-drops-out-of-the-2020-presidential-race -2020-3. The 15 percent threshold is a rule in the Democratic primary that mandates that a candidate receive 15 percent of the vote state wide to receive any state delegates and 15 percent in a congressional district to receive any district level delegates.

45. Ibid.

46. Jacob Pramuk, "Mike Bloomberg Will Transfer $18 Million to the Democratic Party as it Gears Up to Face Trump," *CNBC* Online, March 20, 2020, https://www

.cnbc.com/2020/03/20/mike-bloomberg-to-donate-18-million-to-dnc-in-2020-electio
n.html.

47. Brian Schwartz, "Mike Bloomberg Takes Big Losses after Spending over $100 million in Florida, Ohio and Texas," *CNBC* Online, November 4, 2020, https://ww w.cnbc.com/2020/11/04/bloomberg-sees-losses-after-spending-over-100-million-in-f lorida-ohio-texas.html.

48. "Meet Tom," Tom Steyer, accessed March 4, 2021, https://www.tomsteyer .com/meet-tom/.

49. Ibid.

50. "Presidential Campaign Map, Tom Steyer 2020," Federal Election Commission, accessed March 4, 2021, https://www.fec.gov/data/candidates/president/presidential -map/.

51. "Iowa Democratic Caucus Results," Des Moines Register, February 29, 2020, https://www.desmoinesregister.com/elections/results/primaries/democratic/iowa/.

52. Meg Kinnard, "With Democrats in New Hampshire, Steyer has SC to himself," *Associated Press*, February 10, 2020, https://apnews.com/article/dd9455cc5550f df06a988fa8000ade13.

53. Ibid.

54. Zach Montellaro, "Tom Steyer set to miss Nevada debate," *Politico*, February 18, 2020, https://www.politico.com/news/2020/02/18/tom-steyer-miss-nevada-d ebate-115787.

55. "Reports of Receipts and Disbursements, Tom Steyer 2020, March Monthly," Federal Election Commission, accessed March 4, 2021, https://docquery.fec.gov/ cgi-bin/forms/C00711614/1391924/; "Reports of Receipts and Disbursements, Tom Steyer 2020, February Monthly," Federal Election Commission, accessed March 4, 2021, https://docquery.fec.gov/cgi-bin/forms/C00711614/1391923/.

56. Ibid.

57. "Nevada Caucus Results," *Las Vegas Review-Journal*, accessed March 4, 2021, https://www.reviewjournal.com/nevada-caucus-results-2020/; "South Carolina Primary Results," USA Today, March 2, 2020, https://www.usatoday.com/elections/ results/primaries/democratic/south-carolina/.

58. Juana Summers and Barbara Sprunt, "Tom Steyer Drops Out of the Presidential Race," *NPR* Online, February 29, 2020, https://www.npr.org/2020/02/29/801952931 /tom-steyer-to-drop-out-of-2020-presidential-race.

59. John McCain and Russ Feingold, "A Better Way to Fix Campaign Financing," Washington Post, February 20, 1996, https://www.washingtonpost.com/opinions/ a-better-way-to-fix-campaign-financing/2018/08/26/b45ede68-a935-11e8-a8d7-0 f63ab8b1370_story.html.

60. James Hohmann, "Scott's Self-Funding: $12.8 Million," *Politico*, November 11, 2014, https://www.politico.com/story/2014/11/rick-scott-florida-self-funding -112403.

Chapter 5

Building a War Chest

Trump's Fundraising during Primary Season

Incumbency has certain advantages during a reelection campaign. These advantages include familiarity with the candidate, a preexisting campaign organization, campaign talking points that include candidate accomplishments, and fundraising. In fact, fundraising for an incumbent for a presidential race should have major advantages, especially when the opposition has to go through a competitive primary process where there is no clear front-runner. In 2020, Donald Trump had many of these advantages, but his campaign also had many obstacles to overcome, such as an energized Democratic vote base, criticism over domestic policies including immigration, and the COVID-19 pandemic, which affected both U.S. public health and the economy.

While his politics created polarization between Republicans and Democrats, Trump had a mixed track record going into Republican Convention. One thing in his favor was the Democrats could not decide on a front-runner early on. In fact, their front-runner for the most of 2019 seemed to be independent, Democratic-Socialist Bernie Sanders. His politics were left of many of the other candidates in the party, and it was thought in some circles that in a General Election Sanders would be politically too far left to be electable. However, the sheer size of the Democratic field in 2019 and early 2020 provided Trump an advantage in that Trump was the only known candidate that would definitely be in the General Election in November. He also made political hay out of various candidates and their statements, providing some them with nicknames such as "Sleepy Joe" Joe Biden, "Crazy Bernie" Bernie Sanders, "Pocahontas" Elizabeth Warren, and criticizing their performances and statements during the Democratic primary.[1] While some of these criticisms were offensive to voters, they did gain traction in the media, which allowed Trump some advantage in framing the discussion about Democratic candidates and his future opponent.

Incumbency frequently is a referendum on the president's previous four years. With Trump, that referendum was not as clear because his presidency was highly polarizing, but also because his success rate was mixed. While Trump did accomplish many things in his agenda such as appointing conservative judges (including three U.S. Supreme Court Justices), removing the United States for the Paris Climate Accords, beginning construction of a border wall between Mexico and the United States, and moving the U.S. Embassy in Israel to Jerusalem among others, his success in 2020 really is a contrast between pre-COVID and post-COVID issues surrounding public health and the economy. Trump's economic record was mixed with Trump having success pre-COVID-19 and many economic problems post-COVID. Trump was enjoying a strong economy pre-COVID-19. During his presidency, the Dow Jones Industrial Average (DJIA) broke 25,000 for the first time in 2018, presumably because of a strong jobs report.[2] In fact, the DJIA would break 25,000 three times during the Trump administration, although it would be up-and-down during COVID-19, at one point falling to just above 19,000 in March 2020.[3] Unemployment during Trump's administration was also up-and-down, with unemployment in decline from Trump's inauguration hitting its lowest point in January 2020 at 3.5 percent. However, it would jump to levels higher than those of the Great Recession in April 2020, topping out at 14.8 percent.[4]

Last, Trump had a small, but vocal minority of Republicans, so-called Never Trumpers, who opposed his nomination, and would go on to support the Democratic nominee Joe Biden.[5] The Never Trump Movement began in 2016, and continued into 2020. While it was small, it had some prominent voices, notably George Will and Bill Kristol, and several Republican Party members voted for Democrat or third-party candidates instead of Trump in 2016 and 2020. Related to this movement was a small, yet unsuccessful, challenge to Trump's nomination by William Weld, a former Republican governor of Massachusetts and former vice presidential nominee in 2016 for the Libertarian Party. Other prominent Republicans did not endorse Trump in 2020, creating some fracture in party unity. None of this rose to the level of an interparty fight like those seen by Republicans in 1976 or Democrats in 1980. However, given that the 2020 election was highly polarized, these few votes leaving the party potentially had a greater impact on Trump's reelection efforts, some even saying that this small group actually cost Trump his second term.[6]

This chapter examines the fundraising and campaign of President Donald Trump from when he announced his intention to run for reelection in January 2017 until his nomination at the Republican National Convention in August 2020. The chapter explores both the fundraising efforts of Trump and also examines the context in which the campaign operated. This provides insight into the strengths and weaknesses of Trump's campaign prior to the General Election and provides some insight on the limitation money can play with a political campaign. Specifically, this chapter looks at Trump's campaign from 2017 to 2019, the Trump fundraising and campaign in 2020 prior to the RNC nomination, the Never Trump Movement and its impact on Trump's reelection, and the impact that Trump's fundraising and campaign had on his campaign going into the 2020 General Election.

TRUMP'S REELECTION ANNOUNCEMENT AND FUNDRAISING 2017–2019

Donald Trump's reelection campaign never really started, because it was part of a permanent campaign that was supposed to continue for four years while he was in office. Officially, his first campaign expenditure for the 2020 presidential election occurred on November 24, 2016, when he bought an airplane ticket.[7] Trump also kept his campaign headquarters open after his inauguration, and continued to have staffers work on the 2020 campaign after his 2016 election. This was highly unusual move because most presidents merge their candidate campaign into the party's committee. However, Trump continued working on his campaign post-2016 because of the benefits of data collection and building a strong ground game for 2020.[8] He also declared his candidacy for 2020 much earlier than his predecessors in January of 2017 and began an active fundraising effort for his reelection using the slogan "Keep America Great." Table 5.1 shows that contributions were high for Trump considering in 2017 he was still three years away from the beginning of the primary season for 2020. This was part of the idea of Trump's permanent campaign, which was meant to give him a competitive advantage in 2020. It is worth noting that this January 2017 starting point was even before the first midterm elections during his administration, which would result in the Democrats taking back the House of Representatives and the Republicans gaining two more seats in the U.S. Senate for a balance of fifty-three Republicans, forty-five Democrats, and two independents that caucus with the Democrats.[9]

As table 5.1 shows, Trump steadily increased his cash on hand at the end of each quarter from 2017 through 2019, except for one quarter in 2018 during the months of October through December. However, that quarter was low because Trump had disbursements over $23 million.[10] Cash on hand is important for campaigns, because it is the amount of cash available to spend, and in this case, Trump ended each quarter very strong with million on hand going into 2020. This provided him with a large cash advantage over his Democratic opponents, who were still vying for the nomination. For instance, at the end of the 2019 Year End Quarterly Trump had $102.7 million in cash

Table 5.1   Trump Campaign Cash on Hand 2017–2019[i]

Quarter	Cash on Hand at Close of Reporting Period ($, million)
April 2017	8.36
July 2017	11.9
October 2017	18
Year End 2017	22.1
April 2018	28.3
July 2018	33
October 2018	35.4
Year End 2018	19.2
April 2019	40.7
July 2019	56.7
October 2019	83.2
Year End 2019	102.7

[i]"Report of Receipts and Disbursements, Donald J. Trump for President, April Quarterly 2017 Amended," accessed March 4, 2021, https://docquery.fec.gov/cgi-bin/forms/C00580100/1174081/; "Report of Receipts and Disbursements, Donald J. Trump for President, July Quarterly 2017 Amended," accessed March 4, 2021, https://docquery.fec.gov/cgi-bin/forms/C00580100/1248053/; "Report of Receipts and Disbursements, Donald J. Trump for President, October Quarterly 2017 Amended," accessed March 4, 2021, https://docquery.fec.gov/cgi-bin/forms/C00580100/1193597/; "Report of Receipts and Disbursements, Donald J. Trump for President, Year-End 2017 Amended," accessed March 4, 2021, https://docquery.fec.gov/cgi-bin/forms/C00580100/1219890/; "Report of Receipts and Disbursements, Donald J. Trump for President, April Quarterly 2018 Amended," accessed March 4, 2021, https://docquery.fec.gov/cgi-bin/forms/C00580100/1248056/; "Report of Receipts and Disbursements, Donald J. Trump for President, July 2018 Quarterly Amended," accessed March 4, 2021, https://docquery.fec.gov/cgi-bin/forms/C00580100/1263561/; "Report of Receipts and Disbursements, Donald J. Trump for President, October Quarterly 2018Amended," accessed March 4, 2021, https://docquery.fec.gov/cgi-bin/forms/C00580100/1301594/; "Report of Receipts and Disbursements, Donald J. Trump for President, Year-End 2018 Amended," accessed March 4, 2021,https://docquery.fec.gov/cgi-bin/forms/C00580100/1319152/;"Report of Receipts and Disbursements, Donald J. Trump for President, April Quarterly 2019 Amended," accessed March 4, 2021, https://docquery.fec.gov/cgi-bin/forms/C00580100/1337251/; "Report of Receipts and Disbursements, Donald J. Trump for President, July Quarterly 2019 Amended," accessed March 4, 2021, https://docquery.fec.gov/cgi-bin/forms/C00580100/1351771/; "Report of Receipts and Disbursements, Donald J. Trump for President, October Quarterly 2019 Amended," accessed March 4, 2021, https://docquery.fec.gov/cgi-bin/forms/C00580100/1404772/; "Report of Receipts and Disbursements, Donald J. Trump for President, Year-End 2019 Amended," accessed March 4, 2021, https://docquery.fec.gov/cgi-bin/forms/C00580100/1392271/.

on hand compared with $18.1 million for Bernie 2020, Sanders's campaign committee, and over $8.9 million for Biden for America, Biden's campaign committee.[11]

Part of Trump's success was his ability to use earned media through rallies and his social media to campaign. Hallmarks of Trump's 2016 campaign continued in his early reelection bid. He held rallies across the country, the first being in February 18, 2017, in Melbourne Florida, where over 9,000 people showed up for the president.[12] The rally's content was typical of Trump's rallies in 2017 and 2018. They focused on his election night win, and the media's failure to predict his victory over Hillary Clinton.

However, Trump after the 2018 midterms faced a Democratic majority in the U.S. House with Nancy Pelosi (D-CA) as the Speaker of the House. Now in the majority, Democrats used their subpoena power to investigate the Trump administration. Prior to the midterms, Deputy Attorney General Rod Rosenstein appointed Special Counsel Robert Mueller to investigate Russian interference with the 2016 election.[13] The Mueller investigation into Comey's firing turned into a wide-ranging examination of whether Trump's campaign or any individuals associated with it had colluded with Russia during the 2016 presidential campaign.[14] The investigation would conclude in March 2019 with the highly anticipated Mueller Report, which was released in a redacted form to the public on April 18, 2019. A best-seller, the report was 448 pages long. Attorney General William Barr sent a letter to the House and Senate Judiciary Committees detailing the report's findings.[15] Barr said:

> The Special Counsel states that "while this report does not conclude that the President committed a crime, it also does not exonerate him." The Special Counsel's decision to describe the facts of his obstruction investigation without reaching any legal conclusions leaves into the Attorney General to determine whether the conduct described in the report constitutes a crime. Over the course of the investigation, the Special Counsel's office engaged in discussions with certain Department officials regarding many of the legal and factual matters at issue in the Special Counsel's obstruction investigation. After reviewing the Special Counsel's final report on these issues; consulting with Department officials, including the Office of Legal Counsel; and applying the principles of federal prosecution that guide our charging decisions, Deputy Attorney General Rod Rosenstein and I have concluded that the evidence developed during the Special Counsel's investigation is not sufficient to establish that the President committed an obstruction-of-justice offense.[16]

This conclusion of Barr's letter was used as a fundraising device for the Trump administration. In a fundraising text, Trump said, "NO COLLUSION AND COMPLETE EXONERATION! Dems raised millions off of a lie. Now we FIGHT BACK! Donate in the NEXT HOUR and it'll be QUADRUPLED."[17]

The Mueller Report was not the only political issue Trump was dealing with in 2019. An impeachment inquiry began in September 2019 in House of Representatives, culminating in the House impeachment proceeding in the Judiciary Committee starting in December 4 and was voted out of committee on December 13. The House voted for impeachment on December 18, 2019, mainly along partisan lines for a final vote of 230-197. The impeachment of Trump was part of a fundraising boom for both Democrats and Republicans. Trump used his impeachment as a political issue for the General Election, and in his campaign's Year-End statement of 2019, which showed totals from October 1 to December 31, 2019, showed individual contributions were over $20.2 million.[18]

TRUMP FUNDRAISING DURING PRIMARIES:
FROM IOWA CAUCUSES TO CONVENTION

Impeachment was at fever pitch at the end of 2019. Democratic candidates were affected by the impeachment trial in the Senate because Sanders and Warren had to attend the trial.[19] This was problematic because the Iowa Caucuses were held on January 16, 2020, the day Trump's impeachment trial in the U.S. Senate began. It would last for nearly three weeks, until February 5, 2020, when Trump was acquitted by a vote of 52-48 on abuse of power under Article 1, and 53-47 on Article II obstruction of justice. Normally, such an event would signal trouble for a presidential campaign. However, Trump's campaigning continued with three rallies in Wisconsin, New Jersey, and Iowa. He credited the impeachment with helping his fundraising, with Trump's campaign manager Brad Parscale saying that it helped Trump have record fundraising during late 2019.[20]

As table 5.2 shows, Trump's cash on hand continued to steadily rise in 2020, with him starting out with $92.6 million at the end of January and having over $121 million in cash on hand going into the Republican Convention.

Table 5.2   Trump Campaign Cash on Hand 2020[i]

Month	Cash on Hand at Close of Reporting Period* ($, million)
January	92.6
February	94.4
March	98.4
April	107.6
May	108.1
June	113
July	120.5
August	121

[i]"Report of Receipts and Disbursements, Donald J. Trump for President," Federal Election Commission, February Monthly 2020 Amended," accessed March 4, 2021, https://docquery.fec.gov/cgi-bin/forms/C 00580100/1403600/; "Report of Receipts and Disbursements, Donald J. Trump for President," Federal Election Commission, March Monthly 2020 Amended," accessed March 4, 2021, https://docquery.fec .gov/cgi-bin/forms/C00580100/1405125/; "Report of Receipts and Disbursements, Donald J. Trump for President," Federal Election Commission, April Monthly 2020 Amended," accessed March 4, 2021, https ://docquery.fec.gov/cgi-bin/forms/C00580100/1412555/; "Report of Receipts and Disbursements, Donald J. Trump for President, May Monthly 2020 Amended," Federal Election Commission, accessed March 4, 2021, https://docquery.fec.gov/cgi-bin/forms/C00580100/1428849/; "Report of Receipts and Disburse- ments, Donald J. Trump for President," Federal Election Commission, June Monthly 2020 Amended," accessed March 4, 2021, https://docquery.fec.gov/cgi-bin/forms/C00580100/1435104/; "Report of Receipts and Disbursements, Donald J. Trump for President, July Monthly 2020 Amended," Federal Elec- tion Commission, accessed March 4, 2021 https://docquery.fec.gov/cgi-bin/forms/C00580100/1440916/; "Report of Receipts and Disbursements, Donald J. Trump for President, August Monthly 2020 Amended," Federal Election Commission, accessed March 4, 2021 https://docquery.fec.gov/cgi-bin/forms/C005801 00/1471578/; "Report of Receipts and Disbursements, Donald J. Trump for President, September 2020 Monthly Amended," Federal Election Commission, accessed March 4, 2021 https://docquery.fec.gov/cgi -bin/forms/C00580100/1500199/.
*Millions given to the nearest $100,000.

In fact, in January 2020, Trump's campaign committee began the month with $102.7 million, the fact that Trump credited with his impeachment.[21] Trump's cash on hand grew exponentially because of donations during the primary season where he ran nearly unopposed for the Republican nomination. Despite his lack of competition in the primaries, Trump still had large voter turnout in places like Iowa, New Hampshire, and South Carolina. These large turnouts signaled that Trump's base was strong and that among Republican primary voters there was a high enthusiasm for the president. He set records for primary turnout in Vermont and Minnesota, receiving the most primary votes for an incumbent in forty years, and also had high turnout in Massachusetts, California, and Colorado, which prompted Trump press secretary Kaleigh McEnany to declare that Trump was leading a united GOP in 2020.[22]

Polls in the summer of 2020 were an issue that Trump battled with continually. Fundraising is tied to poll numbers, and sometimes poor polling numbers can result in less enthusiasm for a candidate. So-called suppression polls are also said to be used by campaigns to discourage voters from supporting their opponents. Also at issue are polling standards, which some argue are not standardized, creating different outcomes.[23] Famously in 2016, the presidential polling was wrong and created an election night surprise with Trump's victory. In 2020, Trump seized on this narrative during the summer election cycle, going so far as to demanding CNN to retract a poll that showed Biden up by fourteen points in June 2020.[24]

Trump's summer campaign was harmed by the COVID-19 global pandemic. In February 2020, Trump said that COVID-19 would eventually go away, but cases and mortality kept climbing.[25] Trump would hold his last rally before COVID-19 in February that he thought that the press was in "hysteria mode" over the COVID-19 pandemic.[26] However, the COVID-19 pandemic grew, and Trump's campaign rallies, a tool that he effectively used to boost supporters and gain earned media coverage, were no longer able to be used. Starting in March he began daily press briefings about COVID-19 with a team that included Dr. Anthony Fauci, the director of the National Institute of Allergy and Infectious Diseases, and Dr. Deborah Birx, the White House Coronavirus Response Coordinator. These briefings had high ratings but also provided a forum where Trump's gaffes became political issues including his support of hydroxychloroquine to treat COVID-19, the ingestion of disinfectant to combat the virus, criticizing Democratic governors on COVID responses, sparring with reporters, and minimizing other aspects of the pandemic.[27] In fact, some networks began to question the usefulness of the briefings and felt that they were used to boost Trump's campaign.[28]

Trump began his rallies again in June 2020, with the first one to be held in Tulsa, Oklahoma. Attendance was lower than previous campaigns with only

6,200 attendees, according to the Tulsa Fire Department.[29] He continued with rallies in Arizona, and found a modified way to hold rallies in smaller outdoor venues. His fundraising continued to do well during this time, but he did have some issues with images in campaigns. In June 2020, the Ronald Reagan Presidential Foundation asked the Republican National Committee to have the Trump Make America Great Again Committee to stop using President Reagan's likeness in campaign fundraising materials. Trump previously used the image on a coin that depicted Trump and Reagan on opposite sides as a thank you for a $45 donation.[30]

By August 2020, Trump was preparing to accept the Republican presidential nomination in late August. During his acceptance speech on the South Lawn at the White House Trump he made an issue out of Biden's campaign and their funding of progressive causes. He said:

> During their convention, Joe Biden and his supporters remained completely silent about the rioters and criminals spreading mayhem in Democrat-Run Cities. In the face of left-wing anarchy and mayhem in Minneapolis, Chicago, and other cities, Joe Biden's campaign did not condemn it—they DONATED to it. At least 13 members of Joe Biden's campaign staff donated to a fund to bail out vandals, arsonists, looters, and rioters from jail.[31]

After the convention Trump's campaign continued to raise money at an aggressive rate. At the beginning of August 2020, he had $120.5 million in cash on hand compared with Biden who had $98.8 million.[32] However, Trump's campaign was going into the most important phase of the election, and there were emerging media stories about how Trump used campaign cash on legal fees.[33] Despite this, Trump's pre-convention fundraising was strong, and he still had advantages, despite COVID-19, going into the General Election.

WILLIAM WELD AND NEVER TRUMPERS

The 2020 campaign drew one challenger to Trump's nomination from the Republican Party from former Massachusetts Governor William Weld. A former vice presidential nominee for the Libertarian Party in 2016, Weld challenged Trump in a short-lived campaign lasting from April 2019 until March 2020. Weld never won any Republican primaries, and had little by way of campaign donations. His entire campaign raised over $1.78 million from individuals, and received $281,717 in donations from the candidate.[34] Weld's operating expenditures were slightly over $2 million, and his campaign lacked a high degree of national attention.[35] Weld's candidacy, however, served as a critique of Trump's campaign, and his time as president. Weld's approach to victory was based on a strong showing in the New Hampshire primary, which was something Weld felt was possible because of his campaign manager Paul Spaulding, who was John McCain's campaign manager in the Republican primary in 2000 and 2008.[36] McCain won both of those primaries, which catapulted him as a top-tier candidate, and in 2008 the eventual Republican nominee. Weld, ultimately would not come close to winning in New Hampshire. Trump, like he did in many Republican primaries in 2020, saw a record number of people turn out to support him. Weld's Iowa Caucus showing was low receiving only 1.3 percent of the votes in the state. He received only 13,844 votes compared to Trump's 129,734 votes in New Hampshire, and had similarly weak showings in Vermont (10.1 percent) and Alabama's (1.5 percent) primaries; his campaign was suspended on March 18.

Weld's longshot campaign was actually part of a larger movement within the Republican Party. So-called Never Trumpers emerged during Trump's 2016 presidential campaign, and they saw Trump's nomination as a threat to the party. Their rationales varied, but centered on differences in policy (particularly economic), candidate personal identity, and relationship between Trump and the Republican Party establishment.[37] The Never Trump Movement also gained traction on social media with the hashtag #NeverTrump becoming a rallying cry for Republicans who were not supporting Trump in 2016. This criticism of Trump from Republicans led to some high-level defections in 2016. For instance, George H.W. Bush voted for Hillary Clinton and George W. Bush left the president category blank on his ballot in 2016.[38] Neither president was part of the Never Trump Movement, but again they contributed to the overall feeling among some establishment Republicans that Trump should not be the Republican nominee for president.

Never Trumpers were not a unified organization, but a broader label for Republicans who did not like the influence of Donald Trump in the Republican Party. Among the high profile Never Trumpers included: columnist George Will, Bill Kritol editor of the defunct conservative magazine *The Weekly Standard*, and columnist Jennifer Rubin of *The Washington Post*. However, the stop Trump movement did have some organization in groups such as the Republican Voters Against Trump (RVAT), which described itself as an organization comprised of Republicans, conservatives, and former Trump voters who would not be voting for Trump in 2020.[39] Their efforts included creating short testimonial videos of Republicans and conservatives who would not support Trump in 2020. The group went on to raise $10 million for these efforts and portrayed themselves in the mold of a 1964 Lyndon

Johnson ad of a Republican who criticized the conservative 1964 presidential candidate Senator Barry Goldwater.[40]

Another group tied to stopping President Trump was The Lincoln Project, a PAC, which was formed in 2019 by anti-Trump Republicans to see that Donald Trump was not reelected in 2020 and that "Trumpism" was removed from politics.[41] In a column originally published by the *New York Times*, and reprinted on The Lincoln Project's webpage Republicans, George Conway, husband of Kellyanne Conway, the former chief consultant to President Trump, former Republican campaign manager Steve Schmidt, and Republican strategist Rick Wilson claimed that Trump lacked the ability to be president and that national Republicans were enablers to Trump's policies and behavior.[42] The Lincoln Project raised over $87.4 million from November 5, 2019, to December 16, 2020, from individual and other committee contributions.[43] They went on to spend over $81.9 million in that same time frame.[44] Much of the advertising done by The Lincoln Project was digital ads that used Twitter and other social media to promote its message.[45]

The 2020 election also saw a fair number of Republicans not endorse Donald Trump for president including: Senator Mitt Romney, former Trump Secretary of Defense Richard Mattis, former Trump National Security Advisor John Bolton, and former Trump White House Communications Director Anthony Scaramucci.[46] There were also many George W. Bush administration officials, and there were rumors that George W. Bush would not endorse Trump either. Bush responded that he was retired from politics and did not wish to enter the 2020 election (interestingly George P. Bush, the Texas Land Commissioner and son of Jeb Bush did endorse Trump).[47]

The impact of Never Trump Movement and Republicans who opposed Trump's nomination is hard to gauge. It did create an environment in which members of the Republican Party left and voted for Joe Biden. In fact, these groups created an advantage for Biden to create a broad coalition of voters that ranged from progressives like Sanders to longtime Republicans like Ohio Governor John Kasich (both spoke at the Democratic Convention in August 2020).[48] However, the movement was small and included a select group of Republicans who were at philosophical odds with Trump. This may have been countered by the large number of new voters that Trump brought into the Republican Party, and his very strong and loyal base. The verdict on Never Trumpers is mixed with some progressives wanting them out of the Democratic Party altogether, and pointing to progressive politics as the reason Biden won in 2020. Still, others say that while unsuccessful in depriving Trump the nomination in 2020 and 2016, the group was able to provide enough support to Biden to prevent Trump from having a second term.[49]

TRUMP'S FUNDRAISING'S EFFECT ON
GENERAL ELECTION STRENGTH

Trump entered into the 2020 General Election with a strong fundraising position. He had the benefit of incumbency, and a permanent campaign that was
ongoing since 2017. He also had the benefit of early fundraising that allowed
him to gather aggregate data on voters and position his organization advan-
tageously. Additionally, while vocal, Trump's Republican detractors were
small and also were replaced by new voters to the party. He ended up having
a position by the August RNC Convention of having massive amounts of
Republican support, which included his very devoted base. He also had laid
the groundwork in his campaign rallies in key battleground states including
Florida, Ohio, Pennsylvania, and Michigan (all states he had won in 2016).

However, the issue of COVID-19 defined the presidential race in 2020,
and its impact on the Trump campaign was significant. Like all incumbents
Trump enjoyed daily news coverage, which can help or hurt a candidate.
This earned media was namely in the form of rallies in 2016, but in 2020
the earned media included his COVID-19 press conferences that featured a
variety of people. Moreover, Trump's handling of the virus was something
that was juxtaposed in real time with the COVID-19 infection and hospital
admission trackers, which amplified the crisis. Trump's statements of the
virus were equally problematic for him because some proved to not come to
fruition, such as the country recovering from the virus by Easter 2020. Some
were also panned by the press as uninformed, such as his comments about
household cleaners being used to kill the virus internally. The virus also continued to escalate during the election season making it an issue about Trump's
leadership and ability to lead the nation during a crisis. His robust economy
went into steep decline by April 2020, which also took away his narrative
about his qualifications as a president that was good for the U.S. economy
and unemployment.

Trump's primary campaign also did not benefit from what he perceived
to be one his greatest strengths a protracted Democratic infight that resulted
in Sanders either being the nominee or his supporters bolting from the party.
To be fair, this was not an outcome that was limited to the Trump campaign,
Michael Bloomberg also based his entire presidential strategy under the
assumption that the primaries would end in a dead heat causing a brokered
convention. Even Trump in 2016 had a similar situation in the Republican
primary where there were seventeen major candidates. However, none of that
happened as Joe Biden cinched the Democratic nomination by March, leaving him the ability to fundraise and cast himself as the candidate who could
help with the COVID recovery.

The biggest takeaway from Trump's primary campaign is that he had advantages going into 2020: strong economy, continual campaign, incumbency, a fractured opposition, and a campaign style that garnered a great amount of earned media attention. However, what ultimately harmed his campaign was not the lack of funds, after all he won against Hillary Clinton in 2016 who spent millions more than him, but the issues of the campaign.[50] COVID-19 resulted in the international pandemic dominating all of the news, which, in turn placed Trump in a defensive position. It also limited his campaign strategy of large rallies, and the COVID-19 press briefings were not the substitute for that free media exposure. The larger issue for Trump was that his strategy appealed to his base supporters who would stay with him regardless of what was said. However, swing voters, and energized Democrats signaled trouble for Donald Trump going into the General Election. However, given the misinterpretation of the country's mood and support for Trump in 2016, there was a sense that Trump may win. However, financial support is not the only way to determine if a candidate is going to be successful in an election. In anything, Trump's primary season shows that good fundraising and planning are only part of the necessary elements for election victory.

NOTES

1. Adam Edelman, "A Guide to Trump's Nicknames and Insults about the 2020 Democratic Field," *NBC News* Online, updated May 13, 2019, https://www.nbcnews.com/politics/2020-election/everything-trump-has-said-about-2020-field-insults-all-n998556.

2. Fred Imbert, "Dow Closes Above 25,000 for the First Time After Strong Jobs Data," *CNBC* Online, January 4, 2018, https://www.cnbc.com/2018/01/04/dow-25k-us-stocks-jobs-data-adp-economy.html.

3. "Civilian Unemployment Rate," U.S. Bureau of Statistics, accessed March 4, 2021, https://www.bls.gov/charts/employment-situation/civilian-unemployment-rate.htm.

4. Ibid. These numbers are civilian unemployment rate seasonally adjusted. This rate was even higher for women over twenty who were at 15.5 percent, African Americans at 16.7 percent, and 18.9 percent for Hispanic and Latinos.

5. Olga Khazan, "Never Trump, Forever," *The Atlantic*, November 14, 2020, https://www.theatlantic.com/politics/archive/2020/11/bulwark-never-trump-republicans-biden/617025/

6. Max Boot, "Opinion: Never Trumpers Played a Critical Role in Beating Him. The Numbers Prove It." *Washington Post*, November 12, 2020, https://www.washingtonpost.com/opinions/2020/11/12/did-republicans-vote-against-trump/. The role of Never Trumpers beating Donald Trump is debatable because of their small number, and because Trump's campaign courted new voters at a very high rate. The Never

Trumpers also included former Republicans, such as Colin Powell, who had not endorsed a Republican presidential candidate since 2004.

7. Philip Bump, "Donald Trump Started Spending Money on the 2020 Race on November 24, *Washington Post*, May 1, 2017, https://www.washingtonpost.com /news/politics/wp/2017/05/01/donald-trump-started-spending-money-on-the-2020 -race-on-nov-24/.

8. Alex Isenstadt, "Trump Laying Groundwork for 2020 Bid," *Politico*, January 10, 2017, https://www.politico.com/story/2017/01/donald-trump-campaign-reelectio n-233440

9. The two independent senators were Bernie Sanders (VT) and Angus King (ME).

10. "Reports of Receipts and Disbursements, Donald Trump for President, Inc., Year-End Amendment," Federal Election Commission, accessed March 4, 2021, https://docquery.fec.gov/cgi-bin/forms/C00580100/1319152/.

11. "Reports of Receipts and Disbursements, Donald J. Trump for President, Inc., Year-End Amendment," Federal Election Commission, accessed July 24, 2021, https://docquery.fec.gov/cgi-bin/forms/C00580100/1392271/ ; "Reports of Receipts and Disbursements, Biden for President, Year-End Amendment," Federal Election Commission, accessed March 4, 2021, https://docquery.fec.gov/cgi-bin/forms/C 00703975/1390990/; "Reports of Receipts and Disbursements, Bernie 2020, Year-End Amendment," Federal Election Commission, accessed March 4, 2021, https://do cquery.fec.gov/cgi-bin/forms/C00696948/1392261/.

12. Dan Merica, "Trump Gets What He Wants in Florida: Campaign-Level Adulation, *CNN* Online, February 18, 2017, https://www.cnn.com/2017/02/18/poli tics/donald-trump-florida-campaign-rally/index.html.

13. Rosenstein made the appointment of Robert Mueller because Attorney General Jeff Sessions recused himself from the investigation.

14. Appointment of Special Counsel To Investigate Russian Interference With the 2016 Presidential Election and Related Matters, U.S. Department of Justice, accessed February 18, 2021, https://www.justice.gov/opa/press-release/file/967231/download.

15. "Letter to the House and Senate Judiciary Committees," U.S. Department of Justice, accessed February 18, 2021, https://www.justice.gov/archives/ag/page/file /1147981/download.

16. Ibid.

17. Grace Panette, "'Now We FIGHT BACK!': The Trump Re-Election Campaign is Using the Attorney General's Mueller Summary to Raise Funds," *Business Insider*, March 24, 2019, https://www.businessinsider.com/trump-campaign-is-already-fu ndraising-off-the-mueller-report-barr-2019-3.

18. "Reports of Receipts and Disbursements, Donald Trump for President, Inc., Year-End Amendment," Federal Election Commission, accessed March 4, 2021, https://docquery.fec.gov/cgi-bin/forms/C00580100/1392271/.

19. Rebecca Morin, "As Impeachment Trial Starts, Senator-Jurors Running for President Get Creative, *USA Today*, January 21, 2020, https://www.usatoday.com/ story/news/politics/elections/2020/01/21/impeachment-trial-warren-sanders-klobuc har-bennet-use-surrogates-2020/4530366002/

20. Alex Isenstadt, "Trump Campaign Credits Impeachment for Massive $46 Million Fundraising Haul, Politico, January 2, 2020, https://www.politico.com/news/2020/01/02/trump-campaign-fundraising-46-million-092579; https://docquery.fec.gov/cgi-bin/forms/C00580100/1403600/

21. "Reports of Receipts and Disbursements, Donald Trump for President, Inc., February Monthly Amendment," Federal Election Commission, accessed March 4, 2021, dhttps://docquery.fec.gov/cgi-bin/forms/C00580100/1403600/.

22. Kayleigh McEnany, Trump's Super Tuesday Results: Broad Appeal Beyond a United GOP, *The Hill*, March 4, 2020, https://thehill.com/opinion/campaign/485927-trumps-super-tuesday-results-broad-appeal-beyond-a-united-gop.

23. Dan Nimmo, *Political Persuaders: The Techniques of Modern Election Campaigns* (New Brunswick, NJ: Transaction Publishers, 2002), 136.

24. William Cummings, " Trump Campaign Sends CNN 'Cease and Desist' Letter, Demands It Retract Poll That Found Biden up 14 Points," *USA Today*, June 8, 2020, https://www.usatoday.com/story/news/politics/elections/2020/06/08/president-trump-fumes-cnn-poll-showing-him-trailing-biden-and-approval-down/5317953002/.

25. Philip Bump, Yet Again, Trump Pledges that the Coronavirus Will Simply Go Away," *Washington Post,* April 28, 2020, https://www.washingtonpost.com/politics/2020/04/28/yet-again-trump-pledges-that-coronavirus-will-simply-go-away/.

26. Philip Bump, "Trump Continues to Refuse to Accept the Deadliness of the Coronavirus Pandemic," *Washington Post,* April 28, 2020, https://www.washingtonpost.com/politics/2020/04/28/trump-continues-refuse-accept-deadlines-coronavirus-pandemic/.

27. Michael Grynbaum, "Trump's Briefings Are a Ratings Hit. Should Networks Cover Them Live?," New York Times, updated July 20, 2020, https://www.nytimes.com/2020/03/25/business/media/trump-coronavirus-briefings-ratings.html; https://abcnews.go.com/Politics/controversial-moments-led-trump-stop-white-house-coronavirus/story?id=71899110.

28. Tom Porter, "Journalists are Skipping Trump's Daily Coronavirus Press Briefings, Saying They Don't Have Enough News Value," *Business Insider*, April 1, 2020, https://www.businessinsider.com/trump-coronavirus-briefings-reporters-broadcasters-skip-no-news-value-2020-4.

29. Justin Wise, "Tulsa Fire Department Says Trump Rally Attendance Was about 6,200," *The Hill*, June 21, 2020, https://thehill.com/homenews/campaign/503781-tulsa-fire-department-says-trump-rally-attendance-was-about-6200.

30. Colby Itkowitz, "RNC, Trump Campaign Told to Stop using President Reagan to Raise Money," *Washington Post*, July 25, 2020, https://www.washingtonpost.com/politics/rnc-trump-campaign-told-to-stop-using-president-reagan-to-raise-money/2020/07/25/0a3bf886-cebc-11ea-91f1-28aca4d833a0_story.html. The Ronald Reagan Presidential Foundation had the sole ability to use Reagan's likeness.

31. " Full text: President Trump's 2020 RNC Acceptance Speech," *NBC News*, updated April 28, 2020, https://www.nbcnews.com/politics/2020-election/read-full-text-president-donald-trump-s-acceptance-speech-rnc-n1238636.

32. "Report of Receipts and Disbursements, Donald J. Trump for President, September 2020" Federal Election Commission, accessed March 4, 2021, https

://docquery.fec.gov/cgi-bin/forms/C00580100/1500199/; "Reports of Receipts and Disbursements, Biden for President, September Monthly," Federal Election Commission, accessed March 5, 2021, https://docquery.fec.gov/cgi-bin/forms/C 00703975/1440320/.

33. Tal Axelrod, "Trump and Allies Have Spent $58 Million on Legal Bills and Compliance Work: Report," *The Hill*, September 5, 2020, https://thehill.com/homen ews/campaign/515249-trump-and-allies-have-spent-58-million-on-legal-bills-and-co mpliance.

34. "Presidential Candidate Map, William Weld 2020," Federal Election Commission, accessed March 4, 2021, https://www.fec.gov/data/candidates/president /presidential-map/.

35. Ibid.

36. David Montgomery, "Is William Weld the Hero Never Trumpers Have Been Waiting For?," *Washington Post*, August 19, 2019, https://www.washingtonpost.com /news/magazine/wp/2019/08/19/feature/is-bill-weld-the-hero-never-trumpers-have-b een-waiting-for/

37. Lauren Johnson, Deon McCray, and Jordan Ragusa, "#NeverTrump: Why Republican Members of Congress Refused to Support Their Party's Nominee in the 2016 Presidential Election," *Research and Politics* (Jan.-March 2018): 1–10, 2.

38. Darren Samuelsohn, "George H.W. Bush to Vote for Hillary Clinton," *Politico*, September 19, 2016, https://www.politico.com/story/2016/09/exclusive-g eorge-hw-bush-to-vote-for-hillary-228395; "Neither George Bush voted for Trump, book author tells New York Times," Reuters, November 4, 2017, https://www.reu ters.com/article/us-trump-bush-book/neither-george-bush-voted-for-trump-book-aut hor-tells-new-york-times-idUSKBN1D40TP.

39. Republican Voters against Trump, accessed March 4, 2021, https://rvat.org/.

40. Paul Waldman, "The Never Trumpers Might Be onto Something," *Washington Post*, May 28, 2020, https://www.washingtonpost.com/opinions/2020/05/28/never -trumpers-might-finally-be-something/.

41. "The Lincoln Project," accessed March 4, 2021, https://lincolnproject.us/.

42. George T. Conway III, Steve Schmidt, John Weaver and Rick Wilson, "Opinion: We Are Republicans, and We Want Trump Defeated," *New York Times*, December 17, 2019, https://www.nytimes.com/2019/12/17/opinion/lincoln-project .html.

43. "Financial Summary, The Lincoln Project," Federal Election Commission, accessed March 4, 2021, https://www.fec.gov/data/committee/C00725820/?cycle =2020.

44. Ibid.

45. Tina Nguyen and Elena Schneider, "The Lincoln Project is trolling Trump. But can it sway voters?," *Politico*, June 27, 2020, https://www.politico.com/news/2020/ 06/27/lincoln-project-trolling-trump-sway-voters-341928.

46. Mattis, Bolton, and Scaramucci had all been removed from their White House positions by Trump. Mitt Romney had spoken out against Trump since 2016, and had voted for removal on one count of impeachment, abuse of power, in 2019.

47. Chris Cillizza, "What George P. Bush's endorsement of Donald Trump Tells Us About Republican Politics," *CNN* Online, June 10, 2020, https://www.cnn.com/2020/06/10/politics/george-p-bush-endorsement-donald-trump/index.html.

48. "Democratic National Convention Schedule," Democratic National Committee, accessed March 4, 2021, https://www.demconvention.com/schedule-and-speakers/?_sft_event-day=august-17.

49. Boot, "Opinion: Never Trumpers Played a Critical Role in Beating Him. The Numbers Prove It."

50. Cayce Myers, "Campaign Finance and its Impact in the 2016 Presidential Campaign," in *The 2016 Presidential Campaign: Political Communication and Practice*, ed. Robert Denton (New York: Palgrave McMillan, 2017), 259–283.

Chapter 6

Joe Biden Fundraising

Nomination to General Election

Joe Biden was an unusual candidate for president campaigning in one of the most unusual times. At seventy-eight years old, he was older than any man to ever run for the White House. He also had spent nearly fifty years in federal public service, eight years as the vice president and six terms as U.S. Senator for Delaware. Because of that, Biden had a long legislative history, and his position on campaign finance was firmly established. However, what Biden politically said about campaign finance and what he did in the 2020 election was somewhat contradictory. Beginning in the 1970s when he was a freshman senator (and the youngest at that time), he criticized the role of money in politics and called for greater reforms to campaign finance. He also was willing to support campaign finance reforms in the 1990s when the issue came to the forefront of national politics. However, in 2020 Biden was a very successful fundraiser, and although he advocated for the public funding of elections (in fact, it was part of his candidate statement online), he declined it for the General Election. He also used PACs and super-PACs to help him win in 2020, raising and spending over $1 billion on his campaign. To be fair, Biden was not alone. Trump also used the same campaign finance resources available to him, but Biden differed from Trump in that he had a political position that was firmly articulated for decades. However, Biden's campaign finance reform stance was very robust, much more articulated than Trump's position and was heavily tied to the idea that public funding of elections was an essential ingredient to removing special interests from politics altogether. It was, in many ways, the same stance Biden had in 1973 when he was sworn in one of the youngest U.S. Senators ever elected.[1]

This chapter examines Biden's fundraising during the 2020 General Election. This chapter begins with a look at Biden's past statements and positions on campaign finance, then explores his campaign pledge to reform money in American politics. Next the chapter examines Biden's campaign's fundraising and shows how his campaign coffers grew during the General Election outpacing Trump. Finally, the chapter explores the fundraising by groups outside Biden's campaign including the Democratic Party, Biden's joint fundraising committee, and pro-Biden and Democrat PACs and super-PACs. This analysis shows that the Democrats and Biden had a clearly developed fundraising strategy, which allowed him and Democrats to raise billions in the 2020 election. This analysis is also positioned in the context of the 2020 General Election, specifically focusing on the campaign "stay at home" strategy of Biden, and the issues that created fundraising talking points during the election. Finally, the chapter explores what Biden's fundraising meant to his campaign, and how it potentially created his eventual victory.

CAMPAIGN FUNDRAISING

Campaign finance was a big issue when Joe Biden entered the U.S. Senate in 1973. Nixon was still the president and was embroiled in the Watergate scandal that prompted a wholesale reassessment of money in politics. Biden ran for the U.S. Senate against a Republican incumbent, Caleb Boggs, who was a strong incumbent who had a political network that reached back to his first election in the late 1940s. In his memoir, *Promises to Keep*, Biden notes the difficulty of campaign fundraising, and how his campaign worked hard to raise just $150,000 for his first campaign.[2] That campaign made an impression on Biden's view of money in American politics. During his first term as a U.S. senator, the young recently widowed Joe Biden was the subject of a lengthy profile in *The Washingtonian*, a monthly local D.C. magazine, by reporter Kitty Kelly. In the profile, Biden, then the youngest member of the Senate, detailed the tragedy of losing his wife and daughter, his Senate routine, and his intent to one day get married again. However, Biden also spoke extensively about campaign finance and the difficulties he faced in running for the U.S. Senate from Delaware:

> Politics is a damn expensive business. I had one hell of a time trying to raise money as a candidate. I had to put a second mortgage on our house to get that campaign started, and I ended up spending over $300,000 to get elected. I believe that public financing of federal election campaigns is the only thing that will ensure good candidates and save the two-party system. It is the most degrading thing in the world to go out with your hat in your hand and beg for money, but that's what you have to do if you haven't got your own resources.[3]

Part of the issue, according to Biden in 1974, was that campaign finance required candidates to make compromises on their political positions in order to receive donations. He felt that when he ran for the Senate, he could have received more donations if he were to agree to positions counter to his personal beliefs.[4] In an interview on WGBH Boston in 1974, Biden said that campaign donations was "the most degrading position in the world" and that fundraising needed required candidates to "prostitute themselves" to get funds.[5] As a freshman in the Senate, Biden, along with Dick Clark (D-IA), worked on campaign finance reform and presented their plan to the Senate Democratic Caucus. Biden argued that having a public finance option for elections would allow politicians to be free from the pressure of outside interests, and would provide a type of independence that would result in better governance. Biden recalled that Senator Jim Eastland from Mississippi replied, "Ya'll keep making speeches like you made today . . . and you gonna be the youngest one-term senator in the history of America."[6]

Some forty years later Biden still criticized the role of money in politics. He supported the Bipartisan Campaign Reform Act of 2002, and in 2015 Biden said that the one thing he would do to "increase fairness to the middle class" would be to "get private money out of political process."[7] In his presidential race in 2008, Biden accepted public funding, around $857,000, during the Democratic primaries, only to drop out after a poor showing in the Iowa Caucuses.[8] However, he would later be fined after a FEC audit revealed that he accepted a round-trip flight in 2007 from New Hampshire to Iowa on a jet owned by a hedge fund (Biden would later refund the flight cost, but the FEC determined the cost repaid should have been higher). In 2008, Biden would also be part of Obama's presidential ticket, which was the first to decline public funding, and go on to raise record amounts for a U.S. presidential election.

However, Biden's views of campaign finance remained clearly articulated, particularly in the post-*Citizens United* reality. Part of his concern stemmed from what many feared about *Citizens United v. FEC*, the role of foreign money in U.S. elections.[9] This fear was articulated in Justice John Paul Stevens's dissent, and it was one that was amplified with the concern over foreign influence over the 2016 presidential election. Biden wrote about this issue stating that Russian interference with the 2016 election stemmed from issues in campaign finance law that allowed foreign money into the system. A piece written by Biden and Michael Carpenter for *Foreign Affairs* in 2018 said that Russian, or any foreign nation's interference within U.S. elections, could be seriously limited with campaign finance reform particularly as it relates to so-called ghost corporations, super-PACs, 501(c)(4) groups, and dark money.[10]

By the 2020 election, Joe Biden's political stance on campaign fundraising is in line with most Democrats in the twenty-first century—he criticized it, heavily. In fact, at his 2020 kickoff, he said: "Our Constitution doesn't begin with the phrase, 'We the Democrats' or 'We the Republicans.' And it certainly doesn't begin with the phrase, 'We the Donors.'"[11] Biden also sup-ported public financing of elections, although he did not use that in 2020, and advocated for a change in the election system that would ban large corporate donors. He touted his co-sponsorship of a bill in the late 1990s that would allow for a constitutional amendment that would allow Congress to limit campaign contributions and expenditures (the bill did not pass).[12]

In his 2020 campaign website, Biden put forth a ten-point plan to assist with the problem associated with money in politics. Many of these sug-gestions revolve around the issue of post-*Citizens United v. FEC* campaign fundraising, which is thought to benefit corporations at the expense of indi-viduals.[13] This plan stated Biden would[14]:

- Eliminate private contributions to federal elections through a constitutional amendment, which would, in effect, overturn the decision in *Citizens United v. FEC*.
- Propose a law for federal matching funds for small donor candidates in hopes this supports first-time candidates who cannot afford to get into politics.
- Ban of foreign money in U.S. elections. This proposal would establish a new Commission on Federal Ethics to examine foreign money at all levels of elections in the U.S.[15]
- "Restrict" super-PACs. (These restrictions would be part of the three legal solutions mentioned above.)
- Create a law that says that any group advocating for a particular candidate on social media must disclose its financial supporters. This provision targets the issue of social media posts that foster fake news, and is an attempt to stop dark money groups in elections from using online advertisement with-out disclosing funds. Moreover, Biden's campaign called for the creation of ethics.gov where this information can be easily accessed by the public.
- Ban 503(c)(4) groups from spending money in elections in an attempt to end dark money within all elections. Moreover, any group that spends more than $10,000 during an election must register with the Commission on Federal Ethics.[16]
- A disclosure requirement that made candidates run ads every sixty days disclosing who their donors are up to the last forty-eight hours. This would combat the issue of not knowing how spending was made until after the election cycle because of FEC disclosure dates.
- Ban lobbyists from making donations to politicians who they lobby and require lobbyist fundraisers to disclosure donations and provide a twenty-four-hour notice prior to an event that a fundraiser is being held. Lobbyists would also be required to disclose their contributions within twenty-four hours of the donation.

- Provide public financing of any national party convention for a party who receives 5 percent of the national vote.[17]
- Ban federal contractors from making donations to candidates.[18]

Of course, these are proposals, and the ability to get these reforms through Congress during his administration is highly difficult. But it shows a larger view that for Joe Biden campaign finance reform hinges on many of the talking points of progressive Democrats who dislike the results of *Citizens United v. FEC* and corporate influence within politics. In fact, in 2020 Biden would receive endorsements from End Citizens United and Let America Vote, two groups that advocate for the end of the campaign finance laws ushered in by the 2010 U.S. Supreme Court decision.[19] As a primary candidate Biden needed small donors to help his campaign. At one point in 2019, two-thirds of his campaign funds came from donors making contributions less than $25.[20]

The presidential debates were also interesting since they are usually flashpoints in a president's campaign. Biden raised $10 million within three hours of the first presidential debate.[21] This included 60,000 new donors and a total of over 250,000 donors overall.[22] Even Trump's debate coach said that Trump was "too hot" during the first debate after he peppered Biden with questions and interrupted Biden and the moderator Chris Wallace.[23] The second presidential debate scheduled for October 15 was canceled; Trump was also recovering from COVID-19 that he was diagnosed with on October 2. In lieu of a debate, Biden and Trump held individual televised town halls, Biden on *ABC* and Trump on *NBC*. The ratings for Biden's town hall had 14.1 million viewers, higher than Trump's, and Biden's campaign benefited from the televised event.[24] By the third debate, Biden and Trump had their largest back and forth over campaign cash.

By the third debate Biden was taking in a considerable amount of money from donors. This was an asset to his campaign, but it also became a political liability. In the last presidential debate between Trump and Biden there was a discussion of Biden's Wall Street connections. Biden accused Trump of alerting Wall Street to COVID-19 before the American people, prompting short-sells of stock. However, Trump took the opportunity to link Biden to big corporations, arguing that his forty-seven years in public service provided a path for Biden's family to enrich themselves at the expense of the American people. Responding to Biden, Trump said:

> You're the one that takes all the money from Wall Street. I don't take it. You have raised a lot of money, tremendous amounts of money. And every time you raise money, deals are made. I could raise so much more money. As president and as somebody that knows most of those people, I could call the heads of Wall Street, the heads of every company in America, I would blow away every

record. But I don't want to do that because it puts me in a bad position. And then you bring up Wall Street? You shouldn't be bringing up Wall Street. Because you're the one that takes the money from Wall Street, not me. I could blow away your records like you wouldn't believe. We don't need money. We have plenty of money. In fact, we beat Hillary Clinton with a tiny fraction of the money that she was able to get. Don't tell me about Wall Street.[25]

Biden responded emphasizing his small donors, "Average contribution, $43."[26] When accused of having too close of a relationship with China, particularly in the context of Hunter Biden's business dealings, Biden responded by denying he ever had involvement with a foreign fundraiser. Biden also made an issue out of foreign contributions to U.S. elections and his own relationship with foreign governments saying:

I have not taken a penny from any foreign source ever in my life. We learn that this President paid 50 times the tax in China, as a secret bank account with China, does business in China, and in fact, is talking about me taking money? I have not taken a single penny from any country whatsoever, ever, number one.[27]

However, as a political issue, Biden's son, Hunter, would prove to be a major campaign issue for Trump who equated Hunter's relationships to corporate and political figures in Ukraine, China, and Russia as being part of a larger issue of corruption. The Republican's October surprise was a set of emails from Hunter Biden's laptop, which Trump said showed that Biden was involved with his son's business deals, notably Burisma Holdings, a Ukrainian-based energy company.[28] Despite this, Biden continued fundraising aggressively leading up to the General Election.

BIDEN'S FUNDRAISING DURING
THE POST-CONVENTION

As Obama's running mate in the 2008 presidential election of Barack Obama, Biden was part of a great sea change in campaign financing and donor recruiting. That campaign was a first in many ways, but perhaps one of its most enduring legacy was Obama's ability to raise millions from opting out of public financing. That campaign also demonstrated the importance of digital donations, and how social media and websites could garner large aggregate sums of money for campaigns. Biden's strategy in 2020 mirrored that of Obama's in 2008, if anything Biden was more successful. In 2020 his campaign also opted out of public financing, as did Trump. That way Biden was free to raise millions in individual donations, in addition to the DNC and pro-Democrat and pro-Biden PACs. However, 2020 presented itself with some unique challenges for campaigns. Biden's campaign strategy during the General Election was to make limited appearances.

Starting the summer of 2020, Biden had a "stay at home" strategy, which critics called the basement or bunker strategy that had little interaction with voters. Part of the strategy hinged on allowing the presidential election to be a referendum on Donald Trump, and allowing his handling of COVID-19 to define the presidential election.[29] Another part of the stay at home strategy was to contrast his approach to COVID-19 with Trump. In June 2020, Trump's Tulsa, Oklahoma rally was highly criticized for not providing appropriate social distancing, and media outlets claimed the rally resulted in an increase of COVID-19 cases.[30] Biden staying at his Delaware home made the point that Biden's handling of COVID-19 would be more responsible and adhere to the scientific research on the pandemic. Biden's campaign also benefited from several current events that galvanized Democratic voters. On September 18, 2020, liberal icon and Justice Ruth Bader Ginsberg died, which caused the issue of judicial appointments to become an issue. Progressive fundraising group Act Blue, a group committed to fundraising for progressive and Democratic candidates, had a surge in fundraising after the justice's death.[31]

In table 6.1 Biden's receipts, the sum of all contributions to a campaign committee during a specified time, were very high from August through the Post-General filing period. In August, Biden's campaign took in $212 million in individual contributions. That month included the Democratic National Convention, which was held from August 17 through August 20. The Convention speeches were not held in a rally format because of COVID-19, and instead individual speakers presented their speeches on a set. During

Table 6.1   Biden Total Receipts August–Post-General 2020[i]

Month	Total Receipts ($, million)
August	212.1
September	281.6
Pre-General*	130
Post-General**	112.3

[i]"Report of Receipts and Disbursements, Biden for President, September Monthly," Federal Election Commission, accessed March 4, 2021, HYPERLINK "https://docquery.fec.gov/cgi-bin/forms/C00703975/1440320/" https://docquery.fec.gov/cgi-bin/forms/C00703975/1440320/; "Report of Receipts and Disbursements, Biden for President, October Monthly," Federal Election Commission, accessed March 4, 2021, HYPERLINK "https://docquery.fec.gov/cgi-bin/forms/C00703975/1458940/" https://docquery.fec.gov/cgi-bin/forms/C00703975/1458940/; Report of Receipts and Disbursements, Biden for President, Pre-General," Federal Election Commission, accessed March 4, 2021, https://docquery.fec.gov/cgi-bin/forms/C00703975/1463690/; Report of Receipts and Disbursements, Biden for President, Post General," Federal Election Commission, accessed March 4, 2021, https://docquery.fec.gov/cgi-bin/forms/C00703975/1481223/.

*Pre-General is from October 1 to October 14, 2020. *Note* there is no October figures because they are included in Pre- and Post-General Disclosures.

**Post General is from October 15 to November 23, 2020.

the Convention donations to Democrats increased, with the Democratic fundraiser Act Blue raising $40 million, particularly picking up contributions on the nights that Harris spoke.[32]

Biden's campaign's cash on hand, as shown in table 6.2, also shows that he had large sums of money available to him for campaign expenses. In August, Biden's campaign had over $98.8 million, and nearly doubled that amount by the beginning of September, with $180.6 million. That figure leveled off during September through the election, but the fact that Biden was spending regularly during this time, shows that cash on hand remained steady because of a steady stream of donations. Many of Biden's donations came from both large and small donors. Donors contributing under $200 gave an aggregate of $656.8 million, while donors giving more than $2,000 gave an aggregate of $179.1 million.[33] Moreover, donors giving over $200, but under $2000 gave an aggregate of just over $299.5 million.[34] Biden's campaign would eventually raise over $1 billion for his 2020 presidential election.[35] In fact, as shown in table 6.3 during August through the Post-General reporting period Biden's campaign-operating expenditures were significant.

Compared to Donald Trump's campaign-operating expenditures Biden was handily outspending the president using his campaign contributions. In fact, in September Biden's campaign-operating expenditures were more than double that of Trump, $281 to $125.9 million.

Table 6.2   Biden Beginning and Ending Cash on Hand for Reporting Period August–November 23, 2020[i]

Month	Beginning ($, million)	Close ($, million)
August	98.8	180.6
September	180.6	177.2
Pre-General*	177.2	162
Post-General**	162	1.55

[i]This chart appears in Cayce Myers, "Campaign Finance and its Impact on the 2020 Campaign," in *The 2020 Campaign: Political Communication and Practice*, ed. Robert Denton (Lanham, MD: Roman and Littlefield, 2021, 169).

*Pre-General is from October 1 to October 14, 2020. *Note* there is no October figures because they are included in Pre and Post-General Disclosures.

**Post General is from October 15 to November 23, 2020.

***"Reports of Receipts and Disbursements, September Monthly 2020, Biden for President," Federal Election Commission, accessed January 2, 2021, https://docquery.fec.gov/cgi-bin/forms/C00703975/1440320/ ; "Reports of Receipts and Disbursements, October Monthly 2020, Biden for President," Federal Election Commission, accessed January 2, 2021, https://docquery.fec.gov/cgi-bin/forms/C00703975/1458940/; "Reports of Receipts and Disbursements, Pre-General 2020, Biden for President," Federal Election Commission, accessed January 2, 2021, https://docquery.fec.gov/cgi-bin/forms/C00703975/1463690/; "Reports of Receipts and Disbursements, Post-General 2020, Biden for President," Federal Election Commission, accessed January 2, 2021, https://docquery.fec.gov/cgi-bin/forms/C00703975/1481223/.

Table 6.3 Trump and Biden Total Campaign Operating Expenditures[i]

Month	Biden	Trump
August	$128.8 million	$61.1 million
September	$281 million	$125.9 million
Pre-General*	$143.2 million	$63 million
Post-General**	$269.1 million	$198.6 million

[i]A version of this chart appears in Cayce Myers, "Campaign Finance and its Impact on the 2020 Campaign," in *The 2020 Campaign: Political Communication and Practice*, ed. Robert Denton (Lanham, MD: Roman and Littlefield, 2021, 169).

*Pre-General is from October 1 to October 14, 2020. *Note* there is no October figures because they are included in Pre and Post-General Disclosures.

**Post General is from October 15 to November 23, 2020.

"Reports of Receipts and Disbursements, September Monthly 2020, Biden for President," Federal Election Commission, accessed January 2, 2021, https://docquery.fec.gov/cgi-bin/forms/C00703975/1440320/; "Reports of Receipts and Disbursements, October Monthly 2020, Biden for President," Federal Election Commission, accessed January 2, 2021, https://docquery.fec.gov/cgi-bin/forms/C00703975/1458940/; "Reports of Receipts and Disbursements, Pre-General 2020, Biden for President," Federal Election Commission, accessed January 2, 2021, https://docquery.fec.gov/cgi-bin/forms/C00703975/1463690/; "Reports of Receipts and Disbursements, Post-General 2020, Biden for President," Federal Election Commission, accessed January 2, 2021, https://docquery.fec.gov/cgi-bin/forms/C00703975/1481223/; "Reports of Receipts and Disbursements, September Monthly 2020 Amendment 1, Donald J. Trump for President," Federal Election Commission, accessed January 2, 2021, https://docquery.fec.gov/cgi-bin/forms/C00580100/1484015/ ;"Reports of Receipts and Disbursements, October Monthly 2020, Donald J. Trump for President," Federal Election Commission, accessed January 2, 2021, https://docquery.fec.gov/cgi-bin/forms/C00580100/1458436/; "Reports of Receipts and Disbursements, Pre-General, Donald J. Trump for President," Federal Election Commission, accessed January 2, 2021, https://docquery.fec.gov/cgi-bin/forms/C00580100/1463640/; "Reports of Receipts and Disbursements, Post General Amendment 1, Donald J. Trump for President," Federal Election Commission, accessed January 2, 2021, https://docquery.fec.gov/cgi-bin/forms/C00580100/1483220/.

These fundraising numbers did not mean the election was going to be a foregone conclusion. Starting in September 2020 several lawsuits began to be filed concerning election law, and voting machines.[36] In fact, the specter of a litigated election, like that of 2000, was a fundraising tactic by both campaigns.

Joint Fundraising, PACs and Super-PACs

One of Biden's top campaign aids said that Biden was opposed to the corrupting influence of money in elections. Commenting on Biden's view of PACs in October 2019, she said, "As president, Joe Biden will push to remove private money from our federal elections. He will advocate for a constitutional amendment to overturn *Citizens United* and end the era of unbridled spending by Super PACs."[37] However, acknowledging that Donald Trump would use PAC and super-PAC money she said that Biden had no choice but to utilize funds that were legally allowed to be used in presidential elections.[38] This was a departure for Biden, who one month earlier, when he expressed concern over using a PAC of any kind during the election. After all, progressive opponents like Bernie Sanders criticized the use of outside money in presidential elections. When Biden decided to utilize PAC money he was criticized by Sanders's campaign manager Faiz Shakir, who said the decision to accept PAC money demonstrated that Biden's campaign was willing to "buy the primary."[39] Sanders would go on to say, "I don't need a super-PAC. I am not going to be controlled by a handful of wealthy people. I will be controlled by the working people of this country."[40]

During the General Election Biden did utilize all of the fundraising tools available to him, despite his own campaign's criticism of their existence. In fact, PAC spending helped Biden perhaps more than normal, because their ad purchases were instrumental campaign strategy as Biden's stay at home campaign created a problem for traditional fundraising efforts.[41] Joint Fundraising Committees, PACs, and super-PACs all played a role in raising money for the Democrat's 2020 victory. Biden created his joint fundraising committee, named Biden Victory Fund, in April 2020. A joint fundraising committee pairs a candidate's fundraising with that of a political party, which donors can then donate the legal limits to candidates and party committees, in this case the Democratic National Committee. Biden Victory Fund would go on to raise $659.7 million in 2020 from April 1 until December 31, 2020.[42] Of course, not all of the money in the joint fundraising committee is used by the candidate. Some of it is also used by the party in various states, which may have a net effect of benefiting the presidential ticket.

Biden's PAC support included both super-PACs, which are political committees that can take unlimited donations from individuals, corporations or unions, which can be spent on independent expenditures.[43] These independent expenditures are campaign work that expressly advocates for the election or defeat of a candidate that is not done in consultation or coordination with the candidate. Another type of political action committee that helped Biden in his presidential campaign was hybrid PACs, sometimes referred to as Carey Committees after the court case *Carey v. FEC*.[44] Unlike super-PACs, which can give money only for the stated candidate, a hybrid PAC can give some money to campaign and committees, but must maintain two separate accounts. Biden benefited from both, with two hybrid PACs Future Forward and Priorities USA Action being major supporters of his candidacy in 2020. Future Forward went on to play a major role in Silicon Valley donations in October 2020, with Facebook co-founder Dustin Moskovitz giving $22 million to it to support its large amount of televised advertising.[45] Another hybrid PAC helping Biden was Priorities USA Action, which was developed to support progressive campaign and causes. According to Priorities USA Action, they spent $153 million on advertising buys (radio, television, and digital), and garnered 3.4 billion impressions on their digital advertising. This resulted in 37.4 million voters reached, and an increased support of Biden of 1.25 percent and a decrease of Trump support by 2.4 percent.[46] On November 3, 2020, Priorities USA also declared that it was the largest independent spender in the 2020 election, outspending America First, a pro-Trump super-PAC, by $30 million in television advertising buys.[47]

Biden also benefited from the super-PACs American Bridge to the twenty-first century, Independence USA, and Unite the Country. American Bridge was founded in 2010, and bills itself as the "largest research, video tracking, and rapid response organization in Democratic politics."[48] Independence USA is a super-PAC that was created by Mike Bloomberg to promote gun laws, environmental issues, and education. However, in 2020 the super-PAC provided advertising for Biden's candidacy. On September 29, 2020, Independence USA aired its first pro-Biden advertisement in Florida which touted Biden's middle-class background and how he supports middle-class tax-cuts. Bloomberg had vowed to support Biden in Florida using $100 million (Trump would go on to win the state in the General Election).[49] Other PACs were focused on voter turnout for Democrats generally. For instance, Progressive Turnout Project PAC made a concerted effort to raise money to boost voter turnout in Michigan, a state Trump won in 2016, by spending $4.6 million in the state.[50] While not explicitly pro-Biden, the anti-Trump Lincoln Project was a PAC that created advertising content that did not support Trump's reelection. However, this ad was of the larger defeat-Trump narrative of the Lincoln Project. In December 2019, their leaders, George Conway, Steve Schmit, John Weaver, and Rick Wilson penned an op-ed in the *New York Times* declaring a "common effort" with Democrats.[51]

Looking at PACs in Table 6.4 of all types it is clear that their financial contributions toward Biden's election were helpful, particularly in a large amount of advertising that was purchased. Examining FEC data from 2020 of several high-profile PACs shows the significant amount of fundraising that benefited Biden and the Democrats.

Of course, Biden also benefited from the fundraising of the DNC, which had total receipts of $491.7 million, $231.7 million of which was from individual contributions, from 2019 to 2020.[52] Also, fundraising organizations for Democratic candidates, such as Act Blue also raised money that benefited all Democrats including Biden in 2020. In fact, Act Blue, which prides itself on being an innovative online giving super-PAC, raised, at the time of this writing, over $9 billion for Democrats since its inception in 2004. During 2020, ActBlue PAC raised over $4.3 billion for Democrats, with one-quarter of the money raised by ActBlue coming from donations of $200 or less.[53] Other state-specific super-PACs also emerged such as Blue Texas PAC who raised just over $221,000 to helping Biden win Texas in 2020 (he ultimately lost to Trump).[54]

Table 6.4   Pro-Biden and Pro-Democrat PACs Fundraising Reporting Period 2019–
2020[i]

Political Action Committee	Amount Raised (Total Receipts [$, million])
Unite the Country	49.9
Independence USA PAC	67.7
Priorities USA Action	139.4
The Lincoln Project**	87.4
Progressive Turnout Project	80.6

[i]"Financial Summary, Unite the Country, 2019-2020," Federal Election Commission, accessed March 4, 2021, HYPERLINK "https://www.fec.gov/data/committee/C00701888/" https://www.fec.gov/data/committee/C00701888/; "Financial Summary, Independence USA PAC, 2019-2020," Federal Election Commission, accessed March 4, 2021, HYPERLINK "https://www.fec.gov/data/committee/C00532705/?cycle=2020" https://www.fec.gov/data/committee/C00532705/?cycle=2020; "Financial Summary, Priorities USA Action, 2019-2020," Federal Election Commission, accessed March 4, 2021, HYPERLINK "https://www.fec.gov/data/committee/C00495861/" https://www.fec.gov/data/committee/C00495861/; "Financial Summary, The Lincoln Project, 2019-2020," Federal Election Commission, accessed March 4, 2021, HYPERLINK "https://www.fec.gov/data/committee/C00725820/?cycle=2020" https://www.fec.gov/data/committee/C00725820/?cycle=2020; "Financial Summary, Progressive Turnout Project, 2019-2020," Federal Election Commission, accessed March 4, 2021, HYPERLINK "https://www.fec.gov/data/committee/C00580068/?cycle=2020" https://www.fec.gov/data/committee/C00580068/?cycle=2020.
**The Lincoln Project was more anti-Trump, but in turn Biden benefited from its advertising.

CONCLUSION

Joe Biden's presidential campaign demonstrates the current tension in campaign finance reform in the United States. While his campaign clearly criticized the role of money in politics, and advocated for a public funding model the campaign itself made the practical decision to utilize the funds that were available to him from all legal methods. While this potentially turned away hardcore progressive voters who, like Sanders, view PACs and corporations with total distain, it helped Biden win the election. In fact, during an unconventional campaign these PACs and super-PACs helped Biden articulate his message and frame the election as a referendum on Donald Trump.

Unlike Trump, Biden had forty-seven years in office to articulate his views on the political issue of campaign finance. In fact, his campaign finance views seem to be one of the most important features of his early political career during his first term as a senator from Delaware. Interestingly, he came into politics during the greatest upheaval in U.S. presidential politics with the Watergate scandal and Richard Nixon's resignation. He was present for the greatest development in campaign finance reform with the creation of the Federal Election Commission, and later the Bipartisan Campaign Reform Act of 2002.[55] It is no surprise that his views on campaign finance in 2020 reflect those same values he had in 1973. However, political realities have changed, and, as a result, Biden had to engage in campaign fundraising that is entirely at odds with his own stated political position.

Biden's campaign fundraising opted out of the public financing model he both touted as a young senator and advocates for as a candidate. Interestingly his willingness to opt out in 2020 was really a nonstory in 2020. In fact, Biden had been on the ticket in 2008 that started the trend of opting out of public financing, and no major party nominee accepted public financing in 2012 or 2016. Framing the issue as one of competitive necessities, his campaign went forward to raise unprecedently large sums of money. His total receipts for 2020 in his campaign were over $1 billion, which included contributions over $807 million in donations from individuals.[56] Biden also benefited from the large contributions to his joint fundraising committee and, of course, PACs of all descriptions.

The benefit of party and PAC fundraising is that even if the money is spent on a lower tier race or for the party itself, it has ancillary benefits to the presidential candidate. The DNC from 2019 to 2020 raised over $491.7 million, and ActBlue, one of the biggest fundraising units helping the Democrats, raised over $ 4.3 billion (in fact in 2021 from January 1 to 25 ActBlue raised $55 million).[57] All of this demonstrates that Democrats and Biden had and still do have a very strong fundraising apparatus that provided cash in the billions for 2020. That means that the reforms that Biden is talking about in his campaign platform may be true, but no one is willing to opt-in to a system of public financed elections when the more successful strategy is to opt out. It remains to be seen if Biden will try to uphold his campaign promises on campaign finance reform. While he may be leading the effort in his rhetoric, his party is leading the field in developing a sophisticated donation system in which Democrats have a clear competitive advantage over Republicans.

NOTES

1. Michael Rosenwald, "Biden, Once One of the Nation's Youngest Senators, Will Be Its Oldest President," *Washington Post*, January 11, 2021, https://www.washingtonpost.com/history/2021/01/11/youngest-senators-joe-biden/.

2. Joe Biden, *Promises to Keep* (New York: Random House, 2007), 61.

3. Kitty Kelly, "Death and the All American Boy," *Washingtonian*, June 1, 1974, retrieved from https://www.washingtonian.com/1974/06/01/joe-biden-kitty-kelley-1974-profile-death-and-the-all-american-boy/.

4. Ibid.

5. "Young Joe Biden on Campaign Finance Reform (1974)," YouTube Video, 12:15, August 30, 2017, https://www.youtube.com/watch?v=VIZmZe7fe3E.

6. Biden, *Promises to Keep*, 92. Biden at the time of his election was the second youngest U.S. senator in history. Eastland mistakenly believed he was the youngest.

7. Vice President Biden on Money in Politics, CSPAN, July 17, 2015, https://www.c-span.org/video/?c4544897/user-clip-vice-president-biden-money-politics.

8. Kenneth Vogel, "Biden '08 Campaign Fined $219K," *Politico*, July 17, 2010, https://www.politico.com/story/2010/07/biden-08-campaign-fined-219k-039875.

9. Citizens United v. FEC, 558 U.S. 310 (2010).

10. Joseph Biden and Michael Carpenter, "How to Stand Up to the Kremlin," *Foreign Affairs*, January/February 2018, retrieved from https://www.foreignaffairs.com/articles/russia-fsu/2017-12-05/how-stand-kremlin.

11. "The Biden Plan to Guarantee Government Works for the People," Biden Harris, accessed March 4, 2021, https://joebiden.com/governmentreform/.

12. U.S. Congress, Senate, A joint resolution proposing an amendment to the Constitution of the United States relating to contributions and expenditures intended to affect elections, S.J.Res.18, 105th Cong. https://www.congress.gov/bill/105th-congress/senate-joint-resolution/18/titles.

13. Citizens United v. FEC, 558 U.S. 310 (2010).

14. "The Biden Plan To Guarantee Government Works for the People," Biden Harris, accessed March 4, 2021, https://joebiden.com/governmentreform/.

15. Robert Mutch, *Campaign Finance: What Everyone Needs to Know* (Oxford: Oxford University Press, 2016), 133–134. Foreign money in U.S. elections are at issue because they are a byproduct of the Citizens United v. FEC decision. Dark money groups that do not disclose their donors are thought to be a gateway for foreign money in U.S. elections. FECA bans foreign money from elections, and any dark money in candidate elections is a byproduct of loopholes in dark money campaigns. The ban on foreign money in U.S. campaigns goes back to 1989 when the FEC banned foreign subsidiaries of U.S. companies from forming PACs to spend money in U.S. elections.

16. Dark money is a term used for money raised by groups that is not disclosed to the FEC. This money is not disclosed because there is no legal requirement to do so. However, dark money is raised by three types of organizations 501(c)(4), social welfare organizations, 501(c)(5) unions, and 501(c)(6) trade associations. These names are derived from the section of the U.S. Code they come from, which is 26 U.S.C. §501(c). The holding in Citizens United v. FEC allowed organizations to raise even larger amounts of money that was not required to be reported to the FEC.

17. Public financing for party conventions was once provided, but was stopped in legislation signed by President Obama in 2014.

18. "The Biden Plan to Guarantee Government Works for the People," Biden Harris, accessed March 4, 2021, https://joebiden.com/governmentreform/.

19. Tal Axelrod, "Biden Announces Endorsements from End Citizens United, Let America Vote, *The Hill*, April 16, 2020, https://thehill.com/homenews/campaign/493197-biden-announces-endorsements-from-end-citizens-united-let-america-vote.

20. Brian Slodysko, "Biden Funds Success with Low-Dollar Donors," *PBS News Hour*, May 21, 2019, https://www.pbs.org/newshour/politics/biden-finds-unexpected-success-with-low-dollar-donors.

21. Andrew Solender, "Biden Campaign Raised $10 Million In Three Hours On Night Of First Debate," *Forbes*, September 30, 2020, https://www.forbes.com/sites/andrewsolender/2020/09/30/biden-campaign-raised-10-million-in-three-hours-on-night-of-first-debate/?sh=7903d2976ca2.

22. Elena Schneider, "Biden Smashes Fundraising Records During Chaotic Debate," *Politico*, September 30, 2020, https://www.politico.com/news/2020/09/30/joe-biden-debate-fundraising-423826.

23. Vandana Rambarin, "Trump Debate Coach Chris Christie Says President 'Too Hot' in Biden Showdown," *Fox News* Online, September 30, 2020, https://www.foxnews.com/politics/chris-christie-helped-prep-trump-for-debate-but-said-he-was-too-hot-during-biden-showdown.

24. Elahe Izadi, "Biden's ABC Town Hall Ratings Beat Trump's Three-Network NBC Event," *Washington Post*, October 16, 2020, https://www.washingtonpost.com/media/2020/10/16/biden-trump-townhall-ratings/.

25. "Debate Transcript: Trump, Biden Final Presidential Debate Moderated by Kristen Welker," *USA Today*, accessed March 4, 2021, https://www.usatoday.com/story/news/politics/elections/2020/10/23/debate-transcript-trump-biden-final-presidential-debate-nashville/3740152001/.

26. Ibid.

27. Ibid.

28. Brian Padden, " Trump Campaign Focuses on Hunter Biden Emails as 'October Surprise'," *Voice Of America* Online, October 28, 2020, https://www.voanews.com/2020-usa-votes/trump-campaign-focuses-hunter-biden-emails-october-surprise. The term October surprise originated in 1980 when President Jimmy Carter attempted to gain a release of American hostages held in Iran.

29. Marc Caputo and Christopher Cadelago, "Dems warm to Biden's Bunker Strategy," *Politico*, June 24, 2020, https://www.politico.com/news/2020/06/24/dems-warm-to-bidens-bunker-strategy-338853.

30. Madeleine Carlisle, "Three Weeks after Trump's Tulsa Rally, Oklahoma Reports Record High COVID-19 Numbers," *Time*, July 11, 2020, https://time.com/5865890/oklahoma-covid-19-trump-tulsa-rally/.

31. Andrew Solender, "Biden Campaign Raised $10 Million In Three Hours On Night Of First Debate," *Forbes*, September 30, 2020, https://www.forbes.com/sites/andrewsolender/2020/09/30/biden-campaign-raised-10-million-in-three-hours-on-night-of-first-debate/?sh=7903d2976ca2; "Democrats Smash Fundraising Records after Ruth Bader Ginsburg's Death," *The Guardian*, September 21, 2020, https://www.theguardian.com/us-news/2020/sep/21/democrats-fundraising-records-ruth-bader-ginsburg-death.

32. Brian Schwartz, "Democrats Score a Fundraising Windfall during the DNC, and Biden Bundlers See New Commitments," *CNBC* Online, August 21, 2020, https://www.cnbc.com/2020/08/21/democrats-rack-up-fundraising-windfall-during-the-dnc.html.

33. "Presidential Candidate Map, Joe Biden 2020," Federal Election Commission, accessed March 4, 2021, https://www.fec.gov/data/candidates/president/presidential-map/

34. Ibid.

35. Ibid. The exact figure was $1,051,374,614.

36. Sam Gringlas, Audie Cornish, and Courtney Dorning, "Step Aside Election 2000: This Year's Election May Be The Most Litigated Yet," *NPR* Online, September

22, 2020, https://www.npr.org/2020/09/22/914431067/step-aside-election-2000-this-years-election-may-be-the-most-litigated-yet.

37. Audrey McNamara, "Joe Biden Opens Door to Super PAC Help, Reversing Previous Position," *The Daily Beast,* October 24, 2019, https://www.thedailybeast.com/joe-biden-opens-door-to-super-pac-help-reversing-previous-position.

38. Ibid.

39. Shane Goldmacher, "Biden Campaign Drops Opposition to Super PAC Support," *New York Times*, October 24, 2019, https://www.nytimes.com/2019/10/24/us/politics/joe-biden-super-pac.html.

40. Ibid.

41. Fredreka Schouton, "Democratic Super PACs Race to Fill the Void with Joe Biden off the Trail," CNN, March 25, 2020, https://www.cnn.com/2020/03/25/politics/democratic-super-pacs-attack-trump/index.html.

42. "Financial Summary, Biden Victory Fund 2019-2020," Federal Election Commission, accessed March 4, 2021, https://www.fec.gov/data/committee/C00744946/.

43. Note these super PACs cannot take money from foreign entities, either individuals or corporations. I

44. Carey v. FEC was a 2011 case in the U.S. District Court for the District of Columbia case involving the accounting practices of hybrid PACs. The FEC's response on this was detailed in 2011. See "FEC statement on *Carey v. FEC*: Reporting guidance for political committees that maintain a non-contribution account," Federal Election Commission, October 5, 2011, https://www.fec.gov/updates/fec-statement-on-carey-fec/.

45. Theodore Schleifer, "Silicon Valley Megadonors Unleash a Last-Minute, $100 Million Barrage of Ads against Trump," *Vox*, October 20, 2020, https://www.vox.com/recode/2020/10/20/21523492/future-forward-super-pac-dustin-moskovitz-silicon-valley.

46. "Priorities USA's By the Numbers," Priorities USA, accessed March 4, 2021, https://priorities.org/memos/priorities-usas-2020-by-the-numbers/. These figures are provided by Priorities USA website. Their spending also included eighteen lawsuits that directly dealt with voting rights.

47. "Priorities USA led the charge against Trump and his Allies," Priorities USA, accessed November 3, 2020, https://priorities.org/memos/priorities-usa-led-the-charge-against-trump-and-his-allies/. According to Prioirities USA, America First spent $103 million compared with the $133 million spent by Priorities USA.

48. "American Bridge 21st Century," accessed March 4, 2021, https://american-bridgepac.org/about-us/.

49. "Mike Bloomberg's Independence USA PAC Airs New Ad Touting Vice President's Strength on the Economy," accessed March 4, 2021, https://www.mikebloomberg.com/news/mike-bloombergs-independence-usa-pac-airs-new-ad-touting-vice-presidents-strength-on-the-economy/.

50. Turnout PAC, accessed March 3, 2021, https://www.turnoutpac.org/progressive-turnout-project-congratulates-joe-biden-on-michigan-win/.

51. George T. Conway III, Steve Schmidt, John Weaver and Rick Wilson, "We Are Republicans, and We Want Trump Defeated," *New York Times*, December 17, 2019, https://www.nytimes.com/2019/12/17/opinion/lincoln-project.html. At the time of this writing The Lincoln Project underwent a high-profile scandal that called its organization's founders and management into question. See, Maggie Astor and Danny Hakim, "21 Men Accuse Lincoln Project Co-Founder of Online Harassment," *New York Times*, January 31, 2021, https://www.nytimes.com/2021/01/31/us/politic s/john-weaver-lincoln-project-harassment.html; Michael Isikoff, "George Conway: Lincoln Project Must Give 'full Explanation of What Happened'," YahooNews!, February 15, 2021, https://news.yahoo.com/lincoln-project-co-founder-says-group -must-give-full-explanation-of-what-happened-161913752.html.

52. "Financial Summary, DNC SERVICES CORP / DEMOCRATIC NATIONAL COMMITTEE," Federal Election Commission, accessed March 4, 2021, https://www .fec.gov/data/committee/C00010603/?cycle=2020.

53. "Financial Summary, Act Blue, 2019-2020," Federal Election Commission, accessed March 4, 2021, https://www.fec.gov/data/committee/C00401224/?cycl e=2020; Elena Schneider, "How ActBlue has Transformed Democratic politics," Politico, October 30, 2020, https://www.politico.com/news/2020/10/30/democrats -actblue-fundrasing-elections-433698.

54. "Financial Summary, Blue Texas PAC," Federal Election Commission, accessed March 4, 2021, https://www.fec.gov/data/committee/C00753293/.

55. Bipartisan Campaign Reform Act of 2002, 116 Stat 81, Pub. L. 107-155 (2002).

56. "Presidential Candidate May, Joe Biden," Federal Election Commission, accessed March 4, 2021, https://www.fec.gov/data/candidates/president/presidential -map/.

57. "Financial Summary, DNC SERVICES CORP / DEMOCRATIC NATIONAL COMMITTEE," Federal Election Commission, March 4, 2021, https://www.fec.gov/ data/committee/C00010603/?cycle=2020; "Financial Summary, Act Blue 2021- 2022," Federal Election Commission, March 4, 2021, https://www.fec.gov/data/ committee/C00401224/?cycle=2022; "Financial Summary, Act Blue 2019-2020," Federal Election Commission, March 4, 2021, https://www.fec.gov/data/committee/ C00401224/?cycle=2020.

Chapter 7

Donald Trump's Fundraising in the General Election

The fundraising narrative of 2020 is that Biden raised more money than Trump. However, Trump's 2020 campaign created millions in donations, outperformed both his and his rival Hillary Clinton's totals in 2016 and contributed to what would be the most expensive election in American history. While Biden denounced the excesses of campaign fundraising, while raising astronomical amounts, Trump's fundraising narrative was straightforward. He needed donations because the Democrats, and Biden, already had millions putting him and the every man and woman of MAGA Country at risk of having a Democratic President.

Trump's campaign totals are actually more impressive if one considers the context of how they were raised. Coming off of an acquittal in the U.S. Senate, Trump's administration was plagued with scandals, including one involving campaign finance, Trump attorney Michael Cohen's guilty pleas. However, Trump persevered in raising funds for his reelection taking in more than $789.8 million in receipts.[1] This is not including the millions raised by joint fundraising committees and the RNC. However, Trump's campaign did suffer some setback with fundraising. They were below that of Biden and the Democrats who were able to raise hundreds of millions of dollars; in fact, Biden's campaign committee raised over $1 billion, which outperformed Trump.

PACs and super-PACs also played a large role in Trump's campaign in 2020. Their presence demonstrates the infusion of cash that super-PACs have within the American political sphere. Joint fundraising committees and political party donations have a great impact as well. The RNC and the joint fundraising committee between Trump and the RNC received millions in donations, which benefited Republicans and Trump in the 2020 election. PACs are also playing an important role in the postelection fundraising.

Trump is currently the leader of the Republican Party, and from may seek the party's nomination in 2024. His PAC fundraising can lead to impact in the 2022 election, and gain loyalty of Republican candidates.

This chapter explores all of these aspects of the Trump's fundraising in 2020. The chapter begins with an analysis of Trump's political views on fundraising. Examining his statements from 2016 and 2020 a profile emerges that show Trump's true feeling on campaign finance, and how he uses it as a political talking point against opponents. Next, the chapter examines the campaign donations of Trump's campaign committee, and how he raised millions after the convention despite having a very difficult context in which to run. Finally, the chapter examines how the RNC, joint committees, and PACs benefited Donald Trump's reelection bid. Related to this, the chapter examines the new PAC created by Trump, and how he can use fundraising to position himself within the Republican Party.

CAMPAIGN FUNDRAISING AS A POLITICAL ISSUE

"I think PACs are a horrible thing," said candidate Donald Trump in 2016.[2] His sentiment at that time had more to do with perception that they benefited the establishment Republicans who were trying to keep him from winning the Republican nomination. This attitude is emblematic of Trump's stance on campaign finance. He casts his opponents as the beneficiaries of large donations, and couches himself as an underdog. To be fair, this characterization is not untrue. Hillary Clinton outraised Donald Trump in 2016.[3] His Republican primary opponents in 2016 had access to many donors. Still their political funding could not beat him. That reality was one that Trump must have hoped for in 2020. Biden and the Democrats dominated fundraising, and outperformed Trump's campaign. Democrats had a fundraising apparatus that understood how to harness the aggregate totals of small donors to create multibillion dollar fundraising. Despite being the incumbent, Trump's campaign had less money. However, Trump's fundraising was not bad. He and the Republicans raised millions, and, in turn, made the 2020 presidential election the most expensive in U.S. history.

So, what about campaign finance? Unlike the Democrats, Trump did not have a clear-cut campaign finance reform package. Part of the reason, obviously, is that Trump, unlike Biden, did not have to contend with the discontent among progressive voters regarding corporate donations. However, Trump's comments on campaign finance over the years in some ways mirrors those of people like Sanders, who characterize fundraising as a corrupting influence on politicians. Trump's view on campaign finances is not as nuanced or developed as Joe Biden's. Spending most of his life as a Manhattan businessman and real estate developer, Trump spent more time as a donor than as a politician. In fact, during 2016 his political beliefs came under attack by the media because of his mixed history of supporting both Republicans and Democrats. In fact, prior to 2016, Trump supported Democrats more than Republicans.[4] This is not a surprise given Trump's changing political affiliations over the past thirty years. He was a Republican in 1999 and then registered as a Democrat in 2001 believing that the economy did better under Democrats than Republicans.[5] He was also friendly with many Democratic politicians, notably Bill and Hillary Clinton who attended Trump's 2005 wedding to Melania Trump.[6] Trump would go one to switch back to the Republican Party in 2009.[7]

Trump made political talking points about being a former Democratic donor. In 2016, Trump speaking to the Al Smith Fundraising dinner commented on how he used to donate to many Democrats in the room, saying that they abandoned liking him when he became a Republican.[8] In the past Trump provided campaign donations to Democrats, even contributing $1,000 to Biden in 2001.[9] In a 2016 campaign stop in Iowa, Trump acknowledged this saying that "I've given to Democrats. I've given to Hillary. I've given to everybody! Because that was my job. I gotta [*sic*] give to them. Because when I want something, I get it. When I call, they kiss my ass."[10] In 2020 during the Democratic primary, Trump singled out Kristen Gillibrand stating that she would come to his office "begging" for donations and "would do anything to get them," which set off a firestorm of criticism that Trump was using sexist language.[11]

Trump's view on campaign finance was not something that was part of his campaign. Unlike Democrats in 2020, Trump and Republicans did not make an issue out of the *Citizens United v. FEC* decision or corporate donations one way or another. Instead, the general approach to campaign finance was to criticize opponents' use of donations. In his first election in 2016, Trump was critical toward his opponents' fundraising and suggested that they had legally inappropriate relationships with super-PACs. Legally, PACs and candidate committees cannot coordinate with each other. However, in 2016 Trump said that he knew this was not the case, and that coordination occurred regularly. He said, "First of all, everyone's dealing with their PAC. You know, it's supposed to be like this secret thing. They're all dealing with it."[12] Trump was particularly critical of Jeb Bush, who was a large fundraiser in the 2016 Republican primary. During that primary, a pro-Bush super-PAC, Right to Rise, raised over $121.6 million.[13] However, when Bush dropped out of the primary he stated that he believed that the super-PAC should be banned and the *Citizens United v. FEC* decision should be overturned. Trump heavily criticized what he believed was Bush's hypocrisy on the issue given that Bush had a fundraising advantage and still could not win in the

Republican primary.[14] In fact, Trump used the fact his Republican rivals did not outperform him polls despite their fundraising abilities and well-financed campaigns.[15]

As a political issue, Trump's focus on campaign finance largely focused on criticism of the special interests he claimed his opponents, Clinton and Biden, were beholden to. In 2016 Trump accused Hillary Clinton during the second presidential debate of not implementing the tax code because her friends and political supporters, Warren Buffet and George Soros, were part of the system and benefited from it, and, in turn, donated millions to her campaign so she could buy advertising.[16] He also criticized Clinton for not self-funding part of her campaign, claiming that he intended to self-contribute $100 million (he ended up contributing $66.1 million).[17] In response to her criticism of the impact of the holding in *Citizens United v. FEC* on campaigns Trump said that she should put money in her own campaign.[18] In their final debate Trump said that Clinton's contributions were directly tied to those people who funded her. He said:

> You should have changed the [tax] law, but you won't change the law because you take in so much money. I sat in my apartment today on a very beautiful hotel down the street. I sat there watching ad after ad after ad, all false ads, all paid for by your friends on Wall Street that gave so much money because they know you're going to protect them.[19]

As President Trump's initiatives did not include major campaign finance. In fact, it was not an issue that gained major political traction during the Trump administration aside from some discussion during Justice Neil Gorsuch's confirmation in 2017 and again for Brett Kavanaugh in 2018.[20] Their nominations and subsequent confirmations to the court solidified the conservative majority, and, as a result the likelihood that the *Citizens United v. FEC* decision would be overturned severely diminished.[21] In fact, Kavanaugh was a law clerk to Justice Anthony Kennedy from 1993 to 1994, and later replaced Kennedy on the court. It was Kennedy who wrote the *Citizens United v. FEC* decision.[22] Campaign finance legislation also did not take precedence during the Trump administration. In 2018 he signed one bill, sponsored by Senator John Tester (D-MT), into law requiring electronic filing of campaign disclosures with the FEC making the filings available to the public more quickly.[23]

During the end of Trump's first term, the big campaign finance issue was the accusation of a campaign finance violation surrounding the work of Trump attorney Michael Cohen, who pleaded guilty to eight counts in August 2018. Among his charges was campaign finance violations in which Cohen admitted that he unlawfully accepted a corporate contribution and unlawfully making an excessive campaign contribution at the direction of Trump.[24]

These charges arose from Cohen's involvement with Stephanie Clifford, better known as Stormy Daniels, and have a publishing company pay Karen McDougal for her story so she would not go forward with it in the press.[25] Both the payment for Daniels and the funds received by the publisher were deemed campaign finance violations. Trump denied that he had a relationship with either woman, or that he directed Cohen to pay these sums. That resulted in an investigation by federal prosecutors in the U.S. Attorney's Office for the Southern District of New York, but no charges were filed related to campaign finance violations.[26] Cohen would be sentenced to three years in prison and a $50,000 fine.[27]

Joe Biden was excoriated by Trump for his acceptance of cash, and Hunter Biden's business deals in China, Ukraine, and Russia. During the campaign, Trump said that Biden was beholden to these special interests. Like Biden, Trump would gain million in campaign donations during the presidential debates. At the final debate Trump would haul in $26 million.[28] However, the Democrats and Biden had a clear advantage going into the General Election. However, this is not to say Trump was unsuccessful from a campaign finance perspective—far from it. At the end of 2020 Trump's campaign raised $789.8 million in total receipts and millions more in pro-Trump PACs.[29] Trump's campaign, like Biden's, made use of all of the fundraising tools available under the law. His campaign showed that not only was Trump an effective fundraiser but that as a political figure he is very powerful post election. In 2021, Trump's fundraising shows that his political position is anything but done, and if he continues at the rate he has been going since November, Republicans and Trump will have a cash advantage in 2022 and 2024.

TRUMP'S CAMPAIGN FUNDRAISING
POST-CONVENTION

Donald Trump's campaign was somewhat overshadowed by COVID-19, but his campaign fundraising continued in earnest. While Trump benefited from having no real opposition in the primary, he knew that Biden was going to be a formidable challenger in the General Election starting in March 2020. However, Trump's campaign was dealing with some novel issues that harmed the way Trump's campaigns usually occurred. Because of the pandemic, Trump was unable to hold the same crowded rallies that were popular in 2016. Those rallies were significant from a financial point of view. They allowed Trump to garner millions of dollars of earned media, which gave him an advantage during the election when he had less money that Hillary Clinton. In fact, the *New York Times* figures that in 2016 Trump accumulated around $2 billion in earned media, which boosted his campaign.[30] Trump's strategy in 2020 was to hold smaller rallies, which had limited impact. Consequently, Trump also had fewer rallies covered by the media, which cut into his free earned media that he used to offset campaign cash in 2016.[31]

As shown in table 7.1 Trump had a steady stream of donations starting in August 2020, the same month as the Republican National Convention.[32] Starting in August 2020, Trump campaign's total receipts were $61.7 million, and climbed steadily through September. The Post-General Election period, from October 15 through November 23 saw a surge in donations for Trump's campaign totaling $183.4 million.

Like many politicians, Trump's campaign took in millions from small donations. In fact, he raised over $483.8 million from donors contributing $200 or less.[33] This was actually the largest contribution group in Trump's 2020 campaign. Donors contributing more than $2,000 made up only $99.3 million.[34] However, this was a significant increase from Trump's 2016 campaign. That year donors giving $200 or less made up the largest single contributor group, but only gave $126 million.[35] Donors giving over $2,000 made up only $27.8 million.[36] This small donor trend was not exclusive to Trump or Republicans. Biden's campaign took in $656.8 million in donations $200 or less.[37] That same trend continued for Republicans and Democrats in aggregate. Of all presidential candidates in 2020, the Federal Election Commission shows that over $1.6 billion was raised from donor contributing under $200, compared with only $355 million from donors giving over

Table 7.1   Trump Total Receipts August–Post-General 2020

Month	Total Receipts ($, million)
August	61.7
September	81.3
Pre-General*	43.5
Post-General**	183.4

*Pre-General is from October 1 to October 14, 2020. *Note* there is no October figures because they are included in Pre- and Post-General Disclosures.
**Post General is from October 15 to November 23, 2020.
"Reports of Receipts and Disbursements, September Monthly 2020 Amendment 2, Donald J. Trump for President," Federal Election Commission, accessed February 27, 2021, https://docquery.fec.gov/cgi-bin/forms/C00580100/1500199/; Reports of Receipts and Disbursements, October Monthly 2020 Amendment 1, Donald J. Trump for President," Federal Election Commission, accessed February 27, 2021, https://docquery.fec.gov/cgi-bin/forms/C00580100/1500233/; Reports of Receipts and Disbursements, Pre-General 2020, Donald J. Trump for President," Federal Election Commission, accessed February 27, 2021, https://docquery.fec.gov/cgi-bin/forms/C00580100/1463640/; Reports of Receipts and Disbursements, Post General 2020 Amendment 1, Donald J. Trump for President," Federal Election Commission, accessed February 27, 2021, https://docquery.fec.gov/cgi-bin/forms/C00580100/1483220/.

$2,000.[38] If anything, this shows the power of the small donor is strong for both Republicans and Democrats.

The strength of Trump's campaign was also indicated by his cash on hand. While Trump's spending during the last few months of the campaign increased with disbursements being $61.2 million in August, $139.2 million in September, $63 million from October 1 through the 14, and $208.6 million from October 15 through November 23.[39] This type of spending indicates that Trump had continual cash on hand that allowed him to spend heavily during the General Election. As table 7.2 shows, Trump's cash on hand depleted, as expected declined as the campaign continued. While Biden clearly had an advantage over Trump (see chapter 6) in fundraising Trump's campaign had millions at its disposal.

Trump's cash on hand made him competitive, but it was dwarfed in comparison to Biden. Prior to his COVID-19 diagnosis, Trump held a high dollar fundraiser in Bedminster, New Jersey, where he was present for three events, including a photo session (he was later criticized for hosting this knowing he had been exposed to COVID-19).[40] In his pre-General filing, Biden had $177.2 million compared with Trump's $63 million.[41] In the post General Biden had $162 million compared with $43.6 million for Trump.[42] As these numbers show, Trump had a financial disadvantage to Biden thorough the General Election.

However, Trump had been at a financial disadvantage compared to Hillary Clinton in 2016 and was able to still win. Bill Stepien, Trump's campaign manager in 2020, said that the amount Trump raised still provided him with

Table 7.2 Trump Beginning and Ending Cash on Hand for Reporting Period August–November 23, 2020[i]

Month	Beginning ($, million)	Close ($, million)
August	120.5	121.09
September	121.09	63.1
Pre-General*	63.1	43.6
Post-General**	43.6	18.4

[i]This table appears in Cayce Myers, "Campaign Finance and its Impact on the 2020 Campaign," in *The 2020 Campaign: Political Communication and Practice*, ed. Robert Denton (Lanham, MD: Roman and Littlefield, 2021, 168).

*Pre-General is from October 1 to October 14, 2020. *Note* there is no October figures because they are included in Pre- and Post-General Disclosures.

**Post General is from October 15 to November 23, 2020.

"Reports of Receipts and Disbursements, September Monthly 2020 Amendment 1, Donald J. Trump for President," Federal Election Commission, accessed January 2, 2021, https://docquery.fec.gov/cgi-bin/forms/C00580100/1484015/; "Reports of Receipts and Disbursements, October Monthly 2020, Donald J. Trump for President," Federal Election Commission, accessed January 2, 2021, https://docquery.fec.gov/cgi-bin/forms/C00580100/1458436/; "Reports of Receipts and Disbursements, Pre-General, Donald J. Trump for President," Federal Election Commission, accessed January 2, 2021, https://docquery.fec.gov/cgi-bin/forms/C00580100/1463640/; "Reports of Receipts and Disbursements, Post General Amendment 1, Donald J. Trump for President," Federal Election Commission, accessed January 2, 2021, https://docquery.fec.gov/cgi-bin/forms/C00580100/1483220/ .

"sufficient air cover" to win the General Election. In fact, Trump in 2020 had done far better in his own fundraising activities in 2016. By the end of the election cycle the Trump campaign raised over $789.8 million, compared to only $333.1 million in 2016.[43]

TRUMP'S FUNDRAISING WITH PARTY, JOINT COMMITTEES, AND PACS

Candidate's campaigns are not the only source of contributions, and with the creation of the super-PAC political campaigns benefit from millions given by donors. Like any modern presidential candidate, Trump benefited from fundraising from his joint fundraising committee, Trump Victory, that he formed with the Republican Party. Trump Victory raised over $366.3 million from 2019 through 2020.[44] This was far less than Biden's joint fundraising committee, Biden Victory Fund, which raised $659 million in total receipts during the same time frame.[45] However, Trump's joint fundraising committee Trump Make America Great Again Committee received over $884 million from 2019 through 2020.[46] Trump also benefited from the money raised by the RNC, which is used to support Republican candidates in several offices. The RNC raised $890.4 million in total receipts between 2019 and 2020 compared with the Democratic National Committee which raised $491.7 million during this same timeframe.[47] Part of this strength of the RNC compared to the DNC is the fact there was an incumbent Republican president in 2020. However, looking at all fundraising committees for House races, the Democrats did have an advantage. Biden outraised Trump, and the Democratic Congressional Campaign Committee (DCCC) outraised its Republican counterpart, the National Republican Campaign Committee (NRCC), $345.7 million (DCCC) to $280.9 million (NRCC).[48]

Trump benefited from the donations generated from PACs. These PACs were pro-Trump, pro-Republican, and anti-Biden. Republican PACs have not had the same level of success of those of Democrats, but they gained a large amount of donations during 2020. Perhaps most telling of this Democrat-Republican divide on PAC donations is shown in Win Red versus ActBlue. WinRed, the Republican response to the highly successful Democrats' ActBlue, raised $2.2 billion from 2019 through 2020.[49] However, despite that multibillion dollar amount, ActBlue raised double in the same timeframe, for a total amount of $4.3 billion.[50] Other House-and-Senate-specific PACs also did well in 2020. The Senate Leadership Fund, which supported election of Republicans to the U.S. Senate, took in $475.3 million, and Congressional Leadership Fund, which supports Republican House candidates, took in $165.7 million.[51]

A unique issue emerged in 2020 that may foreshadow campaign finance issues in the future, especially as it relates to candidate brand and identity. The success of PACs has also given rise to PACs that take money, usually from small donors, but have no real affiliation with a candidate's campaign. These groups use merchandise, and other online communications to recruit donors that would otherwise donate to the campaign or the party. Trump's campaign sent out a directive to the FEC and made statements for these outside groups to cease operations, with the exception of America First.[52] However, legally little can be done to combat this issue. This PAC problem is not unique, and with the proliferation of PACs in the 2020s it is an issue that is bound to continue. In sum, these PACs ended up taking in millions in 2020.[53]

Table 7.3 presents the various pro-Republican or pro-Trump PACs that impacted the 2020 presidential election. America First Action was created as a pro-Trump super-PAC, which advocated for Trump's America first policies. It raised over $150.1 million in 2019 to 2020 spending more than $149 million during that time.[54] Preserve America PAC, an anti-Biden PAC also took in $105.3 million in receipts from 2019 to 2020. In fact, businessman Shelton Adelson gave $75 million to the PAC in September, which helped the PAC create a massive amount of advertising in the final month of the election.[55] PACs also raised smaller figures such as Future 45, which was active in the 2016 campaign raising $24.9 million, but only raising $3.8 million in 2020.[56]

The election results in 2020 were finalized with Biden winning 306 electoral votes to Trump's 232. However, these results create a firestorm of

Table 7.3   **Pro-Trump and Pro-Republican PACs Fundraising Reporting Period 2019–2020**

Political Action Committee	Amount Raised (Total Receipts, $)
America First Action	150.1 million
Preserve America PAC	105.3 million
Great America PAC	11.7 million
Future 45	3.8 million
Save America*	31.5 million
WinRed**	2.2 billion

*Save America was a PAC created in October 2020 and largely donated to after the 2020 election. As a leadership PAC Save America can accept a limit of $5,000 of donations per individual, but can accept donations from an unlimited number of individuals.
**WinRed is not a PAC that is just tied to Trump, but is supportive of Republican candidates generally.
Financial Summary, America First Action 2019-2020, Federal Election Commission, accessed February 27, 2021, https://www.fec.gov/data/committee/C00637512/; Financial Summary, Preserve America PAC 2019-2020, Federal Election Commission, accessed February 27, 2021, https://www.fec.gov/data/committee/C00756882/; Financial Summary, Great America PAC, Federal Election Commission, accessed February 27, 2021, https://www.fec.gov/data/committee/C00608489/; Financial Summary, Future 45, Federal Election Commission, accessed March 5, 2021, https://www.fec.gov/data/committee/C00574533/; Financial Summary, Save America, Federal Election Commission, accessed February 27, 2021, https://www.fec.gov/data/committee/C00762591/; Financial Summary, WinRed, Federal Election Commission, accessed February 27, 2021, https://www.fec.gov/data/committee/C00694323/.

criticism and lawsuits from Trump who alleged that election irregularities cost him the election. This, in turn, created a political response by some Trump supporters that resulted in the storming of the U.S. Capitol on January 6, 2021. However, as a political issue the election results provided fodder for fundraising for Republicans and Trump post election.

This fundraising may prove crucial in the future as the Republican Party and Trump strategize for the 2022 midterm elections and the eventual presidential election in 2024. Post election Trump used a new leadership PAC Save America to continue to raise money for potentially another campaign in 2024.[57] Trump indicated that he would be shifting many of his donations to Save America, and the PAC has already endorsed some Republican candidates, notable former White House press secretary Sarah Huckabee Sanders for Arkansas Governor.[58] Conversely the PAC has also targeted Republican Members of Congress who voted for impeachment, specifically Liz Cheney, the Republican Representative from Wyoming.[59] In response, vulnerable Republican Members of Congress who voted for Trump's second impeachment have their own super-PAC, called Americans Keeping Country First. It is described as protecting those Republican Members of Congress who "took votes of conscience to impeach or convict President Trump after rioters stormed the U.S. Capitol on January 6, 2021."[60] This type of fundraising issue could signal an issue for Republicans in 2024. Pro-Trump Republicans remain popular within the party, but those Republicans who opposed Trump, especially after the second impeachment, have created a potential fundraising rift within the party. However, if current events are any indicator, Trump's fundraising abilities are powerful for the current Republicans, and his stature as party leader is still firm. This potentially provides an opportunity for him to run again as the Republican nominee in 2024. In fact, his fundraising activities lead many to speculate that he is positioning himself as the party's standard bearer in 2024 already.

In February 2021, the Conservative Party Action Congress (CPAC) met in Florida to discuss Republican strategies going forward into 2022 and provide a straw poll of support for presidential candidates in 2024. This meeting has been a foreshadowing of the direction of the Republican Party, and it provides the opportunity for Republicans to appear united and decide upon a path moving forward. Trump won the straw poll convincingly for presidential nominee February 28, 2021.[61] This may not be that significant by 2024, but it demonstrates that in 2021 Trump's status among Republicans is very high. In fact, his policies are actually more popular than he is as a candidate with 95 percent of CPAC voters endorsing the Trump agenda.[62] Formed in late 2020, Save America was created as a PAC that would raise money for Republicans meaning Trump would retain power within the Republican Party. At the end of 2020 Save America had raised $31.5 million in total receipts, but had only a little over $343,000 in disbursements at the end of 2020.[63] The Make America Great Again Committee gives money to both Save America and the RNC.[64] Trump's committees and PAC are in a good financial standing for Republicans and Trump going into 2021. Media also speculate that Trump's active political post-presidency will result in the creation of a new super-PAC likely headed by his old 2016 campaign manager Corey Lewandowski.[65] At the time of this writing, Trump seems to be staying active in Republican politics for a potential renomination effort in 2024. He gave the closing speech at CPAC in February 2021, stating that Republicans will take back both houses of Congress and the White House. Commenting on the 2024 presidential election Trump said, "And I wonder who that will be. I wonder who that will be. Who? Who? Who will that be? I wonder."[66] Media speculate that this signals that Trump will be waging a campaign now for the White House in 2024, which will give him four years of building a campaign war chest.

CONCLUSION

Trump's fundraising showed that he was a capable fundraiser, outraising what he did in 2016 against Hillary Clinton. He was able to gain momentum during the primary season by being a strong incumbent and was not hampered by the various scandals and impeachment that would normally plague politicians. In many ways, these types of stories may have helped Trump; it certainly solidified his base. Going into the General Election, Trump's overarching issue was the international COVID-19 pandemic. It is possible that some of Trump's unforced errors, such as his statements about household cleaners treating COVID-19 and the combative exchanges between him and the press, may have cost him some votes. However, from a fundraising perspective Trump remained strong. The one big difference between 2016 and 2020 was that while Trump outperformed his 2016 totals, he did not enjoy the same level of earned media that he received in 2016. That potentially cost him, in some sense, during the General Election. The novelty of his rallies and tweets, along with the reduced crowds may have diminished his message. However, Trump remained strong as a candidate he raised over $789.8 million in his campaign, and his joint fundraising committees were also flush with cash.[67] It is difficult to say that Trump could have done more to raise money for his race, and it is hard to say that raising more would have made a major impact on the outcome of the race.

Compared with Biden, however, Trump's campaign trailed in fundraising totals. Part of this was the organization of the Democrats, and the power of their online donation systems through PACs like ActBlue. However, Biden did outperform Trump in the General Election comparing campaign committees. Biden would raise over $1.05 billion dollars, besting Hillary Clinton's 2016 total of $563.7 million.[68] That in itself raises certain questions about how campaign donations have so dramatically increased in just four years (note that 2016 was at that time the most expensive presidential election). However, Trump and Biden both show that in terms of donations for presidential campaigns the utilization of donations from all donor segments are important. Small donors certainly have an important place within the campaign fundraising model. Trump's fundraising also shows an important point that the narrative that public funding helps Democrats complete against Republicans.

The big concern with *Citizens United v. FEC* was that PAC money from corporations would flood elections making presidential contests costs millions.[69] In fact, that did happen, but the contests ended up costing billions. However, the impact of super-PACs and other PACs is not clear. Trump benefited from PAC money, but something unusual occurred in 2020. The PAC fundraising in 2020 showed the power of using political brands and imagery to raise money. The lack of control over PACs and their real association with candidates illustrates a growing problem in fundraising in which PACS emerge that claim they are supporting a candidate or cause when, in fact, they are not. These types of PACs siphon off contributions from organizations that would have normally benefited Trump. In total, it was estimated that these PACs took $46 million from Trump endorsed PACs, which in political campaign fundraising is a lot of money.[70] This issue signals a bigger issue yet to come in the next elections, and legally options are limited with these types of PACs.

Writing in 2021 it is unclear who will be the Republican nominee for President in 2024. However, what is clear that as of the time of this book's writing, Donald Trump is positioning himself to be in that role. His CPAC straw vote results, and his political fundraising indicate that Trump will not be an inactive former president, but an active leader of the Republican Party. As with all political defeats, parties do some introspection to see how they should change going forward in the future. This happened in 1964 with Goldwater and 1976 with Ford, but in 2021 something unique is happening. Trump's impact on the Republican Party is powerful, despite his electoral defeat. This is not just an illusion created by straw polls or speech attendance, but by the amount of money President Trump raised post election. His ability to use that money to fund Republican candidates in the 2022 midterms will be a value tool to shape the future of the party and position himself within it as its leader.

So, what was the impact of Trump's campaign finance on the 2020 presidential election? Looking back at history there are examples when fundraising probably made a significant impact (think Humphrey in 1968). However, in 2020 the fundraising by Trump positioned him well as an incumbent. Even though he was outperformed by Biden and the Democrats in fundraising, Trump's performance fundraising-wise was strong. It was stronger than both his and Hillary Clinton's fundraising in 2016. However, Trump's loss, as with any political loss, cannot be ascribed to fundraising. It is a mixture of things, and for him notably it was the COVID-19 pandemic and his administration's handling of a worldwide pandemic. He was also curtailed in his ability to generate earned media, which he enjoyed in 2016. And, unlike 2016, Trump was no political outsider; he was the incumbent. As such, his reelection was a referendum on his past four years in office, which resulted in a galvanized Democratic electorate. The big takeaway from 2020 is this: American elections are getting more and more expensive, and without any type of campaign finance control, they will continue to so for the foreseeable future.

NOTES

1. "Presidential Candidate Map, Donald J. Trump, 2020," Federal Election Commission, accessed March 4, 2021, https://www.fec.gov/data/candidates/president/presidential-map/. This figure includes total receipts provided by information at the Federal Election Commission. This total includes total receipts of the candidate from contributions from individuals, the candidate, political committees, and transfers from prior federal campaigns.

2. Bradford Richardson, "Trump Open to Campaign Finance Reform," *The Hill*, January 17, 2016, https://thehill.com/blogs/ballot-box/presidential-races/266189-trump-open-to-campaign-finance-reform.

3. Cayce Myers, "Campaign Finance and Its Impact in the 2016 Presidential Campaign," in *The 2016 Presidential Campaign: Political Communication and Practice*, ed. Robert Denton (New York: Palgrave McMillan, 2017), 259–283.

4. Timothy Noah, "Will the Real Donald Trump Please Stand Up," *Politico*, July 26, 2015, https://www.politico.com/story/2015/07/will-the-real-donald-trump-please-stand-up-120607.

5. Ibid.

6. Trump and the Clintons had a notably amicable relationship prior to his entry into politics. Trump donated to the Clinton Foundation, and Bill Clinton played gold at Trump National Golf Course, which was six miles away from Clinton's home in Westchester, with Trump. See Maureen Dowd, "When Hillary and Donald Were Friends," *New York Times*, November 2, 2016, https://www.nytimes.com/2016/11/06/magazine/when-hillary-and-donald-were-friends.html.

7. Jason Le Miere, "Is Trump Republican? Timeline of President's Shifting Political Views After He Sides With Democrats," Newsweek, September 7, 2017, https://www.newsweek.com/trump-republican-democrats-president-661340.

8. Tara Golshan, "Read the Full Speeches: Clinton and Trump's Awkward Al Smith Charity Dinner Roasts, *Vox*, October 21, 2016, https://www.vox.com/policy-and-politics/2016/10/21/13357412/clinton-trump-al-smith-roasts-full-speeches.

9. Trump's donations to Kamala Harris when she was running for California Attorney General in 2011 and 2013. Ivanka Trump also donated to Harris and held a fundraiser for Corey Booker (D-NJ) in 2013 with a suggested donation of $5,200. In 2015 Harris donated the Trump donation to charity. For a discussion on the Democratic donations made to Harris and Booker see Rebecca Elliot, "Trump to Host Fundraiser for Booker, *Politico*, July 16, 2013, https://www.politico.com/story/2013/07/ivanka-trump-fundraiser-cory-booker-094288 and David Fahrenthold, "Trump previously donated $6,000 to Kamala D. Harris's campaigns, *Washington Post*, August 12, 2020, https://www.washingtonpost.com/politics/trump-harris-campaign-donations/2020/08/12/06eb1f0e-dcdb-11ea-b205-ff838e15a9a6_story.html.

10. Eli Okun, "Awkward: How Trump's Past Donations Could Haunt 2020 Dems," *Politico,* March 5, 2020, https://www.politico.com/story/2019/03/05/2020-presidential-dems-trump-money-1202938.

11. Mallory Shelbourne, "Trump says Gillibrand Begged for Donations 'and Would Do Anything for Them,'" *The Hill*, December 12, 2017, https://thehill.com/homenews/administration/364405-trump-slams-gillibrand-in-tweet-a-total-flunky-for-chuck-schumer.

12. Bradford Richardson, Trump Open to Campaign Finance Reform," *The Hill*, January 17, 2016, https://thehill.com/blogs/ballot-box/presidential-races/266189-trump-open-to-campaign-finance-reform.

13. Nolan McCaskill, "Trump: Bush 'Wasted' Special-Interest Money But Now Wants to End Super PACs," *Politico*, February 8, 2016, https://www.politico.com/story/2016/02/donald-trump-jeb-bush-super-pacs-218962.

14. Ibid.

15. Ibid.

16. "Transcript of Second Debate," *New York Times*, October 10, 2016, https://www.nytimes.com/2016/10/10/us/politics/transcript-second-debate.html.

17. "Presidential Candidate Map, Donald Trump 2016," Federal Election Commission, accessed March 4, 2021, https://www.fec.gov/data/candidates/president/presidential-map/.

18. Ibid.

19. Politico Staff, "Full Transcript: Third 2016 Presidential Debate," *Politico*, October 20, 2016, https://www.politico.com/story/2016/10/full-transcript-third-2016-presidential-debate-230063.

20. Adam Liptak, "How to Tell Where Brett Kavanaugh Stands on Citizens United," *New York Times*, July 23, 2018, https://www.nytimes.com/2018/07/23/us/politics/brett-kavanaugh-citizens-united-campaign-finance.html; David Burke, "With Gorsuch Confirmed, Only An Amendment Can Overturn Citizens United," *Huffington Post*, April 10, 2017, https://www.huffpost.com/entry/with-gorsuch-confirmed-only-an-amendment-can-overturn_b_58eb9457e4b0acd784ca5a4f. Gorsuch's confirmation preserved the conservative seat of Justice Antonin Scalia on the U.S. Supreme Court. In this article Huffington Post stated that with Gorsuch on the court the only thing that would potentially overrule the Citizens United v. FEC decision was a constitutional amendment. In his candidate statements Joe Biden proposed just that along with other reforms to the campaign finance system.

21. Citizens United v. FEC, 558 U.S. 310 (2010).

22. Ibid. Interestingly Kavanaugh had made some decisions on campaign finance while he was a judge on the U.S. Court of Appeals for the D.C. Circuit, in Bluman v. FEC, 800 F.Supp.2d 281 (D.D.C 2011). In that case Kavanaugh upheld the Bipartisan Campaign Reform Act of 2002's prohibition of foreign nationals on temporary work visas donating money in U.S. elections.

23. "Tester's Bill to Shine Light on Campaigns Passes Senate," U.S. Senator for Montana John Tester, June 25, 2018, https://www.tester.senate.gov/?p=press_release &id=6246.

24. "Michael Cohen Pleads Guilty In Manhattan Federal Court to Eight Counts, Including Criminal Tax Evasion and Campaign Finance Violations," U.S. Department of Justice, August 21, 2018, https://www.justice.gov/usao-sdny/pr/michael-cohen-plea ds-guilty-manhattan-federal-court-eight-counts-including-criminal-tax. Cohen's other charges were for tax evasion, five counts, and one count of a false statement to a bank.

25. Geoffrey Guray, "How Michael Cohen broke campaign Finance Law," *PBS News Hour* Online, December 12, 2018, https://www.pbs.org/newshour/politics/how -michael-cohen-broke-campaign-finance-law.

26. William Rashbaum and Ben Protess, "New Charges in Stormy Daniels Hush Money Inquiry Are Unlikely, Prosecutors Signal," *New York Times*, July 18, 2019, https:// www.nytimes.com/2019/07/18/nyregion/stormy-daniels-michael-cohen-documents.html.

27. Cohen was released from prison on May 21, 2020 because of COVID-19. He was ordered to serve the rest of his sentence under house arrest. He was later returned to prison briefly, only to be released again to house arrest. Cohen asserted that his return to prison was prompted by his working on a tell-all book about his experiences with Donald Trump. He would later release his book *Disloyal: A Memoir* in September 2020.

28. Elliot Davis, "Trump Raises $26M around Final Presidential Debate," *US News & World Report*, October 23, 2020, https://www.usnews.com/news/elections/ articles/2020-10-23/trump-raises-26-million-around-final-debate-with-biden.

29. "Presidential Candidate Map, Donald Trump 2020," Federal Election Commission, accessed March 4, 2021, https://www.fec.gov/data/candidates/president /presidential-map/. This figure includes total receipts provided by information at the Federal Election Commission. This total includes total receipts of the candidate from contributions from individuals, the candidate, political committees, and transfers from prior federal campaigns.

30. Nicolas Confessore and Karin Yourish, "$2 Billion Worth of Free Media for Donald Trump," *New York Times*, March 15, 2016, https://www.nytimes.com/2016/0 3/16/upshot/measuring-donald-trumps-mammoth-advantage-in-free-media.html.

31. Jeremy Barr and Elahe Izadi, "We're Seeing a Lot Less of Trump's Rallies on TV News in 2020," *Washington Post,* September 14, 2020, https://www.washingt onpost.com/media/2020/09/14/were-seeing-lot-less-trumps-rallies-tv-news-2020/. Part of the reason for the lack of broadcasts was of COVID-19. Indoor rallies posed health risks to television crews.

32. The 2020 Republican National Convention took place on August 24 through August 27. It was not a convention that was in-person, but rather was a televised event in which Trump gave his acceptance speech at the White House, something that had

not been done before. In fact, Trump received criticism for using the White House as a political backdrop for his acceptance speech.

33. "Presidential Campaign Map, Donald Trump 2020," Federal Election Commission, accessed March 4, 2021, https://www.fec.gov/data/candidates/president /presidential-map/.

34. Ibid.

35. "Presidential Campaign Map, Donald Trump 2016," Federal Election Commission, accessed March 4, 2021, https://www.fec.gov/data/candidates/president /presidential-map/.

36. Ibid.

37. "Presidential Campaign Map, Donald Biden 2020," Federal Election Commission, accessed March 4, 2021, https://www.fec.gov/data/candidates/president /presidential-map/.

38. "Presidential Campaign Map, All Candidates 2020," Federal Election Commission, accessed March 4, 2021, https://www.fec.gov/data/candidates/president /presidential-map/.

39. "Report of Receipts and Disbursements, Donald J. Trump for President, September Monthly Amended," Federal Election Commission, accessed March 4, 2021, https://docquery.fec.gov/cgi-bin/forms/C00580100/1500199/; "Report of Receipts and Disbursements, Donald J. Trump for President, October Monthly Amended," Federal Election Commission, accessed March 4, 2021, https://docquery .fec.gov/cgi-bin/forms/C00580100/1500233/; "Report of Receipts and Disbursements, Donald J. Trump for President, Pre-General," Federal Election Commission, accessed March 4, 2021, https://docquery.fec.gov/cgi-bin/forms/C00580100/146364 0/; "Report of Receipts and Disbursements, Donald J. Trump for President, Post-General Amended," Federal Election Commission, accessed March 4, 2021, https:// docquery.fec.gov/cgi-bin/forms/C00580100/1483220/.

40. Paul Murphy, "Trump Took Photos, Had Roundtable with Donors at Bedminster Fundraiser Hours Before Announcing Covid Diagnosis," *CNN* Online, October 4, 2020, https://www.cnn.com/2020/10/03/politics/bedminister-trump-fu ndraiser-coronavirus/index.html.

41. "Reports and Disbursements, Biden for President, Pre-General," Federal Election Commission, accessed March 4, 2021, https://docquery.fec.gov/cgi-bin /forms/C00703975/1463690/; "Reports and Disbursements, Donald J. Trump for President, Pre-General Amendment," Federal Election Commission, accessed March 4, 2021, https://docquery.fec.gov/cgi-bin/forms/C00580100/1502733/.

42. Reports and Disbursements, Biden for President, Post-General," Federal Election Commission, accessed March 4, 2021, https://docquery.fec.gov/cgi-bin /forms/C00703975/1481223/; Reports and Disbursements, Donald J. Trump for President, Post-General Amendment," Federal Election Commission, accessed March 4, 2021, https://docquery.fec.gov/cgi-bin/forms/C00580100/1483220/.

43. "Presidential Campaign Map, Donald Trump 2020," Federal Election Commission, accessed March 4, 2021, https://www.fec.gov/data/candidates/president/ presidential-map/; "Presidential Campaign Map, Donald Trump 2016," Federal Election Commission, accessed March 4, 2021, https://www.fec.gov/data/candidates/president/ presidential-map/. Both figures includes total receipts provided by information at the

Federal Election Commission. This total includes total receipts of the candidate from contributions from individuals, the candidate, political committees, and transfers from prior federal campaigns. For more information on FEC calculations of total receipts See, https://www.fec.gov/campaign-finance-data/presidential-map-data/.

44. "Financial Summary, Trump Victory, 2019-2020," Federal Election Commission, March 4, 2021, https://www.fec.gov/data/committee/C00618389/. A joint fundraising committee is a joint fundraising committee by Donald Trump's Campaign and the Republican National Committee.

45. "Financial Summary, Biden Victory Fund, 2019-2020," Federal Election Commission, accessed March 4, 2021, https://www.fec.gov/data/committee/C00744946/.

46. "Financial Summary, Trump Make America Great Again Committee," Federal Election Commission, accessed March 4, 2021, https://www.fec.gov/data/committee/C00618371/.

47. "Financial Summary, Republican National Committee, 2019-2020," Federal Election Commission, accessed March 4, 2021, https://www.fec.gov/data/committee/C00003418/?cycle=2020; "Financial Summary, DNC Services Corp./Democratic National Committee," Federal Election Commission, accessed March 4, 2021, https://www.fec.gov/data/committee/C00010603/?cycle=2020.

48. "Financial Summary, NRCC, 2019-2020," Federal Election Commission, accessed March 4, 2021, https://www.fec.gov/data/committee/C00075820/?cycle=2020; "Financial Summary, DCCC, 2019-2020," Federal Election Commission, accessed March 4, 2021, https://www.fec.gov/data/committee/C00000935/?cycle=2020.

49. "Financial Summary, WinRed, 2019-2020," Federal Election Commission, accessed March 4, 2021, https://www.fec.gov/data/committee/C00694323/.

50. "Financial Summary, ActBlue," Federal Election Commission, accessed March 4, 2021, https://www.fec.gov/data/committee/C00401224/?cycle=2020

51. "Financial Summary, Senate Leadership Fund, 2019-2020" Federal Election Commission, accessed March 4, 2021, https://www.fec.gov/data/committee/C00571703/?cycle=2020; "Financial Summary, Congressional Leadership Fund, 2019-2020" Federal Election Commission, accessed March 4, 2021, https://www.fec.gov/data/committee/C00504530/.

52. Maggie Severns, "Trump campaign plagued by groups raising tens of millions in his name," Politico, December 23, 2019, https://www.politico.com/news/2019/12/23/trump-campaign-compete-against-groups-money-089454.

53. Ibid. Part of the issue with these PACs is the use of the Trump likeness and other trademarked and copyrighted material used to promote the PAC to donors.

54. "Financial Summary, America First Action, 2019-2020," Federal Election Commission, accessed March 4, 2021, https://www.fec.gov/data/committee/C00637512/?cycle=2020.

55. Zach Montellaro and Alex Isenstadt, "Adelsons pour $75M into Last-Ditch Effort to Save Trump," *Politico*, October 15, 2020, https://www.politico.com/news/2020/10/15/adelson-trump-super-pac-429688.

56. "Financial Summary, Future 45, 2015-2016," Federal Election Commission, accessed March 4, 2021, https://www.fec.gov/data/committee/C00574533/?cycle=2016; "Financial Summary, Future 45, 2019-2020," Federal Election Commission, accessed March 4, 2021, https://www.fec.gov/data/committee/C00574533/?cycle=2020.

57. Shane Goldmacher and Rachel Shorey, "Trump's Sleight of Hand: Shouting Fraud, Pocketing Donors' Cash for Future," *New York Times*, February 4, 2021, https ://www.nytimes.com/2021/02/01/us/politics/trump-cash.html.

58. Morgan Chalfant, "Trump Likely to Form New Super PAC," *The Hill*, February 26, 2021, https://thehill.com/homenews/campaign/540716-trump-likely-to -form-new-super-pac.

59. Greg Norman, "Trump's Save America PAC starts 2021 with more than $31M, filings show," *Fox Business* Online, February 1, 2021, https://www.foxbusin ess.com/politics/trumps-save-america-pac-starts-2021-with-more-than-31-million.

60. "Americans Keeping Country First," March 4, 2021, https://countryfirst.gop/.

61. Justine Coleman, "Trump Wins CPAC Straw Poll With 55 Percent," The Hill, February 28, 2021, https://thehill.com/homenews/campaign/540909-trump -wins-cpac-straw-poll-with-55-percent. Trump won the straw poll, receiving 55 percent of the vote. The CPAC straw poll has been an indicator of primary strength of Republican candidates. In 2021 Florida Governor Ron DeSantis came in second.

62. Elaina Plott and Shane Goldmacher, "Trump Wins CPAC Straw Poll, but Only 68 Percent Want Him to Run Again," *New York Times*, February 28, 2021, https://ww w.nytimes.com/2021/02/28/us/politics/cpac-straw-poll-2024-presidential-race.html.

63. "Financial Summary, Save America, 2019-2020," Federal Election Commission, accessed March 4, 2021, https://www.fec.gov/data/committee/C0076 2591/?cycle=2020

64. Zach Montellaro and Elena Schneider, "Trump Stocks New PAC with Tens of Millions as He Bids to Retain Control of GOP," *Politico*, January 31, 2021, https:// www.politico.com/news/2021/01/31/donald-trump-pac-millions-gop-464250.

65. Chalfant, "Trump Likely to Form New Super PAC."

66. Maeve Reston, "Trump Teases 2024 Presidential Run In Lie-filled CPAC Speech," *CNN* Online, February 28, 2021, https://www.cnn.com/2021/02/28/politics/ trump-cpac-speech-2021/index.html.

67. "Presidential Candidate Map, Donald J. Trump, 2020," Federal Election Commission, accessed March 4, 2021, https://www.fec.gov/data/candidates/president /presidential-map/. This figure includes total receipts provided by information at the Federal Election Commission. This total includes total receipts of the candidate from contributions from individuals, the candidate, political committees, and transfers from prior federal campaigns.

68. "Campaign Finance Map, Joe Biden 2020," Federal Election Commission," accessed March 4, 2021, https://www.fec.gov/data/candidates/president/presidential-map/; "Campaign Finance Map, Hillary Clinton 2016," Federal Election Commission," accessed March 4, 2021, https://www.fec.gov/data/candidates/president/presidential-map/. These figures include total receipts provided by information at the Federal Election Commission. This total includes total receipts of the candidate from contributions from individuals, the candidate, political committees, and transfers from prior federal campaigns.

69. Citizens United v. FEC, 558 U.S. 310 (2010).

70. Severns, "Trump Campaign Plagued by Groups Raising Tens of Millions in his Name."

Chapter 8

What Is the Value of Money in Politics?

Examining the campaign finance in the 2020 presidential election shows that the U.S. political system is closely tied with fundraising because money is important in maintaining longevity within a race. The 2020 election also shows that in the American campaigns for president, campaign cash is growing at an exponential rate that has nearly doubled since 2016. That signals that the role in American campaigns will likely continue to grow, which begs the question, what is the impact of all this money in campaigns?

The answer to that question is one that is not easily answerable by this analysis. Voter motivation is something that is nuanced, and money paying for advertising and campaign events does not necessarily equate to votes. Certainly, voter enthusiasm and awareness can be impacted by exposure to campaign materials, and in 2020 one of the biggest issues that Democrats and Republicans focused on was voter turnout during the COVID-19 pandemic. Another issue that arises from campaign contributions is the level donors have on the policy and politics of the candidates. Certainly, donors large and small give to candidates who they support, or at least who they think may have some impact on an issue important to them. However, contributions do not work as a direct reflection of political values and aspirations of the donor, and candidates' policies may change once elected.

The one thing that is certain about money in politics from this analysis is that money does not always equate to success. Mike Bloomberg is a prime example of that, but also is the million spent on swing states by both Republicans and Democrats. The other certainty is that as the 2020s progress the rhetoric around campaign finance reform rings a bit hollow when compared to actions. Virtually no candidate argues that PACs and super-PACs are great for democracy, but all of them benefit from them. Both candidates in 2020 opted out of public financing, which also opts them out of certain campaign finance restrictions. Since 2008, there has been a calculated decision at the presidential level that more money is better and that as a political issue, campaign finance reform is a situation where words speak louder than actions.

TRENDS IN CAMPAIGN FINANCE

The 2020 campaign signals that progressive Democrats are eager to pursue changes to the campaign finance system. In fact, the criticism of campaign finance laws led Democratic primary candidates to criticize the current structure of campaigns and used campaign donations as political attacks on others. Nowhere was this more evident than in Warren's attack on Buttigieg for receiving campaign fundraising dollars from wealthy California donors, and many Democrats' attacks on Bloomberg for his position as a billionaire within the Democratic primary. Biden's own campaign finance program suggests that he supports striking down the laws and court cases that have led to the political system that we currently have in the United States, especially as it relates to the *Citizens United v. FEC* decision.[1] In fact, *Citizens United v. FEC* has become a rallying cry of Democrats as the case has come to symbolize the excess of campaign fundraising and the corporate influence in American politics.[2]

However, Democrats have also shown that their rhetoric does not match their actions in campaign finance. In anything, the current campaign finance structure has been taken advantage of the most by Democratic fundraising. Biden was able to outraise Donald Trump by millions of dollars. However, nowhere is the Democratic fundraising skill more obvious than in the online fundraising of the progressive group ActBlue. Although Republicans have their own version of ActBlue with WinRed, they have not caught up on fundraising. Perhaps time will allow for an equalization of campaign finance success between both parties, but 2020 shows that Democrats, and Biden, had a clear advantage.

So, what does this mean for campaign finance reform rhetoric? Currently Democrats dominate the campaign finance reform issue, as they are the only ones really talking about it substantively at a national level. With Democratic success in fundraising, it may be that Republicans need to eventually co-opt the issue because both Biden and Clinton outraised Trump in 2020 and 2016. However, what is clear is that Democrats, like Biden, are using the issue of campaign finance as a political issue, while also stating that the reality of campaign fundraising requires them to take advantage of campaign fundraising laws. Republicans are no different in their actions. After 2008, they have learned that public financing of elections places a candidate at a distinct advantage and that using all of the tools available to them allows for a more level playing field in political campaigns.

In the beginning of the 2020s it seems that political fundraising and campaigns are perfecting how to maximize donations in presidential campaigns. By historical comparison, presidential election years such as 1964, 1968, and 1976 show that presidential campaigns undergo radical changes that reestablish a new norm for politics. In more recent times, 2008 served as a watershed moment for campaigns as it signaled the final end of public financing. The presidential campaign of 2012 was the first presidential election year in which super-PACs existed, and now in 2020 campaign directors see the effects of the new norm of super-PACs and online fundraising. The result is a multibillion-dollar presidential campaign process, which seems to be getting even more expensive with time. However, unique issues are arising. Foremost among these is the super-PACs can emerge and use the mantle of a cause to gain funds that ultimately are not supporting the candidate or cause as suggested. Trump dealt with that reality in 2020, and it is likely a phenomenon that will continue. It is problematic because as campaigns become ever more expensive, ever donation is needed.

MONEY IN 2020: WHAT WERE THE MAIN TAKEAWAYS?

From analyzing campaign finance from the 2020 primary through the general election three things are clear. First, the horse race aspect of campaign fundraising may make for a good media narrative, but it does not tell the entire story. As the Democratic primary in 2019 showed, candidates starting out with a lot of donations do not necessarily end up with the nomination. If that were the case, then Sanders would have been the Democratic nominee. Moreover, the political issue of campaign finance, at least for Democrats, is something that divides the party and potentially the voters. Despite this disagreement, Democrats and Republicans alike need donations to remain in the race. Kamala Harris, the eventual Vice President, did not even make it to the Iowa Caucuses because her funds were running out. That shows that even potential candidates that may have a high level of electability in certain contexts need to have the funds to stay in the race. That means a candidate's fundraising efforts need to utilize fundraising to the best of their ability using all of the tools that are at their disposal.

Second, how much money a candidate has matters, but where a candidate gets his or her money matters too, especially for Democrats. Modern fundraising is a practice that requires getting funds from many sources, large and small. However, where that money comes from has increasingly become a political issue. Buttigieg learned that in his courting of large donors, and Bloomberg learned that during his self-funded primary campaign. In fact, Bloomberg's entry in the race proved that despite all of the changes in politics over the past thirty years, the success rate of a self-funded presidential candidate remains the same.

Third, small donors matter. While these donors have frequently been used in history as evidence of the everyman aspect of presidential campaigns, in 2020 the small donor can provide the necessary means for fundraising. Part of this is the ease of online giving, and part of it is that campaigns have now reached out in meaningful ways through online data collection and platforms with saved credit card information that allow a small donor's contribution to be a quick process. This is not only for campaigns but for any political fundraiser.

TRUMP AND BIDEN 2020: HOW DID FINANCES IMPACT ELECTION OUTCOME?

It is difficult to tell whether money made a difference in 2020's outcome. Unlike previous elections where candidates were strapped for cash and unable to mount a successful campaign (e.g., Humphrey 1968), 2020s candidates were able to raise millions. Moreover, the campaign for Republicans and Democrats had record number voting, which may have been because of voter mobilization, but also the process of early voting and mail-in ballots. In fact, voting in 2020 was the highest it had been since 1900 with 66.3 percent of Americans casting a ballot in 2020 (compare that with 1900 when 73.7 percent of eligible voters voted).[3] Was this increased turnout because campaigns were funded, or for some other reason? While that is beyond the scope of this book, it is reasonable to believe that fundraising played a part in voter participation. However, it is also reasonable to believe that other factors outside of a candidate's campaign galvanized Americans to vote in record numbers.

One thing is clear, both Biden and Trump took advantage of the fundraising efforts afforded to them. So did many groups who started super-PACs to raise money for causes. Of course, this has a trickle-down effect in American politics. Because of the sheer amount of money raised in the presidential election other races became expensive too. For example, the runoff for the two U.S. Senate seats in Georgia set record amounts of fundraising. For example, Georgia Democratic Senate candidate Raphael Warnock raised $125.3 million from January 30 through December 16, 2020.[4] The incumbent Republican Senator Kelly Loeffler would raise $92.2 million from December 4 2019 until December 16, 2020.[5] Note that this was a special election for a Senate seat that would be up again for a full-term election in 2022. This, of course, does not include PAC spending or party spending. The takeaway from this is in order to be a viable candidate in federal races at any level a candidate has to be able to raise money in all amounts from a national pool of donors. Without that support the candidate will not be competitive.

WHAT IS IN THE FUTURE FOR CAMPAIGN FINANCE?

The future of campaign finance seems to be higher amounts of dollars raised, more PAC involvement, greater outreach to small donors, and multibillion-dollar presidential campaigns. As of this writing, Donald Trump is raising money for candidates in upcoming 2022 elections, and positioning himself to perhaps be the Republican nominee for president in 2024. In fact, one aspect of Trump's approach to the presidency is to be prescient of today's political reality—the permanent campaign. Trump did not invent the term, nor was he the first president to engage in the practice. However, his presidency continually used the permanent campaign as a strategy. This tactic may be the future of politics, where political fundraising and campaigning are part of governing. While that is likely bad for good governance, it is the type of reality that the modern U.S. campaign finance laws have created. Without reforms there seems to be no indication that this practice will ever stop, but it will only accelerate.

Reformers, including President Joe Biden, have said that money in politics has bad results. Because of that, the system needs to be reformed, and one way to do that is to take corporate money out of elections. That reform sentiment has been around since Theodore Roosevelt's administration, and the issue seems unchanged. However, the reality of reform is that there seems to be limited not only because of the gridlock in Washington and the slim majorities in Congress but also because under the current system both Republicans and Democrats have filled their campaigns with cash. In some respects, the campaign finance system today perpetuates itself creating ever more expensive campaigns with longer times needed for fundraising. That is the system that created the most expensive presidential election ever in 2020, that is, the most expensive until 2024.

NOTES

1. Citizens United v. FEC, 558 U.S. 310 (2010).
2. Ibid.

3. Kevin Schaul, Kate Rabinowitz, and Ted Mellkin, "2020 Turnout is the Highest in Over a Century," *Washington Post*, last updated December, 28, 2020, https://ww w.washingtonpost.com/graphics/2020/elections/voter-turnout/. It is also important to note the number of eligible voters in 1900 was smaller both due to population and voter restrictions. Note that the 19th Amendment to the U.S. Constitution would be passed twenty years after the 1900 election.

4. "Financial Summary, Raphael Warnock 2020," Federal Election Commission, accessed March 2, 2021, https://www.fec.gov/data/candidate/S0GA00559/?cycle =2020&election_full=false; "Financial Summary, Raphael Warnock 2022," Federal Election Commission, accessed March 2, 2021, https://www.fec.gov/data/candidate/ S0GA00559/?cycle=2020&election_full=false.

5. "Financial Summary, Kelly Loeffler 2020-2021," Federal Election Commission, accessed March 2, 2021, https://www.fec.gov/data/committee/C00729608/?cy cle=2022; "Financial Summary, Kelly Loeffler 2019-2020," Federal Election Commission, accessed March 2, 2021, https://www.fec.gov/data/committee/C0072 9608/?cycle=2020.

Bibliography

Abood v. Detroit Board of Education, 431 U.S. 209 (1977).

Allison, Bill and Mark Niquette. "Bloomberg Tops Half a Billion Dollars in Campaign Advertising." *Bloomberg*, February 24, 2020, https://www.bloomberg.com/news/articles/2020-02-24/bloomberg-tops-half-a-billion-dollars-in-campaign-advertising

Allyn, Bobby. "'Throw Them Against The Wall And Frisk Them': Bloomberg's 2015 Race Talk Stirs Debate." *NPR* Online. February 11, 2020. https://www.npr.org/2020/02/11/804795405/throw-them-against-the-wall-and-frisk-them-bloomberg-s-2015-race-talk-stirs-deba.

American Bridge 21st Century. Accessed March 4, 2021, https://americanbridgepac.org/about-us/.

Americans Keeping Country First. March 4, 2021, https://countryfirst.gop/.

Amper, Richard. "Kefauver Lashes Rivals Over Gift." *New York Times*, October 11, 1956.

Arizona Free Enterprise Club's Freedom Club PAC v. Bennett, 564 U.S. 721 (2011).

Associated Press. "Warren's Souvenir Bottle Pops Up in Buttigieg Wine Cave Debate. *NBC* Online. December 21, 2019. https://www.nbcnews.com/politics/2020-election/warren-s-souvenir-bottle-pops-buttigieg-wine-cave-debate-n1106186.

Astor, Maggie and Katie Glueck. "Elizabeth Warren Endorses Joe Biden: 'When You Disagree, He'll Listen.'" *New York Times*, updated May 22, 2020, https://www.nytimes.com/2020/04/15/us/politics/elizabeth-warren-endorse-biden.html.

Astor, Maggie and Danny Hakim. "21 Men Accuse Lincoln Project Co-Founder of Online Harassment." *New York Times*, January 31, 2021, https://www.nytimes.com/2021/01/31/us/politics/john-weaver-lincoln-project-harassment.html.

Atlanta Constitution. "Incensed Party May Skip Donations." February 26, 1948.

Atlanta Daily World. "Large and Small Donations to President Truman's Campaign." August 18, 1948.

Austin v. Michigan Chamber of Commerce, 494 U.S. 652 (1990).

Atlanta Constitution. "Republicans Spending $3,442,932.22 to Put Over Harding." October 29, 1920.

Axelrod, Tal. "Biden Announces Endorsements from End Citizens United, Let America Vote." *The Hill*, April 16, 2020, https://thehill.com/homenews/campaign /493197-biden-announces-endorsements-from-end-citizens-united-let-america-vote.

Axelrod, Tal. "Trump and Allies Have Spent $58 Million on Legal Bills and Compliance Work: report." *The Hill*, September 5, 2020, https://thehill.com/homen ews/campaign/515249-trump-and-allies-have-spent-58-million-on-legal-bills-and -compliance.

Azzaro, Shannon. "The Hatch Act Modernization Act: Putting the Government Back in Politics." *Fordham Urban Law Journal* 42 (2016): 781–839.

Babcock, Charles and Richard Morin, "Bush's Money Machine." *The Washington Post.* May 15, 1988.

Barr, Jeremy and Elahe Izadi. "We're Seeing a Lot Less of Trump's Rallies on TV News in 2020." *Washington Post,* September 14, 2020, https://www.washingt onpost.com/media/2020/09/14/were-seeing-lot-less-trumps-rallies-tv-news-2020/.

Bernie. "Issues: Get Corporate Money Out of Politics." Accessed March 3, 2021. https://berniesanders.com/issues/money-out-of-politics/.

Barrett, Marsha. "'Millionaires are More Democratic Now': Nelson Rockefeller and the Politics of Wealth in New York." *New York History.* http://www.nysm.nysed .gov/common/nysm/files/barrett_-_millionaires_are_more_democratic_now_a.pdf.

Bennett, Ira. "Hard Facts are Dodged by Colonel." *San Francisco Call*, October 5, 1912.

Bergholz, Richard. "Two Decades Ago." *Los Angeles Times*, May 1, 1973.

Berkes, Richard. "'88 Presidential Candidates Spent $210 Million." *New York Times*, August 27, 1989.

Berke, Richard. "Perot Leads in $40 Million Ad Bliz." *New York Times*, October 27, 1992.

Biden, Joe. *Promises to Keep.* New York: Random House, 2007.

Biden, Joseph and Michael Carpenter. "How to Stand Up to the Kremlin." *Foreign Affairs,* January/February 2018, retrieved from https://www.foreignaffairs.com/arti cles/russia-fsu/2017-12-05/how-stand-kremlin.

Biden Harris. "The Biden Plan to Guarantee Government Works for the People." Accessed March 4, 2021. https://joebiden.com/governmentreform/.

Bipartisan Campaign Reform Act of 2002, 116 Stat 81, Pub L 107-155 (2002).

Bluman v. FEC, 800 F.Supp.2d 281 (D.D.C 2011).

Blood, Michael. "Snubbing the Iowa Caucuses, Michael Bloomberg Charts His Own Path in 2020 contest." *Chicago Tribune*, February 3, 2020, https://www.chicagot ribune.com/election-2020/ct-michael-bloomberg-iowa-caucuses-2020-20200203 -5dab2kp455htxn555oi3tjkvmu-story.html.

Boot, Max. "Opinion: Never Trumpers Played a Critical Role in Beating Him. The Numbers Prove It." *Washington Post*, November 12, 2020, https://www.washingt onpost.com/opinions/2020/11/12/did-republicans-vote-against-trump/.

Bradner, Eric and Paul LeBlanc. "South Carolina Rep. Jim Clyburn Endorses Joe Biden Ahead of Primary." *CNN* Online. February 26, 2020, https://www.cnn.com/ 2020/02/26/politics/jim-clyburn-endorses-joe-biden/index.html.

Brewster, Adam. "Trump's New PAC Raises $30 Million," *CBS News* Online. February 2, 2021. https://www.cbsnews.com/news/save-america-trump-pac-raises -30-million/.

Brownstein, Ronald. "Raising Bucks for Bush." *New York Times*, May 17, 1987.

Buckley v. Valeo, 424 U.S 1, 7 (1976).

Bump, Philip. "Donald Trump Started Spending Money on the 2020 Race on Nov. 24, *Washington Post*, May 1, 2017, https://www.washingtonpost.com/news/poli tics/wp/2017/05/01/donald-trump-started-spending-money-on-the-2020-race-on- nov-24/.

Bump, Philip. "Trump Continues to Refuse to Accept the Deadliness of the Coronavirus Pandemic." *Washington Post*, April 28, 2020, https://www.was hingtonpost.com/politics/2020/04/28/trump-continues-refuse-accept-deadlines-co ronavirus-pandemic/.

Bump, Philip. "Yet again, Trump Pledges that the Coronavirus Will Simply Go Away." *Washington Post*, April 28, 2020, https://www.washingtonpost.com/poli tics/2020/04/28/yet-again-trump-pledges-that-coronavirus-will-simply-go-away/.

Burke, David. "With Gorsuch Confirmed, Only An Amendment Can Overturn Citizens United." *Huffington Post*. April 10, 2017, https://www.huffpost.com/entry /with-gorsuch-confirmed-only-an-amendment-can-overturn_b_58eb9457e4b0a cd784ca5a4f.

Burns, Alexander. "Beto O'Rourke Drops Out of the Presidential Race. *New York Times*, November 1, 2019, https://www.nytimes.com/2019/11/01/us/politics/beto -orourke-drops-out.html.

Burns, Alexander. "Michael Bloomberg Joins 2020 Democratic Field for President." *New York Times*, updated March 4, 2020, https://www.nytimes.com/2019/11/24/us /politics/michael-bloomberg-2020-presidency.html.

Burrough, Bryan and Bethany McLean. "Jon Corzine's Riskiest Business." *Vanity Fair*, February 2012, https://www.vanityfair.com/news/business/2012/02/jon-co rzine-201202.

Burroughs v. U.S., 290 U.S. 534 (1934).

Cannon, Lou. "GOP's Big Game Hunter." *Washington Post*, September 17, 1972.

Caputo, Marc and Scott Bland. "Biden Crushes It in First-Day Fundraising: 6.3 Million." *Politico*, updated April 26, 2019, https://www.politico.com/story/2019 /04/26/biden-fundraising-numbers-2020-1291180.

Caputo, Marc and Holly Otterbein. "Bernie Makes It Official: It's Biden or Bust." *Politico*, Updated April 13, 2020, https://www.politico.com/news/2020/04/13/sand ers-endorses-biden-183961.

Caputo, Marc and Christopher Cadelago. "Dems Warm to Biden's Bunker Strategy." *Politico*, June 24, 2020, https://www.politico.com/news/2020/06/24/dems-warm-to -bidens-bunker-strategy-338853.

Carlisle, Madeleine. "Three Weeks after Trump's Tulsa Rally, Oklahoma Reports Record High COVID-19 Numbers." *Time*, July 11, 2020, https://time.com/586 5890/oklahoma-covid-19-trump-tulsa-rally/.

Chalfant, Morgan. "Trump Likely to Form New Super PAC." *The Hill*, February 26, 2021, https://thehill.com/homenews/campaign/540716-trump-likely-to-form-new- super-pac.

Chambers, John. *A Complete Dictionary of The Law and Practice of Elections of Members of Parliament and of Election Petitions and Committees for England, Scotland, and Ireland.* London: Saunders and Benning, Law Booksellers, 1837. Retrieved from http://books.google.com.

Chicago Daily Tribune. "AFL-CIO Backs Kennedy." August 27, 1960.

Chicago Daily Tribune. "Bill Would Bar Gifts to Campaign Funds." January 26, 1943.

Chicago Daily Tribune. "Donations to Roosevelt Fund Total Million." August 12, 1936.

Chicago Daily Tribune. "Hamon's $18,700 Harding's 1920 Hotel Bill." April 8, 1924.

Chicago Daily Tribune. "Officeholders' Gifts to Wilson Fund Assailed." October 13, 1916.

Chicago Daily Tribune. "Wyman Heads State Bakers of Eisenhower." February 8, 1952.

Citizens United v. FEC, 558 U.S. 310 (2010).

Cillizza, Chris. "What George P. Bush's Endorsement of Donald Trump Tells Us About Republican Politics." *CNN* Online, June 10, 2020, https://www.cnn.com/2020/06/10/politics/george-p-bush-endorsement-donald-trump/index.html.

CNN Online. "Reform Party." Accessed March 3, 2021. https://www.cnn.com/ALLPOLITICS/1996/conventions/long.beach/perot/political.timeline.shtml.

Concha, Joe. "Opinion: The Swift Death of the Media Darlings Known as the Lincoln Project." *The Hill*, February 14, 2021, https://thehill.com/opinion/campaign/538795-the-swift-death-of-the-media-darlings-known-as-the-lincoln-project.

Coleman, Justine. "Trump Wins CPAC Straw Poll With 55 Percent." *The Hill*, February 28, 2021. https://thehill.com/homenews/campaign/540909-trump-wins-cpac-straw-poll-with-55-percent.

Confessore, Nicolas and Karin Yourish. "$2 Billion Worth of Free Media for Donald Trump." *New York Times*, March 15, 2016, https://www.nytimes.com/2016/03/16/upshot/measuring-donald-trumps-mammoth-advantage-in-free-media.html.

Connally, Ceci and Susan Glasser. "Bradley's Campaign Bankroll Nearly Equals Gore's." *Washington Post*, July 16, 1999.

Connelly, Eileen. "Kamala Harris Raises $2M in 24 hours with Help of 'That Little Girl Was Me' Shirts." *New York Post*, June 29, 2019, https://nypost.com/2019/06/29/kamala-harris-raises-2m-in-24-hours-with-help-of-that-little-girl-was-me-shirts/.

Conway III, George T., Steve Schmidt, John Weaver and Rick Wilson. "We Are Republicans, and We Want Trump Defeated." *New York Times*, December 17, 2019, https://www.nytimes.com/2019/12/17/opinion/lincoln-project.html.

Crewdson, John. "Nixon's Taped Remark on Apparent Slush Fund Called Key Evidence in Rebozo Inquiry." *New York Times*, December 9, 1974.

CSPAN Online. "Vice President Biden on Money in Politics." July 17, 2015, https://www.c-span.org/video/?c4544897/user-clip-vice-president-biden-money-politics.

Cummings, Jeanne. "Self Funders Strike Out Big Time." *Politico*, last updated November 10, 2010, https://www.politico.com/story/2010/11/self-funders-strike-o ut-big-time-044677.

Cummings, William. "Trump Campaign Sends CNN 'Cease and Desist' Letter, Demands It Retract Poll that Found Biden up 14 Points." *USA Today*. June 8, 2020, https://www.usatoday.com/story/news/politics/elections/2020/06/08/pres ident-trump-fumes-cnn-poll-showing-him-trailing-biden-and-approval-down/531 7953002/.

D'Elia, Alex. "What Do Democratic Candidates Need to Make the First 2020 Debates?." *PBS NewsHour* Online. April 3, 2019. https://www.pbs.org/newshour/ politics/what-do-democratic-candidates-need-to-make-the-first-2020-debates.

Davis v. FEC, 554 U.S. 724 (2008).

Davis, Elliot. "Trump Raises $26M Around Final Presidential Debate." *US News & World Report*, October 23, 2020, https://www.usnews.com/news/elections/articles /2020-10-23/trump-raises-26-million-around-final-debate-with-biden.

Democratic National Committee. "Democratic National Convention Schedule." Accessed March 4, 2021. https://www.demconvention.com/schedule-and-speaker s/?_sft_event-day=august-17.

Des Moines Register. "Iowa Democratic Caucus Results." February 29, 2020, https:// www.desmoinesregister.com/elections/results/primaries/democratic/iowa/.

Dovere, Edward-Issac. "Democrats are Freaking Out Over Mike Bloomberg." *The Atlantic*, February 3, 2020, https://www.theatlantic.com/politics/archive/2020/02/ mike-bloomberg-democratic-contested-convention/605956/.

Dowd, Maureen. "When Hillary and Donald Were Friends." *New York Times*, November 2, 2016, https://www.nytimes.com/2016/11/06/magazine/when-hillary -and-donald-were-friends.html.

Edelman, Adam. "A Guide to Trump's Nicknames and Insults About the 2020 Democratic Field." *NBC News* Online. Updated May 13, 2019. https://www .nbcnews.com/politics/2020-election/everything-trump-has-said-about-2020-field- insults-all-n998556.

Elliot, Rebecca. "Trump to Host Fundraiser for Booker." *Politico*. July 16, 2013, https://www.politico.com/story/2013/07/ivanka-trump-fundraiser-cory-booker-09 4288.

Elving, Ron. "Joe Biden's Long and Rocky Road to the Democratic Nomination." *NPR* Online, August 16, 2020, https://www.npr.org/2020/08/16/902640265/joe-bi dens-long- and-rocky-road-to-the-democratic-nomination.

Energy Policy Act of 2005, Pub L No 109-58, 119 Stat. 594, codified in 42 U.S.C. §1501 et seq., 16 USC §2601 et seq., 42 USC §13201 et seq.

Epstein, Reid, Sydney Ember, Shane Goldmacher and Katie Glueck. "7 Takeaways From the June 26 Democratic Debate: Castro's Big Night." *New York Times*, June 26, 2019, https://www.nytimes.com/2019/06/26/us/politics/2020-democratic-de bate-tonight.html.

Epstein, Reid and Lisa Lerner. "Warren Says Bloomberg Shouldn't Be Nominee, Citing Redlining Remarks." *New York Times,* February 13, 2020, https://www.nyt imes.com/2020/02/13/us/politics/elizabeth-warren-bloomberg.html.

Epstein, Reid and Trip Gabriel. "Pete Buttigieg Drops Out of Democratic Presidential Race," *New York Times*. March 1, 2020, https://www.nytimes.com/2020/03/01/us/politics/pete-buttigieg-drops-out.html.

Fahrenthold, David. "Trump Previously Donated $6,000 to Kamala D. Harris's Campaigns." *Washington Post*, August 12, 2020, https://www.washingtonpost.com/politics/trump-harris-campaign-donations/2020/08/12/06eb1f0e-dcdb-11ea-b205-ff838e15a9a6_story.html.

FEC v. National Right to Work Committee, 459 U.S. 197 (1982).

FEC v. Massachusetts Citizens for Life, 479 U.S. 238 (1986).

FEC v. Wisconsin Right to Life, 551 U.S. 449 (2007).

Federal Corrupt Practices Act, Pub L. No 61-274, 36 Stat. 822, codified at 2 USC §§241-248 (1910).

Federal Corrupt Practices Act of 1925, 43 Stat. 1053, codified in 2 U.S.C. §241 (1925).

Federal Election Campaign Act of 1971, Pub L 92-225 (1971).

Federal Election Campaign Act Amendments of 1974, Pub L 93-443 (1974).

Federal Election Campaign Act Amendments of 1976, Pub L 94-283 (1976).

Federal Election Commission. "FEC Statement on *Carey v. FEC*: Reporting Guidance for Political Committees that Maintain a Non-Contribution Account." October 5, 2011, https://www.fec.gov/updates/fec-statement-on-carey-fec/.

Federal Election Commission. "Financial Summary, Act Blue, 2019-2020." Accessed March 4, 2021. https://www.fec.gov/data/committee/C00401224/?cycle=2020.

Federal Election Commission. "Financial Summary, Act Blue 2021-2022." Accessed March 4, 2021. https://www.fec.gov/data/committee/C00401224/?cycle=2022.

Federal Election Commission. "Financial Summary, America First Action 2019-2020." Accessed February 27, 2021, https://www.fec.gov/data/committee/C00637512/.

Federal Election Commission. "Financial Summary, Biden Victory Fund 2019-2020." Accessed March 4, 2021. https://www.fec.gov/data/committee/C00744946/.

Federal Election Commission. "Financial Summary, Blue Texas PAC 2019-2020." Accessed March 4, 2021, https://www.fec.gov/data/committee/C00753293/.

Federal Election Commission. "Financial Summary, Congressional Leadership Fund, 2019-2020." Accessed March 4, 2021. https://www.fec.gov/data/committee/C00504530/.

Federal Election Commission. "Financial Summary, DCCC, 2019-2020." Accessed March 4, 2021. https://www.fec.gov/data/committee/C00000935/?cycle=2020.

Federal Election Commission. "Financial Summary, DNC Services Corp./Democratic National Committee 2019-2020." Accessed March 4, 2021. https://www.fec.gov/data/committee/C00010603/?cycle=2020.

Federal Election Commission. "Financial Summary, Future 45, 2015-2016." Accessed March 4, 2021. https://www.fec.gov/data/committee/C00574533/?cycle=2016.

Federal Election Commission. "Financial Summary, Future 45, 2019-2020." Accessed March 4, 2021. https://www.fec.gov/data/committee/C00574533/?cycle=2020.

Federal Election Commission "Financial Summary, Great America PAC 2019-2020." Accessed February 27, 2021. https://www.fec.gov/data/committee/C00608489/.

Federal Election Commission. "Financial Summary, Independence USA PAC, 2019-2020." Accessed March 4, 2021. https://www.fec.gov/data/committee/C00532705/?cycle=2020.

Federal Election Commission. "Financial Summary, Kelly Loeffler 2020-2021." Accessed March 2, 2021, https://www.fec.gov/data/committee/C00729608/?cycle=2022.

Federal Election Commission, "Financial Summary, Kelly Loeffler 2019-2020." Accessed March 2, 2021, https://www.fec.gov/data/committee/C00729608/?cycle=2020.

Federal Election Commission. "Financial Summary, Michael Bloomberg 2020, Inc, 2019-2020." Accessed March 3, 2021. https://www.fec.gov/data/candidate/P00014530/?cycle=2020&election_full=true.

Federal Election Commission. "Financial Summary, NRCC, 2019-2020." Accessed March 4, 2021. https://www.fec.gov/data/committee/C00075820/?cycle=2020

Federal Election Commission. "Financial Summary, Preserve America PAC 2019-2020," accessed February 27, 2021. https://www.fec.gov/data/committee/C00756882/.

Federal Election Commission. "Financial Summary, Priorities USA Action, 2019-2020." Accessed March 4, 2021. https://www.fec.gov/data/committee/C00495861/.

Federal Election Commission. "Financial Summary, Progressive Turnout Project, 2019-2020." Accessed March 4, 2021. https://www.fec.gov/data/committee/C00580068/?cycle=2020.

Federal Election Commission. "Financial Summary, Raphael Warnock 2020." Accessed March 2, 2021, https://www.fec.gov/data/candidate/S0GA00559/?cycle=2020&election_full=false.

Federal Election Commission. "Financial Summary, Raphael Warnock 2022." Accessed March 2, 2021, https://www.fec.gov/data/candidate/S0GA00559/?cycle=2020&election_full=false.

Federal Election Commission. "Financial Summary, Republican National Committee, 2019-2020." Accessed March 4, 2021. https://www.fec.gov/data/committee/C00003418/?cycle=2020.

Federal Election Commission. "Financial Summary, Save America, 2019-2020" Accessed February 27, 2021. https://www.fec.gov/data/committee/C00762591/.

Federal Election Commission. "Financial Summary, Senate Leadership Fund, 2019-2020" Accessed March 4, 2021. https://www.fec.gov/data/committee/C00571703/?cycle=2020.

Federal Election Commission "Financial Summary, The Lincoln Project, 2019-2020." Accessed March 4, 2021. https://www.fec.gov/data/committee/C00725820/?cycle=2020.

Federal Election Commission. "Financial Summary, Trump Make America Great Again Committee 2019-2020." Accessed March 4, 2021. https://www.fec.gov/data/committee/C00618371/.

Federal Election Commission. "Financial Summary, Trump Victory, 2019-2020." Accessed March 4, 2021. https://www.fec.gov/data/committee/C00618389/.

Federal Election Commission "Financial Summary, Unite the Country, 2019-2020." Accessed March 4, 2021. https://www.fec.gov/data/committee/C00701888/.

Federal Election Commission "Financial Summary, WinRed 2019-2020." Accessed February 27, 2021. https://www.fec.gov/data/committee/C00694323/.

Federal Election Commission. "Presidential Campaign Map, All Candidates 2020," Accessed March 4, 2021. https://www.fec.gov/data/candidates/president/presidential-map/.

Federal Election Commission. "Presidential Candidate Map, Bernie Sanders 2020." Accessed March 3, 2021, https://www.fec.gov/data/candidates/president/presidential-map/.

Federal Election Commission. "Presidential Candidate Map, Beto O'Rourke 2020." Accessed March 3, 2021. https://www.fec.gov/data/candidates/president/presidential-map/.

Federal Election Commission. "Presidential Candidate Map, Cory Booker 2020." Accessed March 3, 2021. https://www.fec.gov/data/candidates/president/presidential-map.

Federal Election Commission. "Presidential Campaign Map, Donald Trump 2016." Accessed March 4, 2021. https://www.fec.gov/data/candidates/president/presidential-map/.

Federal Election Commission. "Presidential Campaign Map, Donald Trump 2020." Accessed March 4, 2021. https://www.fec.gov/data/candidates/president/presidential-map/.

Federal Election Commission. "Presidential Candidate Map, Elizabeth Warren 2020." Accessed March 3, 2021. https://www.fec.gov/data/candidates/president/presidential-map/.

Federal Election Commission. "Campaign Finance Map, Hillary Clinton 2016." Accessed March 4, 2021. https://www.fec.gov/data/candidates/president/presidential-map/.

Federal Election Commission. "Campaign Finance Map, Joe Biden 2020." Accessed March 4, 2021. https://www.fec.gov/data/candidates/president/presidential-map/.

Federal Election Commission. "Presidential Campaign Map, Michael Bloomberg, 2020." Accessed March 4, 2021. https://www.fec.gov/data/candidates/president/presidential-map/.

Federal Election Commission. "Presidential Campaign Map, Tom Steyer 2020." Accessed March 4, 2021. https://www.fec.gov/data/candidates/president/presidential-map/.

Federal Election Commission. "Presidential Candidate Map, William Weld 2020." Accessed March 4, 2021. https://www.fec.gov/data/candidates/president/presidential-map/.

Federal Election Commission. "Raising and Spending Funds for the National Party's Nominating Convention, Federal Election Commission." Accessed July 25, 2021. https://www.fec.gov/help-candidates-and-committees/taking-receipts-political-party/national-nominating-convention/.

Federal Election Commission. "Report of Receipts and Disbursements, Amy for America, March Monthly 2020." Accessed March 3, 2021. https://docquery.fec .gov/cgi-bin/forms/C00696419/1424472/.

Federal Election Commission. "Report of Receipts and Disbursements, Bennett for America, October Quarterly 2020." Accessed March 3, 2021, https://docquery.fec .gov/cgi-bin/forms/C00705186/1416743/.

Federal Election Commission. "Report of Receipts and Disbursements, Biden for President, July Quarterly Amended 2019." Accessed March 4, 2021, https://do cquery.fec.gov/cgi-bin/forms/C00703975/1360571/.

Federal Election Commission, "Report of Receipts and Disbursements, Biden for President, October Quarterly Amended 2019." Accessed March 4, 2021, https://do cquery.fec.gov/cgi-bin/forms/C00703975/1366605/.

Federal Election Commission, "Report of Receipts and Disbursements, Biden for President, Year-End 2019." Accessed March 4, 2021, https://docquery.fec.gov/cgi -bin/forms/C00703975/1390990/.

Federal Election Commission. "Report of Receipts and Disbursements, Biden for President, September Monthly 2020." Accessed March 4, 2021, https://docquery .fec.gov/cgi-bin/forms/C00703975/1440320/.

Federal Election Commission. "Report of Receipts and Disbursements, Biden for President, October Monthly 2020." Accessed March 4, 2021. https://docquery.fec .gov/cgi-bin/forms/C00703975/1458940/.

Federal Election Commission. "Report of Receipts and Disbursements, Biden for President, Pre General 2020." Accessed March 4, 2021. https://docquery.fec.gov/ cgi-bin/forms/C00703975/1463690/.

Federal Election Commission. "Report of Receipts and Disbursements, Biden for President, Post General 2020." Accessed March 4, 2021, https://docquery.fec.gov/ cgi-bin/forms/C00703975/1481223/.

Federal Election Commission. "Report of Receipts and Disbursements, Bernie 2020, April Quarterly 2019." Accessed March 4, 2021, https://docquery.fec.gov/cgi-bin/ forms/C00696948/1326070/

Federal Election Commission. "Report of Receipts and Disbursements, Bernie 2020, July Quarterly 2019 Amended." Accessed March 4, 2021, https://docquery.fec .gov/cgi-bin/forms/C00696948/1354560/.

Federal Election Commission. "Report of Receipts and Disbursements, Bernie 2020, October Quarterly 2019Amended." Accessed March 4, 2021, https://docquery.fec .gov/cgi-bin/forms/C00696948/1367132/.

Federal Election Commission. "Report of Receipts and Disbursements, Bernie 2020, Year-End 2019 Amended." Accessed March 4, 2021.https://docquery.fec.gov/cgi -bin/forms/C00696948/1392261/.

Federal Election Commission. "Report of Receipts and Disbursements, de Blasio 2020, October 2019 Quarterly." Accessed March 3, 2021, https://docquery.fec.gov/ cgi-bin/forms/C00706697/1414451/.

Federal Election Commission. "Report of Receipts and Disbursements, Donald J. Trump for President, April Quarterly 2017 Amended." Accessed March 4, 2021. https://docquery.fec.gov/cgi-bin/forms/C00580100/1174081/.

Federal Election Commission. "Report of Receipts and Disbursements, Donald J. Trump for President, July Quarterly 2017 Amended." Accessed March 4, 2021. https://docquery.fec.gov/cgi-bin/forms/C00580100/1248053/.

Federal Election Commission. "Report of Receipts and Disbursements, Donald J. Trump for President, October Quarterly 2017 Amended." Accessed March 4, 2021. https://docquery.fec.gov/cgi-bin/forms/C00580100/1193597/.

Federal Election Commission. "Report of Receipts and Disbursements, Donald J. Trump for President, Year-End 2017 Amended." Accessed March 4, 2021. https://docquery.fec.gov/cgi-bin/forms/C00580100/1219890/.

Federal Election Commission. "Report of Receipts and Disbursements, Donald J. Trump for President, April Quarterly 2018 Amended." Accessed March 4, 2021. https://docquery.fec.gov/cgi-bin/forms/C00580100/1248056/.

Federal Election Commission. "Report of Receipts and Disbursements, Donald J. Trump for President, July 2018, Quarterly Amended." Accessed March 4, 2021. https://docquery.fec.gov/cgi-bin/forms/C00580100/1263561/

Federal Election Commission. "Report of Receipts and Disbursements, Donald J. Trump for President, October Quarterly 2018 Amended." Accessed March 4, 2021, https://docquery.fec.gov/cgi-bin/forms/C00580100/1301594/.

Federal Election Commission. "Report of Receipts and Disbursements, Donald J. Trump for President, Year-End 2018 Amended." Accessed March 4, 2021. https://docquery.fec.gov/cgi-bin/forms/C00580100/1319152/.

Federal Election Commission. "Report of Receipts and Disbursements, Donald J. Trump for President, April Quarterly 2019 Amended." Accessed March 4, 2021. https://docquery.fec.gov/cgi-bin/forms/C00580100/1337251/.

Federal Election Commission. "Report of Receipts and Disbursements, Donald J. Trump for President, July Quarterly 2019 Amended." Accessed March 4, 2021. https://docquery.fec.gov/cgi-bin/forms/C00580100/1351771/.

Federal Election Commission. "Report of Receipts and Disbursements, Donald J. Trump for President, October Quarterly 2019 Amended." Accessed March 4, 2021. https://docquery.fec.gov/cgi-bin/forms/C00580100/1404772/.

Federal Election Commission. "Report of Receipts and Disbursements, Donald J. Trump for President, Year-End 2019 Amended." accessed March 4, 2021. https://docquery.fec.gov/cgi-bin/forms/C00580100/1392271/.

Federal Election Commission. "Report of Receipts and Disbursements, Donald J. Trump for President February Monthly 2020 Amended." Accessed March 4, 2021. https://docquery.fec.gov/cgi-bin/forms/C00580100/1403600/.

Federal Election Commission. "Report of Receipts and Disbursements, Donald J. Trump for President, March Monthly 2020 Amended." Accessed March 4, 2021. https://docquery.fec.gov/cgi-bin/forms/C00580100/1405125/.

Federal Election Commission. "Report of Receipts and Disbursements, Donald J. Trump for President, April Monthly 2020 Amended." Accessed March 4, 2021. https://docquery.fec.gov/cgi-bin/forms/C00580100/1412555/.

Federal Election Commission. "Report of Receipts and Disbursements, Donald J. Trump for President, May Monthly 2020 Amended." Accessed March 4, 2021, https://docquery.fec.gov/cgi-bin/forms/C00580100/1428849/.

Federal Election Commission. "Report of Receipts and Disbursements, Donald J. Trump for President, June Monthly 2020 Amended." Accessed March 4, 2021. https://docquery.fec.gov/cgi-bin/forms/C00580100/1435104/.

Federal Election Commission. "Report of Receipts and Disbursements, Donald J. Trump for President, July Monthly 2020 Amended." Accessed March 4, 2021 https ://docquery.fec.gov/cgi-bin/forms/C00580100/1440916/.

Federal Election Commission. "Report of Receipts and Disbursements, Donald J. Trump for President, August Monthly 2020 Amended." Accessed March 4, 2021. https://docquery.fec.gov/cgi-bin/forms/C00580100/1471578/.

Federal Election Commission. "Report of Receipts and Disbursements, Donald J. Trump for President, September Monthly 2020 Amended." Accessed March 4, 2021. https://docquery.fec.gov/cgi-bin/forms/C00580100/1500199/.

Federal Election Commission. "Reports of Receipts and Disbursements, Donald J. Trump for President, September Monthly 2020 Amendment 1" Federal Election Commission. Accessed January 2, 2021, https://docquery.fec.gov/cgi-bin/forms/C 00580100/1484015/.

Federal Election Commission. "Reports of Receipts and Disbursements, Donald J. Trump for President, October Monthly 2020." Accessed January 2, 2021, https:// docquery.fec.gov/cgi-bin/forms/C00580100/1458436/.

Federal Election Commission. "Reports of Receipts and Disbursements, Donald J. Trump for President, Pre-General 2020," Accessed January 2, 2021, https://do cquery.fec.gov/cgi-bin/forms/C00580100/1463640/.

Federal Election Commission. "Reports of Receipts and Disbursements, September Monthly 2020 Amendment 2, Donald J. Trump for President." Accessed February 27, 2021, https://docquery.fec.gov/cgi-bin/forms/C00580100/1500199/.

Federal Election Commission. "Report of Receipts and Disbursements, Friends of Andrew Yang, October Quarterly 2019." Accessed March 3, 2021, https://docquer y.fec.gov/cgi-bin/forms/C00659938/1371212/.

Federal Election Commission. "Report of Receipts and Disbursements, Friends of Andrew Yang, July Quarterly 2019." Accessed March 3, 2021. https://docquery .fec.gov/cgi-bin/forms/C00659938/1369581/.

Federal Election Commission. "Report of Receipts and Disbursements, Friends of Andrew Yang, Year-End 2019." Accessed March 3, 2021. https://docquery.fec .gov/cgi-bin/forms/C00659938/1391831/.

Federal Elections Commission, "Report of Receipts and Reimbursements, Gillibrand 2020, April Quarterly 2019." Accessed February 7, 2021, https://docquery.fec.gov/ cgi-bin/forms/C00694018/1326061/.

Federal Election Commission. "Report of Receipts and Disbursements, Gillibrand 2020." July Quarterly 2019." Accessed March 3, 2021, https://docquery.fec.gov/ cgi-bin/forms/C00694018/1340492/.

Federal Election Commission. "Report of Receipts and Disbursements, Gillibrand 2020, Year-End 2019." Accessed March 3, 2021. https://docquery.fec.gov/cgi-bin /forms/C00694018/1378930/.

Federal Election Commission. "Report of Receipts and Disbursements, Hickenlooper 2020, October Quarterly 2019." Accessed March 3, 2021. https://docquery.fec.gov/ cgi-bin/forms/C00698258/1367731/.

Federal Election Commission. "Report of Receipts and Disbursements, Kamala Harris for the People, April Quarterly Amended 2019." Accessed March 4, 2020, https://docquery.fec.gov/cgi-bin/forms/C00694455/1391946/.

Federal Election Commission. "Report of Receipts and Disbursements Kamala Harris for the People, July Quarterly Amended 2019." Accessed March 4, 2020, https://docquery.fec.gov/cgi-bin/forms/C00694455/1391947/.

Federal Election Commission. "Report of Receipts and Disbursements Kamala Harris for the People, October Quarterly Amended 2019." Accessed March 4, 2020, https://docquery.fec.gov/cgi-bin/forms/C00694455/1391948/.

Federal Election Commission. "Report of Receipts and Disbursements Kamala Harris for the People, Year-End Amended 2019." Accessed March 4, 2020, https://docquery.fec.gov/cgi-bin/forms/C00694455/1391949/.

Federal Election Commission. "Report of Receipts and Disbursements, Marianne Williamson for President, October Quarterly 2019." Accessed March 3, 2021, https://docquery.fec.gov/cgi-bin/forms/C00696054/1379354/.

Federal Election Commission. "Report of Receipts and Disbursements, Mike Bloomberg 2020, Year-End Amended 2019." Accessed March 4, 2021, https://docquery.fec.gov/cgi-bin/forms/C00728154/1392145/.

Federal Election Commission. "Report of Receipts and Disbursements, Mike Bloomberg 2020, February Monthly Amended 2020." Accessed March 4, 2021, https://docquery.fec.gov/cgi-bin/forms/C00728154/1392150/.

Federal Election Commission. "Report of Receipts and Disbursements, Mike Bloomberg 2020, March Monthly Amended 2020." Accessed March 4, 2021, https://docquery.fec.gov/cgi-bin/forms/C00728154/1407504/.

Federal Election Commission. "Report of Receipts and Disbursements, Mike Bloomberg 2020, April Monthly Amended 2020." Accessed March 4, 2021, https://docquery.fec.gov/cgi-bin/forms/C00728154/1413718/.

Federal Election Commission. "Report of Receipts and Disbursements, Mike Bloomberg 2020, Year-End Amended 2020." Accessed March 4, 2021, https://docquery.fec.gov/cgi-bin/forms/C00728154/1392145/

Federal Election Commission, "Termination Report, Swalwell for America," Accessed March 3, 2021. https://docquery.fec.gov/cgi-bin/forms/C00701698/1376364/.

Federal Election Commission. "Reports of Receipts and Disbursements, Tom Steyer 2020, February Monthly 2020." Accessed March 4, 2021. https://docquery.fec.gov/cgi-bin/forms/C00711614/1391923/.

Federal Election Commission. "Reports of Receipts and Disbursements, Tom Steyer 2020, March Monthly 2020." Accessed March 4, 2021. https://docquery.fec.gov/cgi-bin/forms/C00711614/1391924/.

Federal Election Commission. "Reports of Receipts and Disbursements, Tom Steyer 2020, October Quarterly." Accessed September 28, 2021, https://docquery.fec.gov/cgi-bin/forms/C00711614/1521517/.

Federal Election Commission. "Reports of Receipts and Disbursements, Tom Steyer 2020, Year-End 2019." Accessed March 3, 2021. https://docquery.fec.gov/cgi-bin/forms/C00711614/1379864/.

Federal Election Commission. "Reports of Receipts and Disbursements, Trump Make America Great Again Committee, Year-End 2020" Accessed March 4, 2021. https://docquery.fec.gov/cgi-bin/forms/C00618371/1497174//.

Federal Election Commission. "Reports of Receipts and Disbursements, Warren for President, April Quarterly Amended 2019." Accessed March 4, 2021, https://do cquery.fec.gov/cgi-bin/forms/C00693234/1343914/.

Federal Election Commission. "Reports of Receipts and Disbursements, Warren for President, July Quarterly Amended 2019." Accessed March 4, 2021, https://do cquery.fec.gov/cgi-bin/forms/C00693234/1350879/.

Federal Election Commission. "Reports of Receipts and Disbursements, Warren for President, October Quarterly Amended 2019," Accessed March 4, 2021, https://do cquery.fec.gov/cgi-bin/forms/C00693234/1366132/

Federal Election Commission. "Reports of Receipts and Disbursements, Warren for President, Year End 2019." Accessed March 4, 2021, https://docquery.fec.gov/cgi -bin/forms/C00693234/1378669/.

Federal Election Commission. "The Federal Election Campaign Laws: A Short History." Accessed January 31, 2021. https://transition.fec.gov/info/appfour.htm.

Federal Election Commission. "Using the Personal Funds of a Candidate." Accessed February 9, 2021. https://www.fec.gov/help-candidates-and-committees/candidate -taking-receipts/using-personal-funds-candidate/.

First National Bank of Boston v. Bellotti, 435 U.S. 765 (1978).

Folliard, Edward. "Ike Delays Cleveland Speech to Hear Nixon on Television." *Washington Post*, September 24, 1952.

Forbes. "#14 Michael Bloomberg." March 4, 2021, https://www.forbes.com/profile/ michael-bloomberg/?sh=727b8f871417.

Ford, Gerald. "Remarks on Signing the Federal Election Campaign Act Amendments of 1974." The American Presidency Project, accessed March 2, 2021, https://ww w.presidency.ucsb.edu/documents/remarks-signing-the-federal-election-campaign -act-amendments-1974.

Fortier, Marc. "Bloomberg Beat 2 Well-Known Democrats in the NH Primary. He Wasn't Even on the Ballot." *NBC Boston* Online. February 13, 2020. https://ww w.nbcboston.com/news/local/bloomberg-beat-2-well-known-democrats-in-the-nh- primary-he-wasnt-even-on-the-ballot/2076566/.

Freidrichs v., California Teachers Association, 578 U.S. ___(2016).

Fuller, Jaime. "From George Washington to Shaun McCutcheon: A Brief-ish History of Campaign Finance Reform." *Washington Post*. April 3, 2014, https://www .washingtonpost.com/news/the-fix/wp/2014/04/03/a-history-of-campaign-finance -reform-from-george-washington-to-shaun-mccutcheon/.

Gabriella Miller Kids First Research Act, 128 Stat. 1086, Pub L 113-94, codified in 26 USC §9008 (2014).

Ga. Const. art. I, §2, pt V.

Gambino, Lauren, "Bernie Sanders Raises $5.9m in 24 hours after ANNOUNCING 2020 Campaign." *The Guardian*, February 20, 2019, https://www.theguard ian.com/us-news/2019/feb/20/bernie-sanders-2020-presidential-campaign-fund raising.

Goldmacher, Shane. "Biden Campaign Drops Opposition to Super PAC Support." *New York Times*, October 24, 2019, https://www.nytimes.com/2019/10/24/us/po litics/joe-biden-super-pac.html.

Goldmacher, Shane and Rachel Shorey. "Trump's Sleight of Hand: Shouting Fraud, Pocketing Donors' Cash for Future." *New York Times*, February 4, 2021, https://www.nytimes.com/2021/02/01/us/politics/trump-cash.html.

Golshan, Tara. "Read the full speeches: Clinton and Trump's Awkward Al Smith Charity Dinner Roasts." *Vox.* October 21, 2016, https://www.vox.com/policy-and-politics/2016/10/21/13357412/clinton-trump-al-smith-roasts-full-speeches.

Graham, David. "The Lie of Trump's Self Funding Campaign." *The Atlantic,* May 13, 2016, https://www.theatlantic.com/politics/archive/2016/05/trumps-self-funding-lie/482691/.

Greenwood, Max. "O'Rourke Raises $3.6 Million in Second Quarter." *The Hill,* last updated July 15, 2019, https://thehill.com/homenews/campaign/453213-orourke-raises-36-million-in-second-quarter.

Gringlas, Sam, Audie Cornish, and Courtney Dorning. "Step Aside Election 2000: This Year's Election May Be The Most Litigated Yet." *NPR* Online. September 22, 2020. https://www.npr.org/2020/09/22/914431067/step-aside-election-2000-this-years-election-may-be-the-most-litigated-yet.

Grynbaum, Michael. "Trump's Briefings Are a Ratings Hit. Should Networks Cover Them Live?," *New York Times*, updated July 20, 2020, https://www.nytimes.com/2020/03/25/business/media/trump-coronavirus-briefings-ratings.html.

Libby Cathey, "9 Controversial Moments That Led Trump to Stop His White House CORONAVIRUS briefings," *ABC News* Online, July 21, 2020 https://abcnews.go.com/Politics/controversial-moments-led-trump-stop-white-house-coronavirus/story?id=71899110.

Guardian. "Democrats Smash Fundraising Records after Ruth Bader Ginsburg's Death." September 21, 2020, https://www.theguardian.com/us-news/2020/sep/21/democrats-fundraising-records-ruth-bader-ginsburg-death.

Guray, Geoffrey. "How Michael Cohen Broke Campaign Finance Law," *PBS News Hour* Online. December 12, 2018. https://www.pbs.org/newshour/politics/how-michael-cohen-broke-campaign-finance-law.

Hamilton, David. "Herbert Hoover: Campaigns and Elections." The Miller Center, accessed March 1, 2021. https://millercenter.org/president/hoover/campaigns-and-elections.

Heard, Alexander. "A New Approach to Campaign Finances." *New York Times*, October 6, 1963.

Hess, Abagail. "Kamala Harris Suspends Campaign, Says: 'I'm Not a Billionaire. I Can't Fund My own Campaign.'" *CNBC* Online. Updated December 3, 2019. https://www.cnbc.com/2019/12/03/kamala-harris-suspends-campaign-over-finances-im-not-a-billionaire.html.

Hiltzik, Michael. "Column: How Michael Bloomberg's Presidential Candidacy Harms Journalism." *Los Angeles Times* https://www.latimes.com/business/story/2019-11-24/bloomberg-news-coverage-presidential-race.

Hirsch, Lauren. "With Mike Bloomberg Out of Presidential Race, Bloomberg Journalists Resume Normal Political Coverage." *CNBC* Online. Updated March 4, 2020. https://www.cnbc.com/2020/03/04/bloomberg-journalists-free-to-resume-normal-political-coverage.html.

Hirsch, Lauren and Brian Schwartz. "Bloomberg News Will Not Investigate Mike Bloomberg or His Democratic Rivals During Primary." *CNBC* Online. November 24, 2019. https://www.cnbc.com/2019/11/24/bloomberg-news-will-not-investigate-mike-bloomberg-or-his-democratic-rivals-during-primary.html.

Hohmann, James. "Scott's Self-Funding: $12.8 Million." *Politico*. November 11, 2014, https://www.politico.com/story/2014/11/rick-scott-florida-self-funding-112403.

Huebner, Lee. "The Checkers Speech after 60 Years." *The Atlantic*. September 22, 2012, retrieved from https://www.theatlantic.com/politics/archive/2012/09/the-checkers-speech-after-60-years/262172/.

Imbert, Fred. "Dow Closes above 25,000 for the First Time after Strong Jobs Data," *CNBC* Online. January 4, 2018. https://www.cnbc.com/2018/01/04/dow-25k-us-stocks-jobs-data-adp-economy.html.

International Association of Machinists v. Street, 367 U.S. 740 (1961).

Isikoff, Michael. "George Conway: Lincoln Project Must Give 'full Explanation of What Happened.'" YahooNews!, February 15, 2021, https://news.yahoo.com/lincoln-project-co-founder-says-group-must-give-full-explanation-of-what-happened-161913752.html.

Isenstadt, Alex "Trump Campaign Credits Impeachment for Massive $46 Million Fundraising Haul." *Politico*. January 2, 2020, https://www.politico.com/news/2020/01/02/trump-campaign-fundraising-46-million-092579.

Isenstadt, Alex. "Trump Laying Groundwork for 2020 Bid." *Politico*, January 10, 2017, https://www.politico.com/story/2017/01/donald-trump-campaign-reelection-233440.

Itkowitz, Colby. "RNC, Trump Campaign Told to Stop using President Reagan to Raise Money." *Washington Post*, July 25, 2020, https://www.washingtonpost.com/politics/rnc-trump-campaign-told-to-stop-using-president-reagan-to-raise-money/2020/07/25/0a3bf886-cebc-11ea-91f1-28aca4d833a0_story.html.

Izadi, Elahe. "Biden's ABC Town Hall Ratings Beat Trump's Three-Network NBC Event," *Washington Post*, October 16, 2020, https://www.washingtonpost.com/media/2020/10/16/biden-trump-townhall-ratings/.

Jacobson, Louis. "The Record-Setting 2020 Democratic Primary Field: What You Need to Know." *Politico*, last updated January 31, 2020, https://www.politifact.com/article/2019/may/02/big-democratic-primary-field-what-need/.

Jamerson, Joshua and Julie Bykowicz. "2020 Democrats Call for End to Self-Fundraising, Private Donors." *Wall Street Journal,* December 13, 2019, https://www.wsj.com/articles/2020-democrats-split-on-whether-self-funding-should-be-legal-11576243674.

Johnson, Lauren, Deon McCray, and Jordan Ragusa. "#NeverTrump: Why Republican Members of Congress Refused to Support Their Party's Nominee in the 2016 Presidential Election." *Research and Politics* (Jan.-March 2018): 1–10.

Kallenbach, Joseph. "The Taft-Hartley Act and Union Political Contributions and Expenditures." *Minnesota Law Review* 33 (1948): 1–27.

Khazan, Olga. "Never Trump, Forever." *The Atlantic*. November 14, 2020, https://www.theatlantic.com/politics/archive/2020/11/bulwark-never-trump-republicans-biden/617025/.

Kelly, Kitty. "Death and the All American Boy." *The Washingtonian*, June 1, 1974, https://www.washingtonian.com/1974/06/01/joe-biden-kitty-kelley-1974-profile -death-and-the-all-american-boy/.

Kennedy, John. Remarks of Senator John F. Kennedy at the Gridiron Club, Washington, D.C., March 15, 1958. John F. Kennedy Library. Accessed March 3, 2021, https://www.jfklibrary.org/archives/other-resources/john-f-kennedy-spe eches/washington-dc-19580315.

Kenworthy, E.W. "Kennedy Asks Tax Break for Campaign Donors." *Atlanta Constitution*, May 30, 1962.

Kinnard, Meg. "With Democrats in New Hampshire, Steyer has SC to Himself," *Associated Press*, February 10, 2020, https://apnews.com/article/dd9455cc5550f df06a988fa8000ade13.

Labor Management Relations Act of 1947 ("Taft-Hartley Act"), Pub L No 100, 61 Stat. 136, 159, codified at 29 USC §§ 151-66 (1947).

Labor Management Relations Act of 1947, Pub L No 80-101, 61 Stat. 136, codified in 29 USC §§ 141-197 (1947).

Langlois, Shawn. "'I'm Not a Billionaire': Kamala Harris Receives Internet Consolation After Dropping Out of Presidential Race." *Market Watch*, December 3, 2019, https://www.marketwatch.com/story/non-billionaire-kamala-harris-feels-the-internet-love-after-dropping-out-of-race-2019-12-03.

Las Vegas Review-Journal. "Nevada Caucus Results." Accessed March 4, 2021. https ://www.reviewjournal.com/nevada-caucus-results-2020/.

Le Miere, Jason. "Is Trump Republican? Timeline of President's Shifting Political Views After He Sides With Democrats." *Newsweek*, September 7, 2017, https://ww w.newsweek.com/trump-republican-democrats-president-661340.

Lemelin, Bernard. "The U.S. Presidential Election in 1948: The Causes of Truman's 'Astonishing' Victory." *Revue française d'études américaines* 97 (2001): 38–61.

Leslie, Wayne. "Forbes Spends Millions, but for Little Gain." *New York Times*, February 10, 2000.

Levin, Doron. "Billionaire in Texas Is Attracting Calls to Run, and $5 Donation." *New York Times*, March 7, 1992, 11.

Liptak, Adam. "How to Tell Where Brett Kavanaugh Stands on Citizens United." *New York Times*. July 23, 2018, https://www.nytimes.com/2018/07/23/us/politics/ brett-kavanaugh-citizens-united-campaign-finance.html.

Los Angeles Times. "Angelino Cash Aiding Hoover." October 27, 1928.

Luo, Michael and Jeff Zelensky. "Obama, in Shift, Says He'll Reject Public Financing." *New York Times*, June 20, 2008, https://www.nytimes.com/2008/06 /20/us/politics/20obama.html.

Luo, Michael. "Obama Hauls in Record $750 Million for Campaign." *New York Times*, December 4, 2008, https://www.nytimes.com/2008/12/05/us/politics/05d onate.html.

Mackinnon, Douglas. "Bloomberg Made a Yuge Mistake Dropping Out." *The Hill*, March 7, 2020, https://thehill.com/opinion/white-house/486269-bloomberg-made -a-yuge-mistake-dropping-out.

Martin, Jonathan. "Beto O'Rourke Raised $6.1 Million Online in First 24 Hours." *New York Times,* last updated March 18, 2019, https://www.nytimes.com/2019/03 /18/us/politics/beto-o-rourke-fundraising.html.

Martin, John. "Self Funded Campaigns and the Current (Lack Of?) Limits On Candidate Contributions to Political Parties." *Columbia Law Review Forum* 120 (2020): 178–197.

Mass. Gen. Laws Ann. ch 5 § 8 (West Supp. 1977).

Mazo, Earl. "Politics Cost Put $200 Million." *New York Times*, October 27, 1963.

McEnany, Kayleigh. "Trump's Super Tuesday Results: Broad Appeal beyond a United GOP." *The Hill.* March 4, 2020, https://thehill.com/opinion/campaign/485 927-trumps-super-tuesday-results-broad-appeal-beyond-a-united-gop.

McCain, John and Russ Feingold. "A Better Way to Fix Campaign Financing." *Washington Post.* February 20, 1996, https://www.washingtonpost.com/opinions/ a-better-way-to-fix-campaign-financing/2018/08/26/b45ede68-a935-11e8-a8d7-0 f63ab8b1370_story.html.

McCaskill, Nolan. "Trump: Bush 'Wasted' Special-Interest Money but Now Wants to End Super PACs." *Politico.* February 8, 2016, https://www.politico.com/story /2016/02/donald-trump-jeb-bush-super-pacs-218962.

McConnell v. FEC, 540 U.S. 93 (2003).

McCutcheon v. FEC, 572 U.S. 185 (2014).

McKellar, Kenneth. "Campaign Fund Evils Beset Both Parties." *New York Times.* March 30, 1924.

McNamara, Audrey. "Joe Biden Opens Door to Super PAC Help, Reversing Previous Position." *The Daily Beast,* October 24, 2019, https://www.thedailybeast.com/joe -biden-opens-door-to-super-pac-help-reversing-previous-position.

Merica, Dan. "Windfall at Bernie's: Sanders Raises $1.5 Million in 24 Hours." *CNN* online. Updated May 1, 2015. https://www.cnn.com/2015/05/01/politics/bernie -sanders-fundraising/index.html.

Merica, Dan. "Trump Gets What He Wants in Florida: Campaign-Level Adulation," *CNN* Online, February 18, 2017, https://www.cnn.com/2017/02/18/politics/donald -trump-florida-campaign-rally/index.html.

Merica, Dan Cristina Alesci, and Jake Tapper. "Mike Bloomberg is the Latest 2020 Hopeful." *CNN* Online. Updated November 24, 2019. https://www.cnn.com/2019/ 11/24/politics/michael-bloomberg-2020-election/index.html.

Merica, Dan and Caroline Kenny. "Michael Bloomberg Said in 2008 that End of 'Redlining' Was to Blame for Financial Crisis." *CNN* Online February 14, 2020. https://www.cnn.com/2020/02/13/politics/michael-bloomberg-redlining-housing-c risis/index.html.

Mike Bloomberg. "Mike Bloomberg's Independence USA PAC Airs New Ad Touting Vice President's Strength on the Economy." Accessed March 4, 2021, https://www.mikebloomberg.com/news/mike-bloombergs-independence-usa-pac -airs-new-ad-touting-vice-presidents-strength-on-the-economy/.

Montellaro, Zach. "Tom Steyer Set to Miss Nevada Debate." *Politico*, February 18, 2020, https://www.politico.com/news/2020/02/18/tom-steyer-miss-nevada-debate -115787.

Montellaro, Zach and Alex Isenstadt. "Adelsons pour $75M into Last-Ditch Effort to Save Trump." *Politico*. October 15, 2020, https://www.politico.com/news/2020/10/15/adelson-trump-super-pac-429688.

Montellaro, Zach and Elena Schneider. "Trump Stocks New PAC with Tens of Millions as he Bids to Retain Control of GOP." *Politico*, January 31, 2021, https://www.politico.com/news/2021/01/31/donald-trump-pac-millions-gop-464250.

Montgomery, David. "Is William Weld the Hero Never Trumpers Have Been Waiting For?," *Washington Post*, August 19, 2019, https://www.washingtonpost.com/news/magazine/wp/2019/08/19/feature/is-bill-weld-the-hero-never-trumpers-have-been-waiting-for/.

Morin, Rebecca. "As Impeachment Trial Starts, Senator-Jurors Running for President Get Creative. *USA Today*. January 21, 2020, https://www.usatoday.com/story/news/politics/elections/2020/01/21/impeachment-trial-warren-sanders-klobuchar-bennet-use-surrogates-2020/4530366002/.

Murphy, Paul. "Trump Took Photos, had Roundtable with Donors at Bedminster Fundraiser Hours Before Announcing Covid Diagnosis." *CNN* Online. October 4, 2020. https://www.cnn.com/2020/10/03/politics/bedminster-trump-fundraiser-coronavirus/index.html.

Mutch, Robert. *Campaign Finance: What Everyone Needs to Know*. New York: Oxford University Press, 2016.

Myers, Cayce. "Campaign Finance and Its Impact in the 2016 Presidential Campaign." In *The 2016 U.S. Presidential Campaign*, edited by Robert Denton, 259–283. London: Palgrave MacMillan, 2017.

Myers, Cayce. "Campaign Finance and Its Impact in the 2020 Presidential Campaign." In *The 2020 U.S. Presidential Campaign*, edited by Robert Denton, 155–171. Lanham, MD: Rowman and Littlefield, 2021.

Nagourney, Adam and Jeff Zeleny. "Obama Forgoes Public Funding in a First for Major Candidate." *New York Times*, June 20, 2008, https://www.nytimes.com/2008/06/20/us/politics/20obamacnd.html.

Niquette, Marc. "Bloomberg's Path Clouded by Biden's South Carolina Win." *Bloomberg*, March 1, 2020, https://www.bloomberg.com/news/articles/2020-03-01/bloomberg-s-path-clouded-by-biden-s-decisive-south-carolina-win.

Nimmo, Dan. *Political Persuaders: The Techniques of Modern Election Campaign*. New Brunswick, NJ: Transaction Publishers, 2001.

Nixon, Richard. "Statement on Signing the Federal Election Campaign Act of 1971." The American Presidency Project, accessed March 2, 2021, https://www.presidency.ucsb.edu/documents/statement-signing-the-federal-election-campaign-act-1971.

National War Labor Relations Act, 57 Stat. 163, codified in 50 USC §1501 et seq. (1943).

NBC News Online. "New Hampshire Results." February 14, 2020, https://www.nbcnews.com/politics/2020-primary-elections/new-hampshire-results.

NBC News Online. "Full Transcript: Ninth Democratic Debate in Las Vegas." February 20, 2020, https://www.nbcnews.com/politics/2020-election/full-transcript-ninth-democratic-debate-las-vegas-n1139546.

NBC News Online. "Full Text: President Trump's 2020 RNC Acceptance Speech." Updated April 28, 2020. https://www.nbcnews.com/politics/2020-election/read-full-text-president-donald-trump-s-acceptance-speech-rnc-n1238636.

Newberry v. U.S., 256 U.S. 232 (1921).

New York Times. "Borah Denounces Corrupt Politics." January 7, 1927.

New York Times. "Buying the President." October 1, 1904.

New York Times. "Cox Aimed at Nixon Fundraising." October 25, 1973.

New York Times. "First Lady Pleads for Alert Women." April 19, 1944.

New York Times. "Harding Confers on the Campaign with General Wood." July 11 1920.

New York Times. "Gov. Roosevelt Asks Many Small Gifts to Run His Campaign." August 26, 1932.

New York Times. "Raskob Opens Drive to Lift Party Debts." October 6, 1931.

New York Times. "Reagan Leading Ford in Donations." January 7, 1976.

New York Times. "Republicans Get $529,551 in Month." October 29, 1940.

New York Times. "Transcript of Second Debate." October 10, 2016, https://www.nyt imes.com/2016/10/10/us/politics/transcript-second-debate.html.

Nguyen, Tina and Elena Schneider. "The Lincoln Project is Trolling Trump. But Can It Sway voters?" *Politico*, June 27, 2020, https://www.politico.com/news/2020/06 /27/lincolnproject-trolling-trump-sway-voters-341928.

Noah, Timothy. "Will the Real Donald Trump Please Stand Up." *Politico*. July 26, 2015, https://www.politico.com/story/2015/07/will-the-real-donald-trump-please -stand-up-120607.

Norman, Greg. "Trump's Save America PAC Starts 2021 with More Than $31M, Filings Show." *Fox Business* Online. February 1, 2021. https://www.foxbusiness.c om/politics/trumps-save-america-pac-starts-2021-with-more-than-31-million.

Panette, Grace. "'Now We FIGHT BACK!': The Trump Re-Election Campaign Is Using the Attorney General's Mueller Summary to Raise Funds." *Business Insider.* March 24, 2019, https://www.businessinsider.com/trump-campaign-is-already-fu ndraising-off-the-mueller-report-barr-2019-3.

Pratt, Henry. *Personal Finances of Abraham Lincoln.* Chicago: Lakeside Press, 1943. https://quod.lib.umich.edu/l/lincoln2/5250244.0001.001/1:17.2?rgn=div2 ;view=fulltext.

Oberdorfer, Don. "Ford Fund Appeal Nets $1 Million." *Washington Post*, December 13, 1975.

Oliphant, James and Joseph Ax. "Democrat Joe Biden Chooses Kamala Harris for White House Running House." *Reuters*, August 11, 2020, https://www.reuters.com /article/us-usa-election-biden-harris/democrat-joe-biden-chooses-senator-kamala -harris-for-white-house-running-mate-idUSKCN2572MZ.

Okun, Eli. "Awkward: How Trump's Past Donations Could Haunt 2020 Dems." *Politico.* March 5, 2020, https://www.politico.com/story/2019/03/05/2020-pre sidential-dems-trump-money-1202938.

Padden, Brian. "Trump Campaign Focuses on Hunter Biden Emails as 'October Surprise.'" Voice of America Online. October 28, 2020. https://www.voanews.com /2020-usa-votes/trump-campaign-focuses-hunter-biden-emails-october-surprise.

PBS Online. "Nixon's Checkers Speech, September 23, 1952." Accessed March 1, 2021. https://www.pbs.org/wgbh/americanexperience/features/eisenhower -checkers/.

Permissible Non-Campaign Use of Funds, 11 C.F.R. § 113.2 (2016).

Pezenik, Sasha and Will McDuffie. "Warren Slams Bloomberg for His News Organization Not Covering Democrats." *ABC News* Online. January 23, 2020. https://abcnews.go.com/Politics/warren-slams-bloomberg-news-organization-co vering-democrats/story?id=68464104.

Pincus, Walter. "21 Million Raised for Nixon Bid." *Washington Post*, January 3, 1969.

Pipefitters Local Union No. 562 v. U.S., 407 U.S. 385 (1972).

Plott, Elaina and Shane Goldmacher. "Trump Wins CPAC Straw Poll, But Only 68 Percent Want Him to Run Again." *New York Times*, February 28, 2021, https:// www.nytimes.com/2021/02/28/us/politics/cpac-straw-poll-2024-presidential-race .html.

Politico. "Full Transcript: Third 2016 Presidential Debate." October 20, 2016. https ://www.politico.com/story/2016/10/full-transcript-third-2016-presidential-debate -230063.

Porter, Tom. "Journalists Are Skipping Trump's Daily Coronavirus Press Briefings, Saying They Don't Have Enough News Value." *Business Insider*, April 1, 2020, https://www.businessinsider.com/trump-coronavirus-briefings-reporters-broad casters-skip-no-news-value-2020-4.

Pramuk, Jacob. "Mike Bloomberg will transfer $18 million to the Democratic Party as it gears up to face Trump." *CNBC* Online. March 20, 2020. https://www.cnbc.com /2020/03/20/mike-bloomberg-to-donate-18-million-to-dnc-in-2020-election.html.

Presidential Election Campaign Fund Act of 1966, 80 Stat. 1553, Pub. L. 89-809 (1966).

Priorities USA. "Priorities USA's By the Numbers." Accessed March 4, 2021. https ://priorities.org/memos/priorities-usas-2020-by-the-numbers/.

Priorities USA. "Priorities USA Led the Charge against Trump and His Allies." accessed November 3, 2020. https://priorities.org/memos/priorities-usa-led-the-cha rge-against-trump-and-his-allies/.

Public Utility Holding Act of 1935, Pub L. No. 74-333, codified in 15 UCC §79 (1935).

Railway Clerks v. Allen, 373 U.S. 113 (1963).

Rambarin, Vandana. "Trump Debate Coach Chris Christie Says President 'too Hot' in biden showdown," *Fox News* Online, September 30, 2020, https://www.foxnews. com/politics/chris-christie-helped-prep-trump-for-debate-but-said-he-was-too-hot -during-biden-showdown.

Rashbaum, William and Ben Protess. "New Charges in Stormy Daniels Hush Money Inquiry Are Unlikely, Prosecutors Signal." *New York Times*, July 18, 2019, https:/ /www.nytimes.com/2019/07/18/nyregion/stormy-daniels-michael-cohen-documen ts.html.

Real, Evan. "Kamala Harris Campaign Selling T-Shirts Inspired by Viral Joe Biden Moment." *Hollywood Reporter.* June 28, 2019, https://www.hollywoodreporter. com/news/kamala- harris-selling-t-shirts-inspired-by-viral-biden-debate-momen t-1221674.

Reed, Roy. "Humphrey Donations have Dropped Since Kennedy's Death." *New York Times*, June 20, 1968.

Reich, Kenneth. "Carter Campaign Doubles Its Fundraising Projection." *Los Angeles Times*, June 29, 1976.

Reid, Tim and Michael Martina. "Democrat Warren Accuses Rival Bloomberg of Trying to Buy U.S. Presidential Election." *Reuters*, November 25, 2019, https://www.reuters.com/article/us-usa-election-warren/democrat-warren-accuses-rival-bloomberg-of-trying-to-buy-u-s-presidential-election-idUSKBN1XZ2G0.

Relman, Eliza and Sonam Sheth. "Mike Bloomberg Drops Out of the 2020 Presidential Race and Endorses Joe Biden." *Business Insider*, March 4, 2020, https://www.businessinsider.com/mike-bloomberg-drops-out-of-the-2020-presidential-race-2020-3.

Republican Voters against Trump. Accessed March 4, 2021. https://rvat.org/.

Reston, Maeve. "Trump Teases 2024 Presidential Run in Lie-Filled CPAC Speech." *CNN* Online. February 28, 2021. https://www.cnn.com/2021/02/28/politics/trump-cpac-speech-2021/index.html.

Reuters. "Neither George Bush Voted for Trump, Book Author Tells New York Times." November 4, 2017. https://www.reuters.com/article/us-trump-bush-book/neither-george-bush-voted-for-trump-book-author-tells-new-york-times-idUSKBN1D40TP.

Richardson, Bradford. "Trump Open to Campaign Finance Reform." *The Hill*. January 17, 2016, https://thehill.com/blogs/ballot-box/presidential-races/266189-trump-open-to-campaign-finance-reform.

Roosevelt, Theodore. "Fifth Annual Message, December 5, 1905." The Miller Center, University of Virginia. Accessed January 15, 2021, https://millercenter.org/the-presidency/presidential-speeches/december-5-1905-fifth-annual-message.

Roosevelt, Theodore. "Seventh Annual Message, December 3, 1907." The Miller Center, University of Virginia. Accessed January 15, 2021, https://millercenter.org/the-presidency/presidential-speeches/december-3-1907-seventh-annual-message.

Rosenwald, Michael. "Biden, Once One of the Nation's Youngest Senators, Will Be Its Oldest President." *The Washington Post*, January 11, 2021, https://www.washingtonpost.com/history/2021/01/11/youngest-senators-joe-biden/.

Russonello, Giovanni. "Why Warren Supporters Aren't a Lock to Get Behind Sanders." *New York Times*, March 6, 2020, https://www.nytimes.com/2020/03/06/us/politics/elizabeth-warren-bernie-sanders-voters.html.

Sanders, Bernie. *Our Revolution: A Future to Believe In*. New York: St. Martin's Press, 2016.

Samuelsohn, Darren. "Georgee H.W. Bush to Vote for Hillary Clinton." *Politico*. September 19, 2016, https://www.politico.com/story/2016/09/exclusive-george-hw-bush-to-vote-for-hillary-228395.

Schaul, Kevin, Kevin Uhrmacher, and Anu Narayanswamy, "Bloomberg's Immense Spending Gets Him 30,000 Online Ads a Minute, and a Whole Lot More." *Washington Post*, February 19, 2020, https://www.washingtonpost.com/graphics/2020/politics/bloomberg-ad-spending-scale/.

Schaul, Kevin, Kate Rabinowitz, and Ted Mellkin. "2020 Turnout Is the Highest in Over a Century." *Washington Post*, last updated December, 28, 2020, https://www.washingtonpost.com/graphics/2020/elections/voter-turnout/.

Schneider, Elena. "Biden Smashes Fundraising Records During Chaotic Debate." *Politico*, September 30, 2020, https://www.politico.com/news/2020/09/30/joe-biden-debate-fundraising-423826.

Schneider, Elena. "How ActBlue Has Transformed Democratic Politics." *Politico*, October 30, 2020, https://www.politico.com/news/2020/10/30/democrats-actblue-f undrasing-elections-433698.

Schouton, Fredreka. "Democratic Super PACs Race to Fill the Void with Joe Biden off the Trail." *CNN* Online. March 25, 2020. https://www.cnn.com/2020/03/25/poli tics/democratic-super-pacs-attack-trump/index.html.

Schwartz, Brian. "Democrats Score a Fundraising Windfall during the DNC, and Biden Bundlers See New Commitments." *CNBC* Online. August 21, 2020. https ://www.cnbc.com/2020/08/21/democrats-rack-up-fundraising-windfall-during-the -dnc.html.

Schwartz, Brian. "Mike Bloomberg Takes Big Losses after Spending Over $100 Million in Florida, Ohio and Texas." *CNBC* Online. November 4, 2020. https://ww w.cnbc.com/2020/11/04/bloomberg-sees-losses-after-spending-over-100-million -in-florida-ohio-texas.html.

Sen Rep. No. 151, 75th Cong., 1st Sess. 127-133 (1937).

Severns, Maggie. "Trump Campaign Plagued by Groups Raising Tens of Millions in His Name," *Politico*. December 23, 2019, https://www.politico.com/news/2019/12 /23/trump-campaign-compete-against-groups-money-089454.

Shelbourne, Mallory. "Trump says Gillibrand Begged for Donations 'And Would Do Anything for Them'." *The Hill*. December 12, 2017, https://thehill.com/homenews /administration/364405-trump-slams-gillibrand-in-tweet-a-total-flunky-for-chuck -schumer.

Schleifer, Theodore. "Silicon Valley Megadonors Unleash a Last-Minute, $100 Million Barrage of Ads Against Trump." *Vox*, October 20, 2020, https://www.vox .com/recode/2020/10/20/21523492/future-forward-super-pac-dustin-moskovitz-s ilicon-valley.

Shogan, Robert. "Ford's Campaign Hurt By Watergate." *Los Angeles Times*, October 9, 1975.

Smith v. Allwright, 321 U.S. 649 (1944).

Siders, David. "Beto O'Rourke Fundraising Fell to 3.6 Million in Second Quarter." Politico, last updated July 15, 2019, https://www.politico.com/story/2019/07/15/ beto-orourke-fundraising-second-quarter-1416486.

Sitkoff, Robert. "Political Speech, Political Extortion, and the Competition for Corporate Charters." *The University of Chicago Law Review* 69 (2002): 1103–1166.

Slodysko, Brian. "Biden Funds Success With Low-Dollar Donors." *PBS News Hour* Online, May 21, 2019, https://www.pbs.org/newshour/politics/biden-finds-unexp ected-success-with-low-dollar-donors.

Smithsonian National Portrait Museum. "John Wanamaker Portrait" Accessed January 15, 2021. https://postalmuseum.si.edu/collections/object-spotlight/john -wanamaker-portrait.

Solender, Andrew. "Biden Campaign Raised $10 Million In Three Hours On Night Of First Debate." *Forbes*, September 30, 2020, https://www.forbes.com/sites/

andrewsolender/2020/09/30/biden-campaign-raised-10-million-in-three-hours-on
-night-of-first-debate/?sh=7903d2976ca2.

Speechnow.org v. FEC, 599 F.3d 686 (DC Cir. 2010).

Stark, Louis. "CIO Sets Up Group on Election Funds." *New York Times*, June 18, 1944.

Summers, Juana and Barbara Sprunt. "Tom Steyer Drops Out of the Presidential Race." *NPR* Online, February 29, 2020, https://www.npr.org/2020/02/29/8019 52931/tom-steyer-to-drop-out-of-2020-presidential-race.

Svitek, Patrick and Abby Livingston. "How the Race between Ted Cruz and Beto O'Rourke Became the Closest in Texas History in 40 Years." *The Texas Tribune*, last updated November 9, 2018, https://www.texastribune.org/2018/11/09/ted-cruz -beto-orourke-closest-texas-race-40-years/.

Terry v. Ohio, 392 U.S. 1 (1968).

The Commission on Presidential Debates. "Presidential Debate at Washington University in St. Louis Missouri." October 9, 2016. https://www.debates.org/voter-education/debate-transcripts/october-9-2016-debate-transcript/.

The Lincoln Project. Accessed March 4, 2021. https://lincolnproject.us/.

The Hatch Act of 1939, Pub L 76-252, 53 Stat. 1147, codified in 5 USC §§7321-7326 (1939).

The Smithsonian. "Woodrow Wilson Federal Segregation." Accessed March 3, 2021, https://postalmuseum.si.edu/research-articles/the-history-and-experience-of -african-americans-in-america%E2%80%99s-postal-service-3.

Thompson, Alex. "Oprah Pal and Spirituality Guru Plans 2020 Run." *Politico*, November 16, 2018, https://www.politico.com/story/2018/11/16/oprah-pal-wil liamson-2020-run-996174.

Thompson, Alex. "Andrew Yang Announces $120,000 Giveaway During Debate." *Politico*, updated September 12, 2019, https://www.politico.com/story/2019/09/12 /andrew-yang-120000-giveaway-for-ubi-pilot-program-1493622.

Tillman Act of 1907, Pub L No 59-36, 34 Stat. 864, chap. 420 (1907).

Tom Steyer. "Meet Tom." Accessed March 4, 2021. https://www.tomsteyer.com/ meet-tom/.

Trist v. Child, 88. U.S. 441 (1875).

Turnout PAC. Accessed March 3, 2021, https://www.turnoutpac.org/progressive-t urnout-project-congratulates-joe-biden-on-michigan-win/.

U.S. Department of State, Office of the Historian. "Message of the President December 5, 1905." Accessed February 1, 2021. https://history.state.gov/historica ldocuments/frus1905/message-of-the-president.

U.S. Department of State, Office of the Historian. "Annual Message of the President Transmitted To Congress, December 3, 1906." Accessed March 2, 2021, https://hi story.state.gov/historicaldocuments/frus1906p1/annual.

U.S. Department of State, Office of the Historian. "Message of the President, Annual, December 3, 1907." Accessed March 2, 2021. https://history.state.gov/historica ldocuments/frus1907p1/message-of-the-president.

USA Today. "Debate Transcript: Trump, Biden Final Presidential Debate Moderated by Kristen Welker." Accessed March 4, 2021. https://www.usatoday.com/story

/news/politics/elections/2020/10/23/debate-transcript-trump-biden-final-presiden tial-debate-nashville/3740152001/.

USA Today. "South Carolina Primary Results." March 2, 2020. https://www.usatoday .com/elections/results/primaries/democratic/south-carolina/.

U.S. v. Congress of Industrial Organizations, 335 U.S. 106 (1948).

U.S. v. UAW-CIO, 352 U.S. 567, 570-571 (1957).

U.S. Bureau of Statistics. "Civilian Unemployment Rate." Accessed March 4, 2021. https://www.bls.gov/charts/employment-situation/civilian-unemployment -rate.htm.

U.S. Customs and Border Protection. ""Did You Know . . . Samuel Swartwout Skimmed Staggering Sums?." Last Modified December 20, 2019. https://www.cbp .gov/about/history/did-you-know/samuel-swartwout.

U.S. Department of Justice. "Michael Cohen Pleads Guilty In Manhattan Federal Court To Eight Counts, Including Criminal Tax Evasion and Campaign Finance Violations." August 21, 2018. https://www.justice.gov/usao-sdny/pr/michael-cohen-pleads-guilty-manhattan-federal-court-eight-counts-including-criminal-tax.

U.S. Department of Justice. "Appointment of Special Counsel to Investigate Russian Interference with the 2016 Presidential Election and Related Matters." Accessed February 18, 2021. https://www.justice.gov/opa/press-release/file/967231 /download.

U.S. Department of Justice. "Letter to the House and Senate Judiciary Committees." Accessed February 18, 2021. https://www.justice.gov/archives/ag/page/file/1147 981/download.

U.S. Senator for Montana John Tester. "Tester's Bill to Shine Light on Campaigns Passes Senate." June 25, 2018. https://www.tester.senate.gov/?p=press_release &id=6246.

Vogel, Kenneth and David Levinthal. "Obama, Romney Both Top $1B." *Politico*, December 7, 2012, https://www.politico.com/story/2012/12/barack-obama-mitt -romney-both-topped-1-billion-in-2012-084737.

Waldman, Paul. "The Never Trumpers Might Be Onto Something." *Washington Post*, May 28, 2020, https://www.washingtonpost.com/opinions/2020/05/28/never-tru mpers-might-finally-be-something/.

Wall Street Journal. "Washington Wire." September 24, 1948.

Warren Democrats. "Getting Big Money Out of Politics." Accessed March 3, 2021. https://elizabethwarren.com/plans/campaign-finance-reform.

Washington Post. "2020 Iowa Democratic Caucuses Live Results." February 27, 2020, https://www.washingtonpost.com/elections/election-results/iowa/.

Washington Post. "Bars Big Donations." June 26, 1920.

Washington Post. "Live Results: Super Tuesday 2020." Accessed March 3, 2021, https://www.washingtonpost.com/elections/election-results/super-tuesday/.

Washington Post. "Maryland Money Flows to Nixon." September 30, 1972.

Washington Post. "Political Arena: Senate Probing Ads for Willkie." September 13, 1940.

Washington Post. "Roosevelt's Campaign Fund." December 3, 1905.

Washington Post. "Wilson in New York." August 25, 1912.

White, Richard. "The Bullmoose and the Bear: Theodore Roosevelt and John Wannamaker Struggled Over the Spoils." *Pennsylvania History: A Journal of Mid-Atlantic Studies* 71 (2004): 1–24.

Wise, Justin. "Tulsa Fire Department Says Trump rally Attendance Was About 6,200." *The Hill*, June 21, 2020, https://thehill.com/homenews/campaign/503781-tulsa-fire-department-says-trump-rally-attendance-was-about-6200.

Wright, David. "Kamala Harris Touts $1.5 Million Haul in 24 hours After Campaign Announcement. *CNN* Online. January 22, 2019. https://www.cnn.com/2019/01/22/politics/kamala-harris-fundraising-announcement/index.html.

"Young Joe Biden on Campaign Finance Reform (1974)." YouTube Video, 12:15, August 30, 2017. https://www.youtube.com/watch?v=VIZmZe7fe3E.

Index

About the Author

Cayce Myers, PhD, LLM, JD, APR is the director of graduate studies and an associate professor at Virginia Tech's School of Communication where he teaches public relations and communication law. His research focuses on public relations history and laws that influence public relations practice. He is the author of *Public Relations History: Theory, Practice, and Profession* and the coauthor of *Mass Communication Law in Virginia*, fourth edition. His work has appeared in numerous academic journals and trade presses. He is also an accredited member of Public Relations Society of America, the legal research editor for the Institute for Public Relations, and a member of the Arthur W. Page Society.

www.ingramcontent.com/pod-product-compliance
Lightning Source LLC
Chambersburg PA
CBHW022318280326
41932CB00010B/1148